Writing Methods in Theological Reflection

Writing Methods in Theological Reflection

Heather Walton

scm press

© Heather Walton 2014

Published in 2014 by SCM Press
Editorial Office
3rd Floor, Invicta House
108–114 Golden Lane
London EC1Y 0TG

SCM Press is an imprint of Hymns Ancient & Modern Ltd
(a registered charity)
13A Hellesdon Park Road
Norwich NR6 5DR, UK

www.scmpress.co.uk

British Library Cataloguing in Publication data

A catalogue record for this book is available
from the British Library

978 0 334 05185 5

Typeset by Manila Typesetting Company
Printed and bound in Great Britain by
CPI Group (UK) Ltd, Croydon

For my sister Helen

Contents

Acknowledgements

This book is dedicated to Helen, my kind, wise and lovely sister. It comes with love and thanks to my partner, Reinier, who proof read with great 'patience' all its pages. And with love and gratitude to our daughter, who inspired so much of what is written here.

There are a number of people who have encouraged me in reflective theological writing over the years. First, my mother Hazel, a gifted and original preacher, inspired me to be daring when I spoke about God. Colleagues and friends from the Northern Federation for Training in Ministry in Manchester were the first to support me in the shared development of our reflective writing; special thanks go to Richard Kidd, Susan Durber, Mary Cotes and Frances Ward. In Glasgow, David and Alison Jasper have patiently listened to many of these works and offered valuable insights into their revision. I have benefited so much from the critical companionship of members of the Centre for Literature, Theology and the Arts at Glasgow during the past 16 years. I count myself very fortunate to have been part of this radical and inclusive community. Many of the postgraduate researchers associated with the Centre have made important contributions to my writing, but especial thanks are due to Anna Fisk, Elizabeth Anderson, Jennifer Reek, Mark Godin and Alana Vincent. My colleagues in Practical Theology at Glasgow University have also significantly shaped my understanding of theology and practice; thanks go to Doug Gay, Vicky Gunn and Leah Robinson. I am grateful for the perceptive research assistance of Ioulia Kolovou and also to Meg MacDonald for her continuing support.

The Development of the Doctorate in Practical Theology, under the auspices of the British and Irish Association for Practical Theology, has enabled me to work closely with colleagues from a number of universities in developing theological reflection among doctoral researchers. I have received important challenges and much kindness from my friends Stephen Pattison and Zoe Bennett. Elaine Graham's friendship over many years has been a continuing source of energy, inspiration and new ideas.

Further afield I would like to thank Will Storrar for enabling me to attend the Writing Theology Workshop held at the Center for Theological Inquiry in Princeton in 2010. Bonnie Miller-McLemore has encouraged me to keep writing in my peculiar way, and Pam Couture and Claire Wolfteich have been keen advocates for the establishment of poetics as a vital resource in practical theology.

I would also like to thank a number of publishers for permission to reprint versions of previously published work. 'Calls to Preach' was originally published as 'Calls to Preach: Constructing Vocational Theology' in *Practical Theology* 2:1 (2009), and 'Seeking Wisdom in Practical Theology: *Phronesis*, Poetics and Everyday Life' was originally given as a plenary lecture to the British and Irish Association for Practical Theology and later published in *Practical Theology* 7:1 (2014); Maney Publishing gave permission for their republication here. 'Desiring Things' was originally published as 'Desiring Things: Practical Theology and the New Materialisms' in Bonnie Miller-McLemore, Ruard Ganzevoort and Rein Brouwer (eds), *City of Desires: A Place for God*; Lit Verlag granted permission for reuse. 'The Course Outline: Teaching Theology through Creative Writing' was originally published in *The Journal of Adult Theological Education* 9:2 (2013), and permission was granted for reuse by Acumen. 'Poetics and Practical Theology' was originally published as 'Poetics' in Bonnie Miller-McLemore's edited collection *The Wiley-Blackwell Companion to Practical Theology*, and permission was granted by Wiley-Blackwell for its inclusion here. 'Poetics and Public Theology' was originally published as 'You Have to Say You Cannot Speak: Feminist Reflections upon Public Theology' in *The International Journal of Public Theology* 4:1 (2010), and permission was given to reprint here by Brill. 'Poetics and Pastoral Care' was originally published as 'Speaking in Signs: Narrative and Trauma in Practical Theology', in the *Scottish Journal of Healthcare Chaplaincy* 5:2 (2002). Ian Stirling kindly granted editorial permission for its reuse. Natalie Watson, at SCM Press, has supported this project throughout with kindness, wit and good advice.

Heather Walton
Glasgow, January 2014

Introduction

Reflective Theological Writing

The Challenge to Write from Life

The requirement to reflect and write about experience from a theological perspective has increasingly become a cornerstone of practice-based learning and theological education. This is part of a shift in emphasis away from traditional pedagogical models founded upon knowledge acquisition and skills training. The intention is to foster a perception and awareness of God in the midst of life which will enable people of faith to orientate their practice according to their beliefs and values – and also to communicate their convictions in ways that are rooted in and relevant to the cultural context in which we live.

However, in my teaching, examining and engagement with pastoral practitioners, I have encountered a great deal of confusion and anxiety about what form this reflective writing should take; what a text of theological reflection should actually look, sound and read like. The guidance varies, and frequently there is little advice given at all. It is assumed that theological reflection will develop organically from the life of faith and find its way unmediated onto the written page. In my experience this is never the case. There is thus a growing and urgent need to provide tools to support this work. It is equally important to undergird the growing interest in reflective writing with a theoretical interrogation of both its principles and its purposes. These practical and critical ambitions are both equally present within this text.

This book is also born out of my own reflective writing practice over many years. In response to various personal and professional challenges I have learnt to write 'on-the-job' in many different genres, each with its own distinct conventions. I have kept spiritual journals and journals to support projects of social research. I have written sermons and liturgies. I have published academic books and articles and penned papers to be 'performed' in classrooms, church assemblies and conference halls. I have produced works of life writing that have enabled me to negotiate difficult periods in my personal life, and I have also published texts as acts of political commitment. My conviction that good writing is always contextually located and painstakingly constructed, however natural and artless it appears to be, has been born directly out of these various productive processes. It is my hope that through discussing and displaying my own work some of the implicit 'rules' at work in writing for theological reflection will become clearer, and that this will prove helpful to emerging theological writers, whether they be students, practitioners, spiritual seekers or academics.

For the challenge to write experiences as a means of articulating faith or values is a daunting one. The fact that it now routinely appears as an integral part of the theological curriculum by no means lessens its fierce demands. When a researcher chooses reflective writing as the form in which to present a thesis, the risks this entails are evident. It is less easy to determine what constitutes 'good' reflective writing[1] than what is acceptable academic writing, and cautious supervisors often feel compelled to advise against this choice. When the writing goal is to construct worship, engage in spiritual direction or professional supervision the task is still formidable. The requirements of craft and authenticity often appear irreconcilable, and behind them lies the greater challenge – to speak about what is deeply sensed but not easily articulated.

In this Introduction, therefore, I will endeavour to make the processes of theological writing more transparent by addressing a number of key questions. These will include:

- Where are the historical roots of reflective theological writing?
- What has prompted the current move towards reflexivity in theological reflection?
- How should we frame the relationship between modes of writing and theological reflection methods?
- What personal and ethical choices must be made in theological writing – and what are their consequences?
- What writing techniques can aid us in the construction of our reflective accounts?
- How can differing traditions of reflective writing (in this text I focus upon autoethnography, journalling and life writing) help in structuring theological reflection?

---

1 The terms 'reflective' and 'reflexive' are overlapping and sometimes used interchangeably. However, strictly speaking, reflective processes are characterized by acute observation and analysis of roles and context. Reflexivity takes this critical work a step further and also interrogates the position of the 'self' who observes. I use both terms in this work but in theological discourse 'reflective' occurs more frequently.

Before progressing further, however, it is perhaps best to decide now how you wish to read this book. Some people will prefer to engage directly with examples of theological writing before considering issues of theory and practice. If you are the kind of reader who likes to discover their own meanings rather than be guided in interpretation, then it is probably best that you proceed directly to the chapters themselves and come back to this Introduction at a later stage if need be. However, if you are the type of person who likes things to be structured and clear, particularly in such a potentially misty area as reflective writing, then it will be worth taking the time to work through this introductory chapter, as it may alert you to what to look out for as you read on and begin to make your own responses to the writing challenge.

Traditions of Theological Writing

People have always used their experiences, whether these be in the natural world, in familiar human relationships or amid challenging historical events, as a vivid source of theological understanding. The Bible is full of examples of such work. In the Psalms, in particular, we can find the full range of mundane and dramatic events that constitute our common life shaped into poetic invocations of a God whose glory is declared in the starry heavens (Ps. 19), who is a shelter and refuge in trouble (Ps. 46.1) and who dispenses justice to the nations (Ps. 67). Furthermore, the Bible is replete with narratives, dramas and laments that shape religious reflection according to the conventions of particular genres and 'literary' traditions. A considerable part of their power lies in the fact that they function according to well-understood conventions that enable hearers and readers to respond appropriately to the various elements of the tradition and creatively re-employ them when navigating their own personal or corporate journeys through life.

From this perspective there is nothing at all novel about the crafted use of experience in theological reflection. Furthermore, a literary culture of devotion has been part of the Christian tradition since earliest times. The testimonies of martyrs and visionaries, the narratives of pilgrims, the earthy texts of spiritual guidance that flowered in monastic communities, and the imaginative processes of the Ignatian spiritual exercises have contributed greatly to our spiritual traditions and also shaped our theological sense-making. Protestant practices of personal testimony, confessional preaching and self-examination have made their own contributions to this rich literary resource, extending its reach into popular spiritual practice. The historian Christopher Hill argues that from the late seventeenth century we can trace a gradual democratization of spiritual writing due to increased literacy, pietistic religion, political circumstances and technological development. 'Anticipation of spiritual autobiographies can be found in diaries (spiritual balance sheets), prefaces to the collected writing of preachers or biographical appendices to funeral sermons. The revolutionary decades saw the publication of this new genre. Spiritual biographies of ordinary people' (1988, p. 64).

The emergence of Romanticism a century later further stimulated an intense concern with the interior life and its dramatic challenges. Romanticism was not simply an elite movement of poets, artists and philosophers. It struck a note that resounded deeply in emerging industrial societies and was quickly assimilated into many cultural forms. Romanticism,[2] when translated into a religious quest, sought God within the depths of subjective experience, and writing about this became a form of exploration in which the adventurous soul attended deeply to its own imaginative and emotive engagements with spiritual reality. It deeply influenced popular devotion, hymnody and the language forms in which spirituality was cast. This was the case among people of all classes and throughout the western world (see for example Santmire and Cobb 2006).

Many scholars believe that contemporary religion in the West, both in traditional denominational settings and within new religious movements, is still deeply influenced by Romanticism with its search for personal authenticity, self-expression and the divine who dwells within (see Heelas 2008). Our contemporary interest in reflective theological writing thus stands within an ancient tradition, but one that is adaptive and responsive to cultural change. Indeed, the self-interrogating spirit of Pietism, as it interacted with Romanticism, is held by some to be one of the major shapers of our contemporary cultural landscape in the late modern or postmodern world.

---

2 Many romantic poets and philosophers were not conventionally religious and some outspokenly rejected all religious systems. Nevertheless, the symbolic forms they used and their emphasis upon the sublime capacities of mind and spirit generated a discourse that was easily and eagerly appended to the discourses of popular piety.

The Current Context

Postmodernism

There are many ways of characterizing postmodernism. Some of these describe a loss of faith in all grand systems of knowledge and belief (Lyotard 1984). Others chart a shift within late capitalism towards a communication economy and the triumphant domination of virtual reality, a world of signs and immaterial wonders, over other cultural forms (Baudrillard 1994). Perhaps of most relevance to us here are the analyses that highlight the importance of self-construction within postmodernity – an endeavour that Anthony Giddens (1991) describes as the 'reflexive project of the self'. According to Giddens, in contemporary culture individuals feel themselves to be held accountable for the work of fashioning an identity, a self-narrative, which demonstrates how they have achieved self-actualization and attained a position of personal authenticity. This project of 'being true to oneself' entails an organic integration of values and lifestyle (Giddens 1991, pp. 75–80). In a development beyond the conceptual frame of previous eras, this narrative identity is now presented as a deeply embodied story that seeks to combine emotions, ideas and relationships within a holistic frame. Other commentators have spoken of a 'subjective turn' in modern culture in which the individual no longer seeks to conform to moral ideals and principles imposed from outside but struggles to find truth in authentic living. 'The goal is not to defer to higher authority but to have the courage to become one's own authority' (Heelas and Woodhead 2005, p. 4).

To argue that the turn to reflective writing in theology has to be placed within this wider context is not to imply an uncritical acceptance of this cultural development. Giddens himself talks about the work of self-policing that takes place as we seek to construct acceptable stories in the face of ambiguous circumstances. This he views as an 'extension of the control systems of modernity to the self . . . a morally stunted process' (1991, p. 9). It is rather to alert us to the fact that self-narration and the quest to tell stories conveying our authentic identity are part of the way we live now and influence the chatroom host, the Facebook user and the spiritual director alike. When people set out to write theologically, they will do so in a context in which the dominant discourses of authenticity and self-actualization are powerfully at play. This is one reason why it appears natural and appropriate to undertake this kind of self-reflexive work. But it is also why the compulsion to narrate our lives should be continually and carefully examined.

Attention to life experience in a spiritual frame may bring us close to the heart of the Christian mystery – but it can also be a problematic process that owes as much to the questionable forms of idealism that are part of the romantic movement as it does to prayerful devotion or curious theological creativity.

Reflexivity

When Giddens refers to reflexivity in the terms used above, he is highlighting the role the self plays in the construction of identities that appear to be made and chosen rather than inherited or enforced. However, the concept of reflexivity is used much more widely than this. It is an important concept within current debates about epistemology (ways of knowing), where it is used to highlight the role that the self plays in the generation of all forms of knowledge about the world. It is now widely acknowledged that the knower is not related to knowledge as a coherent bounded subject to a separate object. A much more complex interplay takes place between the observer and the observed that changes both of them and challenges views of reasoning as a process of rational and unbiased observation (see Sandywell 1996).

So reflexivity in this frame refers to the interrogative processes that enable us to understand all our meaning-making, even in the most abstract spheres, as relational, provisional, embodied and located. The types of questions that reflexive inquirers ask of themselves thus include:

- How does my personal history generate presuppositions that influence my approach to this topic?
- How does my gender/class/ethnicity/sexual identity/cultural location influence my understanding?
- Where do my allegiances lie and how do my commitments guide my approach to inquiry?
- What can my body and my emotional responses contribute to generating the knowledge I seek?

When these questions are posed, the intention is not simply to generate self-knowledge (although this remains important), but rather to understand the self within the context of the political and social world through which it is being continually shaped and formed.

A major contribution to this reflexive approach has come from the development of feminist theory over the past half-century. One of the founding principles of feminism is that the world looks different according to the place from which it is viewed. If that place is a woman's body, then much of the dominant understandings of what a person is, what the good life is, what a moral decision is, how the sacred is to be addressed, can be challenged. The point that women's experience does not parallel that of men was well made in Simone de Beauvoir's *The Second Sex* (1972 [1949]). In many key areas of our social life women's perspectives are marginalized and muted, and male experience informs the cultural norm. This fact has led women scholars to present new paradigms of what constitutes 'good' ways of knowing. Sandra Harding (1991), for example, advocates an approach to objectivity that does not assume a neutral perspective. She argues that those most painfully affected by an issue gain a privileged understanding of its parameters – she who wears the shoe best understands how it pinches! However, this experiential knowledge should be tried and tested through dialogue with others who view the same problem from a different location. Through such dialogical processes a 'stronger' objectivity emerges which in turn can inform action – action that is both appropriate and transforming.

Many of the key tenets of feminist epistemology have now become part of the mainstream and exercise considerable influence on current scholarly practice. Deepened by the insights of postcolonial theory and queer theory, reflexive understandings have now been assimilated into many processes of social research in anthropology, sociology, human geography and organizational studies – the type of research, in fact, that is routinely used in theological reflection. Even researchers who have a realist understanding of the social world and are seeking 'hard evidence' to support their theoretical perspectives now frequently 'locate' themselves within their research findings as a widely recognized mark of good practice.

This brief exploration of reflexivity and epistemology highlights another reason why there has been a turn towards reflective writing in theology. Reflexivity, in the broader sense in which we have examined it here, is an invaluable critical tool. Its affirmation of the location and value base through which knowledge is produced, and its affirmation of bodily and emotional knowledge, are all important aspects of a pastorally astute and theologically aware approach. When a student or practitioner is requested to write reflexively, it is this kind of rigorous interrogative process they are being invited to pursue.

Reflective Practice

As I have attempted to demonstrate, cultural shifts are felt at many levels, and it is clear that changing understandings of knowledge go hand in hand with a correspondingly changed approach to pedagogy. Within the world of theological education this has certainly been the case. There have been a number of key contributors to our re-visioning of pedagogical practice.

The tremendous impact of liberation theology upon all forms of theological thinking from the 1970s onwards was accompanied by an interest in the work of the Brazilian educationalist Paulo Freire, whose approach firmly linked growth in personal awareness with a transforming theological vision and an emphasis upon political agency:

> Freire's method prioritized the concrete and immediate experience of the student and encouraged them to reflect critically on their experience, challenge the status quo and take control of their own destiny. It starts from the concrete problems of immediate concern, and is knowledge directed towards reversing the cycles of fatality and passivity and moving toward empowerment. (Graham, Walton and Ward 2005, p. 183)

Freire's work inspired experimentation and renewal within the work of many theological educators – myself included, as I participated with colleagues in the development of a community-based programme of ministerial training in a deprived part of Manchester. It was both moving and challenging to engage with the experiences of students, as they wrestled with social problems and sought to preach to and care for those most affected by those problems. Often our reflective and storytelling sessions were unbearably poignant – both disturbing and renewing.

Rebecca Chopp (1995) brought feminist perspectives into dialogue with liberation theology in her investigation of theological education practices in the United States. The theological training communities she encountered were no longer composed of young, white, heterosexual men with conventional academic training. They were now constituted of people from diverse backgrounds and included a growing number of women. These new theological inquirers were often somewhat alienated from the authoritative traditions they were studying. She noted that narrative practices (focused storytelling using a range of resources) were the ones that seemed most able to spark intellectual engagement, generate theological competencies and evidence the social relevance of Christian believing. As these students engaged in practices of theological 'storytelling' they were empowered in their wider learning and developed a more critical, but also more appreciative, understanding of the legacy of faith.

The impact of such emancipatory approaches to education has been consolidated within theological education through an increased interest in the processes through which adults learn. David Kolb (1984), for example, presented learning as a reflective journey that begins with concrete experience and moves in a cyclical way[3] through observation and reflection to revised practice. The work of Donald Schön, who focused upon the way professional practitioners respond to challenges in their working lives, has also made a very considerable impact upon the curriculum as his advocacy of reflective practice has been enthusiastically embraced.

Schön spent more than 20 years researching the relationship between professional identity and the tasks professionals performed. He observed that what characterizes professional life is the multiplicity and variety of roles professionals are called upon to play. He also identified that many professionals felt there was a chasm between the initial academic training they had received and the very messy realities of their working lives. Schön described this as a gap between the high ground of theory and the swampy lowlands of practice. In order to overcome this gap, it was necessary to foster the reflective abilities of practitioners to learn in and through their own active engagement with the real challenges they encountered on an everyday basis. Interestingly in the context of this book, Schön viewed the learning processes that take place in reflective practice as one of risk taking, adventure and artistry. We fashion knowledge creatively when faced by the challenge of the unknown, and, following the poet Coleridge, he argued that the 'willing suspension of disbelief' is a necessary part of the process of opening ourselves up to new possibilities and ways of thinking/acting (in Schön 1983, p. 296). As Gillie Bolton puts this, 'uncertainty or lack of knowledge is an educative space for insight, intuition and credulity' (2005, p. 33).

Writing reflective accounts of pastoral practice according to Schön's frame should thus be an imaginative and creative process facilitating radical thinking and new forms of acting. Unfortunately, however, as frequently happens when new ideas become orthodoxy, the elements of Schön's vision for reflective practice that could be easily assimilated

---

3 Readers are likely to be familiar with similar models derived from liberation theology. The 'pastoral cycle' and the 'hermeneutical circle' are frequently used methods of theological reflection (see Graham, Walton and Ward 2005, pp. 188–9).

are now frequently used rather mechanically and formulaically. The requirement to 'become reflective' can often mean 'become reflective in the way we desire you to be' rather than 'dare to contemplate doing things differently'.

Writing with Theological Intent

Methods of Reflection

In the previous section I attempted to show how the turn to reflective writing within theology can be seen as part of a larger cultural, epistemological and pedagogical shift. One that has helpfully served to remind us that reflection upon human experience has always been a significant ingredient in the theological mix. Various models have been proposed for understanding the role that our experience plays alongside Scripture, tradition and reason in the generation of theological thinking. In *Theological Reflection: Methods* (2005) I worked with my friends Elaine Graham and Frances Ward to identify and explain some of these. We named seven major trajectories currently observable in theological reflection. These are briefly summarized below:

- *Writing the Living Human Document*: God is experienced in intimate personal communion speaking through interiority. The records of journalling, autobiography and therapeutic accounts of the self become vehicles for theological discovery.
- *Constructive Narrative Theology*: The narratives that form the foundational traditions of faith are woven together with the stories that believers tell of encounters with God in their own lives. These vividly constructed, interwoven narratives tell of experiences that have become revelatory for us, and link them back to the Christian tradition.
- *Canonical Narrative Theology*: Believers seek to place their own stories within the framework of the story the Church tells about Jesus in order to discover and perform their own parts in this great drama.
- *Corporate Theological Reflection*: The community generates corporate narratives in the course of life together that function to describe the community to itself and articulate its sense of purpose and mission. Theological reflection identifies and interprets these shared stories.

- *Critical Correlation*: Theological reflection emerges out of a conversation (or correlation) between Christian revelation and human experience expressed through contemporary culture. The products of culture (including the arts and sciences as well as popular modes of expression) are seen as having revelatory potential alongside the faith tradition. The theology emerges out of the interaction between them.
- *The Praxis Method*: The emphasis here is on the importance of practice as a source of theological understanding, and this model proposes processes of action-and-reflection (or praxis) as a mode of Christian obedience in an unjust world.
- *Local Theology*: The emphasis of this method is upon the challenge to express the gospel in the context of cultural, historical, geographical and ethnic difference. It must be re-imagined and re-expressed in the vernacular forms of local 'languages'.

(Adapted from Graham, Walton and Ward 2005, pp. 13–14)

Theoretically at least, these seven models of theological reflection could be expressed through the writing practices that have been traditionally used in an academic setting. That is, theological accounts could be written analytically, with a claim to objectivity, and constructed in the abstract and impersonal styles that are still prevalent within some forms of theological discourse. Stories do sometimes have their claws removed in this way so that they appear tame and docile.

Had I but space enough and time, it would be fun at this point to identify some of the submerged myths and metaphors that are present in even the most abstract forms of analytic reasoning (see Le Doeuff 2002 and Anderson 1998) and present a case that no form of reflection is ever actually perfectly story-sterile. But this would be a diversion. For in the case of the methods of theological reflection outlined above, those who use them are very actively encouraged to become storytellers and story-hearers in order to fulfil their theological task. For some this is a liberating challenge. For others constructing a story on paper is something they have avoided since primary school and seems to be achievable only with childish ineptitude. Fortunately, once the process is embarked upon 'childish' quickly becomes 'child-like', and many practitioners find themselves rediscovering the joy of creative processes that appear to be integrally part of our human constitution.

The Elements of a Story

In a fascinating account of children's linguistic development Julia Gillen (2006) explores how at the very start of language acquisition art, play, jokes, plotting and narrating exist alongside the desire to communicate – and are integral to this. I particularly enjoyed reading extracts from transcripts of children talking to themselves as they played with toys or murmured alone in bed at night. In one of these transcripts two-year-old Emily tells the same story repeatedly, as she reflects on an unusual experience. The narrative she speaks describes how she fell asleep at a friend's house and was awakened by her mother and brought home. What is particularly touching is the way this little child, reflecting alone at night, hones and shapes her story. Through the retelling it increases in sophistication and in rhythmic resonance, events become sequentially ordered, time and tense are introduced, and causality is inferred. Emily takes on the role of an active narrator, and her mother and herself become actors in a tiny drama. It is very small but beautifully formed, and it gives Emily the satisfaction of agency, control, location and comfort.

It is my hope that this book will be of use to students and practitioners from a wide range of backgrounds, who face very different challenges. Some will be confronting the task of producing apparently simple accounts of pastoral encounters, often stripped back to the bare bones of pastoral conversations recalled 'verbatim'. Others will be required to reflect on 'critical incidents', and the presupposition is often that the report of an incident will be made with determined brevity, clarity and objectivity. However, it is important to be aware that even in these instances, as Emily's case reveals, an artful story is being told. We do not simply recall. We cannot help but construct accounts that are story-shaped. Furthermore, no one is able to present the fullness of an incident or conversation textually. So in the accounts we present, much is excluded. As our accounts are never innocent, what questions should the reflector ask about their storytelling? These might include:

- How do I position myself as narrator in this text?
- How have I framed the action (by choosing a start and end point, including contextual details, abstracting a particular interaction from a stream of life)?
- How have I developed characters through ways of presenting speech and strategically including aspects of background information?
- What is the plot here?

- How have I made an 'ending'?
- What values and beliefs are implicit in my storytelling?
- WHAT HAVE I LEFT OUT? This may be the most important question!

Addressing these basic issues is a mark of reflexivity in theological reflection. Even before verbatims and critical incidents are discussed or presented, we can discover a great deal through attending to them. However, many theological writers want to progress far beyond the stage of constructing a basic account for group analysis or supervision. In this case, the challenge becomes to actively use the elements of storytelling to create narratives that are rich, engaging and disclosive of faith. It is no longer the case that we are simply recognizing the classic elements of narration within our text; it is rather that we are purposefully occupying a particular narrative space and assuming responsibility for characterization, plotting and value attribution. In this case, rather different questions arise. Some of these may be:

- What sort of narrator am I? Do I assume omniscience or am I a 'blind guide'? Am I a coherent self or do I display splits and fractures in my identity? Is my reflexivity made explicit or do I display it implicitly through evolving story lines? Is my 'voice' consistent throughout or does it serve the narration to write with different voices in order to thicken the account?
- What decisions have I made about the frame of my story? Do I choose particular starting and end points to control the narration, and what would happen if these were challenged through including memory and anticipation in the text?
- Is my plot both interesting and convincing? Does it twist and thicken? Does it engage with the mysterious and the unexpected?
- Am I giving too much information because I want to remain in control of interpretation rather than allowing the reader a creative role?
- Have I sought closure in my story rather than allowing it to remain a disturbingly open-ended creation?
- How do I display the characters in this story? What tokens of identity do I give them? Do I offer explicit judgements – such as 'Bill was a kind man', for example? Or do I describe characters acting in particular ways? What is the role of physical description in character development? Am I implicitly assigning some characters to minor roles, and why?

- In what ways should my beliefs and values structure this storytelling? Am I seeking to draw out a moral or to challenge my own preconceptions? Am I telling a story that affirms what I believe to be true, or in order to celebrate a new insight or perception? How do I engage with elements of my faith tradition that I regard as authoritative without closing down interpretative potential? What is the role of metaphor, image or symbol in highlighting the sacred elements in this story?
- WHAT HAVE I LEFT OUT? This still may be the most important question!

As will be evident, once these questions come to structure our writing we are simultaneously moving both towards a greater understanding of the meaning in the story being told, and further away from a 'factual' account. Gillie Bolton describes this as a 'creative leap' that both widens and deepens perspective:

> The professional arena can be opened up to observation and reflections through the lens of artistic scrutiny . . . perspectives will be artistically and creatively enhanced . . . Artistic processes such as writing can . . . enable a harnessing of, for example, material such as memories which we did not know we remember, and greater access into the possible thoughts and experiences of others. The perspectival nature of such writing is acknowledged . . . and the many skills they use are those of literature. (2005, p. 11)

Poetics and Theology

What Bolton describes as a creative leap into the arms of literature will undoubtedly be seen by some as a fall from the grace of truth into the misty murk of imagination. To be clear, neither Bolton nor I are suggesting that in reflective writing about experience authors should deliberately distort or deceive. What I am arguing, however, is that narrative technique is unavoidable, and that it is better to consciously acknowledge this rather than naïvely assume it is not important. Furthermore, reflective accounts can be deeply enhanced through what Bolton names as artistry and I would call poetics.

Poetics is the term used to refer to those devices through which authors create their texts. We have already named some of these in relation to significant aspects of storytelling: narration, characterization and plot. However, there are other (more ghostly) elements to consider, such as genre, form, symbol and metaphor.

I remember the first time I understood that it was possible to preach in different registers. Up till then, my sermons had all been constructed as exhortations with increasingly lengthy illustrations. They had been cast in 'everyday' language. And then one day I stood up in the pulpit and dramatically called upon my 'sisters and brothers' to 'Listen!'. I used archaic speech forms and biblical imagery to deliver a visionary message with no apology and no explanation. The work was deeply rhetorical and surprisingly effective. At that point, I must admit, I had no theories to explain what I was doing but had somehow grasped that certain messages require certain modes of expression. They function well within them and are inexpressible without them.

If we are constructing a reflective account, it is important to consider what genre it should be cast in. What type of narrative is it? Most frequently we will employ the familiar conventions of autobiographical 'non-fiction', and these are the ones that are focused upon within this book. But is important to realize that this is as constructed a mode of expression as fantasy fiction. Non-fiction is also 'fictive', and all storytelling employs literary genres. At times we will wish to consciously draw upon these powerful traditions to frame our experience as, for example, a 'quest story' in which the dramatic action leads to a discovery (most PhDs are thinly disguised quest narratives and none the worse for that). We may wish to deliberately employ mythological or parabolic frameworks to add extra weight to our work. Fable, fairy tale and folklore carry homely and familiar associations that can be artfully exploited, and comedy and satire are hugely effective – if rather underused in theological reflection. When we choose a particular genre to express our own experiences, we are activating resonances from other stories that already carry deep associations for our readers. It is very helpful to allow echoes from differing genres to enter otherwise 'realistic' texts. This literary device will heighten intensity at points in the story and indicate to readers that they are being called upon to make a different kind of interpretative response.

Form is very closely related to genre. I use the term here to refer to the 'physical' form of the writing; the heartbeat and contours of a textual body – its flesh. Reflective writing can be constructed as a poem with rhythms and rhymes or stamped by the cadences of liturgical memory – as we believe many passages in the Bible to have been constructed. In such cases embodied associations will certainly be added to cognitive ones as we detect deep shapes and musicality in the text. As we shall discuss later in this book, reflective writers are increasingly being challenged to view their texts as performative – whether they are articulated in public or not. A performative text is dramatic. It stages a narrative, and one of the ways it does so is by heightening language for the sake of impact – just as happens in a theatrical performance.

It might be assumed that 'heightened language' carries us beyond the everyday and places us on some more exalted plane. When we seek to express holy things, we might also seek to escape the mundane world and reach for symbols to express what it is not possible to talk about directly. However, as we discover in reading great literature, the most powerful symbols are those taken from daily life. In reflective theological writing this is where our best resources lie. Instead of reaching for ethereal terms, it is helpful to employ concrete nouns and simple words that have a tough, resisting, gritty tangibility to them. Robert Alter (2000) and David Norton (2000) are among the many literary scholars who have explored the ways in which biblical prose has been so enduring and effective a medium of expression. They conclude that it is so, partly at least, because the words through which theological meaning is conveyed refer us back to the common stuff of life – blood, heart, flesh, bone, seed, fruit, rock, bread, wine. Such words are powerful because they function to link the material world to the symbolic realm. That is to say, in their constant everyday use they have gathered to themselves a whole range of associations and these are deep-wired into our responsive systems. As such they are able to assume a sacramental function.

So symbolic language does not need to be esoteric or exotic to be powerful. It may be best drawn from the common currency of a culture. It is effective, because it recalls to us deep and half-acknowledged understandings that appear fundamental. Something rather different happens in metaphor, however. We should be startled by metaphoric language.

A metaphor brings together two different and distinct things in an unusual and creative combination to provoke thought and enable us to see the world differently. Some literary theorists believe that the capability to construct metaphors is actually how we human beings invent and change our world. Paul Ricoeur, for example, states that 'metaphor shatters not only the previous structures of our language but also the previous structures of what we call reality' (Ricoeur in Valdès 1991, p. 85). This is particularly important in theological reflection. Theology is a deeply metaphoric discourse; when we speak about God we have to reach for impossible conjunctions in language: 'The word was made flesh and dwelt among us' (John 1.14) is a metaphoric declaration of a strange meeting. Some metaphors, like this one, are so profoundly important that their resonance endures. They have changed our way of thinking fundamentally. However, most metaphors are apt to become stale through convention. They become 'dead', because they have lost their power to transmit the shock of an encounter with otherness. Describing Christ as a lamb should, but does not, raise an eyebrow, which is probably why T. S. Eliot (1974 [1920], p. 39), following William Blake, found it necessary to employ the metaphor of Christ as a devouring tiger in his poem 'Gerontion'. Many theologians now understand that one of the most important tasks in their work is to find new metaphors to facilitate divine encounters. As theologians are not routinely celebrated for their poetic creativity, these new discoveries are often made with the aid of literature – that is, literary works are employed in theological contexts. However, new metaphors can also be forged through reflective writing that employs literary conventions – the sort of work this book seeks to nourish and provoke.

This has been a long section and has covered a considerable amount of ground. There are many good and helpful books on creative and life writing that will offer further help and guidance on the terms and processes I have highlighted here. It is my hope that reading the reflective chapters in this text will also help to demonstrate how poetics is implicated in reflective writing. However, I should like to stress that writing is both craft and art. There are techniques, 'tricks of the trade', that are very helpful to reflective writers of all kinds. The following list should be printed out and stuck on your fridge or above your mirror when you are attempting a reflective writing task:

- Show, don't tell. It is always more effective to invite the reader to 'see' a situation than explain it to them.
- Less is more. Cut away what is not needed. Excess is never helpful.
- Signpost your path. Allow the reader to find their own way through a narrative, but provide them with the way-markers they need to do so.
- Do not fear the personal or the particular. These are your gift to your reader. They will have had intense experiences of their own that will enable them to enter into yours.
- Small is beautiful. It really is possible to see a world in a grain of sand – although it may take a little practice!

- Always revise, rewrite, revise. And then do so again.
- Rules are made to be broken.

Being Vulnerable and Caring for Others

The Self in the Text

One of the most common worries that people have when embarking on a process of reflective writing is that in displaying themselves 'on the page' they will be opening up areas of their lives that are usually, and appropriately, regarded as private. At best, they fear this might be self-indulgent; at worst, they worry it may be dangerous. There are real causes for concern, if deeply painful experiences are being expressed without any of the safeguards that usually prevail in a therapeutic setting.

I was caught off balance recently when a highly creative doctoral student, intending to construct their PhD using autoethnographic techniques, asked me if there were any ethical guidelines about the way such a text should be read. The placing of ethical responsibility upon the reader in this way was an issue I had not really considered previously – and the challenge is worth contemplating. However, the hard facts are that readers do make judgements, they will form an image about a writer from what they read; and when we write from experience, we are giving unprecedented access to our personal worlds.

However, we are not required to abandon all protective mechanisms in order to become reflective writers. There are safeguards. Some of these come from generally accepted forms of professional ethics. In an educational context, where writing from experience is required as part of training, teachers should be, and usually are, aware of the need for confidentiality, personal boundaries and appropriate care. The same applies to pastoral supervision and to the facilitation of reflective groups in which experience is shared. If you are uncertain at all about what boundaries prevail in your personal context, it is important to check these out for yourself. But it is also important to take responsibility for your own writing practice.

Reflective writing does not function like a game of 'Truth or Dare' in which participants are invited to tell all or pay a terrible forfeit. No one wants you to spill your soul onto the page. This is not conducive to good writing or good reflection. Our culture, as I have already argued, is one in which we are encouraged to construct an 'authentic self'. However, it quite liberating to realize that there is no authentic self on the page. There is only the self that you are presenting through your words. You are in control of this situation. The first duty of ethical responsibility is self-care, and this involves self-control. It is important to cultivate the wisdom of restraint.

I would always urge caution in deciding what you wish to address through your writing. As we are increasingly aware through our use of the internet, it is impossible to take back something once it has entered the public sphere. This being the case, we must be as confident as we can be in all forms of communication that we can live with what we have expressed. There is a great deal of difference between writing something for personal benefit in a diary or spiritual journal and the act of sending it out into the world. I have published extensively over the years on the experience of infertility. However, I was not able to do so in the first few years of this experience. It was too painful, and my feelings about it were too strong and chaotic. It was only when I had achieved some kind of perspective that I was ready to begin communicating. Having achieved this 'distance' I found that the writing process did not make me feel vulnerable or miserable – it was actually empowering. While I have been able to draw deeply upon the journals and records that I kept 'at the time' (throughout my years of diagnosis and fertility treatment), I am so glad that I delayed publication until the moment was right.

Even if the stakes are not very high, self-expression always requires a certain amount of courage. But there may be times when we take brave decisions to share experiences that are painful to us, because their telling may be of benefit to others. Even in these cases there are ways of lessening the risks to ourselves. Some forms of writing are more disclosive than others. We don't need to go into every painful aspect of an experience in order to communicate powerfully about what it has entailed. There are always blanks and absences in writing. This is acceptable. As I wrote earlier, the decision about what we leave out can be the most important one of all in the construction of a narrative.

Other People's Stories

The traditions that guide reflective writing in theology come to us through a number of interdisciplinary encounters. We have been deeply influenced by writing practices in the social sciences and in literature, as well as through traditions that can be identified as distinctly theological in origin.

Within the social sciences there is an acute awareness of the need to make ethical judgements when writing about other people. There are strong conventions about informed consent and the right not to participate in research. The requirement to ensure confidentiality and anonymity is emphasized, as is the general prohibition on disseminating work that could unduly affect the wellbeing or damage the reputation of people identifiable within the text. All research covering vulnerable groups (such as the sick, the bereaved, children or people in mental distress) is subjected to high levels of ethical scrutiny before it can take place.

Theological writers have much to learn from absorbing these general protocols along with the spirit of respectful care that lies behind them. In an educational setting gaining ethical consent is a mandatory part of any research process that involves human subjects, and writers whose primary focus is on their own experience are not exempted from customary ethical procedures. As Chang writes,

> if your focus lies upon yourself, you may feel that ethical issues involving human subjects do not apply . . . This assumption is incorrect. Whichever format you may take, you still need to keep in mind that other people are always present in self-narratives, either as active participants in the story or as associates in the background. (2008, p. 68)

These are challenging words and should be taken very seriously. However, those engaged in theological reflection are often keen to explore precisely those difficult and challenging areas that many social researchers consider to be off limits. Pastoral encounters are frequently with vulnerable people experiencing distress and trauma, but it remains important that we find ways to write about these in order to improve our practice and generate understanding while preserving the safety of all those involved. This is a very difficult task, particularly because as reflective writers we are often motivated by a strong desire to testify to the truth as we see it.

Beyond the social sciences there has been a recent growth in interest in the ethics of literary and biographical writing (e.g. Eakin 2004), but it remains the case that creative writers frequently insist on their right, or indeed their unavoidable duty, to tell their stories – despite the threat this poses to others. It could be argued that obligations exist, not only to the 'characters' in the text, but to ourselves 'as authors' and also to readers who may benefit in many ways from the sharing of a story. Reflecting upon her own autobiographical work, Nancy K. Miller writes:

> It is not my wish to do harm, but I am forced to acknowledge that I may well cause pain – or embarrassment to others – if I also believe, as I do, in my right to tell my story. I can engage to make the memoir as honest as I can . . . but by the rules – or, rather, the realities – of

the genre, I can't promise not to impinge on the lives of others in the process. (2004, p. 157)

There may seem to be irresolvable tensions here. Certainly, there are some painful decisions to be made. Perhaps this is one of those occasions when it is appropriate to turn to our own religious traditions for guidance. There is a special quality to the spiritual writing that endures, which comes not from confidence in its own legitimacy but from its sense of prayerful self-examination. To adapt Paul's great hymn in 1 Corinthians 13, our theological writing should never be haughty or proud. It should be patient, believing, hopeful and kind, braving and bearing all things. But this does not mean that it should be never be angry or outspoken. It should rightly seek justice and thirst for truth. One of the best translations of these principles into an ethics of writing that I have come across is in the words of David Gardner, who explores the moral function of literature as it:

> clarifies life, establishes models for human action, casts nets towards the future, carefully judges our right and wrong directions, celebrates and mourns. It does not rant. It does not sneer or giggle in the face of death, it invents prayers and weapons. It designs visions worth trying to make fact. (quoted in Frank 2004, p. 182).

Autoethnography, Journalling and Life Writing

This introductory chapter has been ambitious in its scope. We have travelled from epistemology to ethics and noted many other significant matters in between. I have been at pains to set out signposts for future exploration but also to make clear that in the business of reflective writing much remains ambiguous, untidy and creatively muddled. In this last section I introduce the three categories in which my own reflective writing is presented in this book: autoethnography, journalling and life writing. These categories represent differing ways of writing, but it is only in a heuristic sense that they can be separated out as distinct methods. They overlap and interact at very many points. Nevertheless, it is useful to distinguish between them as each has particular emphases and can be used to serve different purposes:

- *Autoethnography is a way of using personal experience to investigate a particular issue or concern that has wider cultural or religious significance.* The experience here acts as a lens that allows us to see and interrogate aspects of the concern in question that might be missed in a more abstract discussion of ethics or values. The method comes to us from the disciplines of social research, where it has been growing in significance in recent years. It is particularly effective in reflective theological writing because it allows us to look with fresh eyes at familiar beliefs and practices.

- *Journalling is a way of using experience that allows us to see changes taking place over time.* Integral to the structure of journal writing are processes of recall and reflection that allow the gradual incorporation of ideas and events into a personal journey. Because reflective writing in journal form is in motion through time, it is fluid, provisional and exploratory. It is valued in spiritual reflection because it intimately records how we wrestle with challenges in the life of faith and also enables us to register the deepening of commitment and understanding.
- *Life writing is a way of reflecting upon how experience shapes identity.* The key challenge of this method of writing is to understand how we became who we are. What experiences in life have contributed to forming aspects of our personality and worldviews? In theological terms life writing opens another challenge. Reflection upon own identity inevitably leads us to think about how we have come to 'know' God. It also helps us to address questions of gifts and calling as well as to seek healing and reconciliation.

These three forms of writing are also the ones that you are most likely to encounter in a training context. *Autoethnography* is becoming an increasingly important form of writing at masters and doctoral level when a researcher seeks to address an issue of importance that has emerged for them out of personal experience. *Journalling* is a very common method in professional education and is especially suitable for recording stages of a learning process. *Life writing* is often employed in formative contexts where reflection is needed on the next stage of a vocational journey.

Understanding why you have been asked to use one of these forms may itself help you decide how you should begin to write. There are also specific introductory chapters relating to each one at the start of the respective parts of this book dedicated to the three categories. It is likely that you will respond more positively to one particular method than the others, but they are all inviting and capacious – capable of carrying a great deal of theological weight within a rather slender structure. It is my hope that you will feel invited to try them all out for yourself.

The final Part of the book is rather different from the others. In this I do not present a method of writing but begin to reflect in greater depth upon the relationship between theology, practice and poetics in public testimony, pastoral care and everyday life. Although forms of life writing are increasingly used in theological reflection, we are only at the beginning of a process of reflecting critically upon our own efforts in this field. There is a very long way to go! This book is a small step forward on that journey.

PART I

Autoethnography

I

Approaching Autoethnography

What is Autoethnography?

Autoethnography can be defined as 'an approach to research and writing that seeks to describe and systematically analyse (*graphy*) personal experience (*auto*) in order to understand cultural experience (*ethno*)' (Ellis, Adams and Bochner 2011). The emphasis upon both 'analysis' and 'cultural experience' places autoethnography alongside other forms of social research that seek to observe and interpret cultural life.

The echoing of the word 'ethnography' within the term is an important marker of its meaning. Ethnography is the multi-layered study of cultural forms as they exist in everyday contexts. Its use links the autoethnographic project back to traditions of social investigation developed by pioneering anthropologists such as Franz Boas (1858–1942) and Bronislaw Malinowski (1884–1942). They developed traditions of inquiry based upon acute observational and interpretative skills in order to categorize and represent the 'ways of life' they encountered in their early ethnographic studies. A key part of this approach to research has always been the self-conscious use of the self as research instrument – indeed the acute, observing self is the guarantor of the authenticity of data. However, autoethnography takes this process a good deal further. Instead of the researcher being a disciplined observer of social processes 'out there', the project is brought much closer to home. The focus in autoethnography is upon the analysis and communication of those experiences that have shaped the researcher. Personal experience becomes a data source for 'a critically reflexive methodology . . . [that] provides a framework to critically reflect upon the ways in which our personal lives intersect, collide and commune with others in the body politic' (Spry 2011, p. 54).

This recognition of the significance of particular, located and embodied experience has been made possible by the postmodern reflexive turn in epistemology. It is critically linked to liberative movements such as feminism, postcolonialism and queer theory, which have all emphasized the

3

importance of the standpoint from which we view the world (see previous chapter). Although autoethnography has taken a defined shape only within the past 20 years, it has been enthusiastically embraced by an emerging generation of researchers who are keen to write themselves 'into a deeper critical understanding . . . of the ways in which our lives intersect with larger sociocultural pains and privileges' (Spry 2011, p. 51). One reason why it has proved so attractive is that it has sought to communicate these 'pains and privileges' in strong, evocative ways that provoke empathetic responses. In so doing it has breached many of the boundaries between art and the social sciences and generated controversy and critique (see, for example, Denzin 2006). Although it is such a young movement, it is already possible to identify divergent streams within it that represent different interpretations of the 'claims to truth' made in autoethnographical texts (see Ellis, Adams and Bochner 2011). I have chosen to explore three of the main currents of contemporary autoethnographic research that have particular relevance to the reflective theological researcher.

Forms of Autoethnography

Telling Evocative Stories

This is the vision for autoethnography that is powerfully articulated in the work of two of its most well-known advocates: Caroline Ellis and Art Bochner. It was their essay in the second edition of the Sage Handbook of Qualitative Research entitled *Collecting and Interpreting Qualitative Materials* (Ellis and Bochner 2003) that heralded the emergence of autoethnography onto the world stage. In this early 'manifesto' they state quite clearly that the aim of autoethnography is to provoke feeling in order to generate an empathetic response to:

> a self or some aspect of a life lived in a cultural context. In personal narrative texts authors become 'I', readers become 'you,'. . . [and] take more active roles as they are invited into the author's world [and e]voked to a feeling level about the events described . . .The goal is to write meaningfully and evocatively about things that matter and may make a difference . . . and to write from an ethic of care and concern. (Ellis and Bochner 2003, p. 213)

It is important to note that an emphasis still remains upon the interpretation of 'cultural context'. Indeed, Ellis and Bochner show a particular interest in those areas of social life that are rarely publicly narrated or

4

addressed. But this cultural analysis is made possible through recounting experiences of personal transformation,

> 'epiphanies' – remembered moments perceived to have significantly impacted the trajectory of a person's life ... times of existential crises that forced a person to attend to and analyze lived experience ... and events after which life does not seem quite the same. (Ellis, Adams and Bochner 2011)

The hope is that the constructing narratives of such life-changing events (including, for example, bullying, bereavement, work challenges, consciousness of ethnic identity, sexual practice, abuse, childbirth, abortion, cancer treatment) will enable deeper perceptions to emerge. As generating these changed understandings has now become a major research goal, considerable attention has to be paid to constructing the autoethnographic text. It must be carefully crafted and is often written in narrative form, employing a variety of literary techniques to move hearts and change minds. 'Autoethnography wants the reader to care, to feel, to empathize and to do something, to act' (Ellis and Bochner 2006, p. 433).

This is not to say that the experiences being recounted and the events surrounding them have no significance beyond their emotive power. I think it is very interesting that, despite her frequent affirmations of the importance of literary style, Ellis is a very 'realistic', no-nonsense sort of writer who wants to make very clear that people's actions and life choices take place within specific social contexts. It is, rather, that there is a frank acknowledgement of the importance of the writing process to research. Questions of the truth and reliability of an autoethnographic text are thus intimately bundled together with issues of style and representation. Those who advocate evocative autoethnography would argue that this has in fact always been the case even in traditional forms of ethnographic research. Ultimately, we are always drawn back to questions concerning our trust in a narrator and our response to the narrator's voice.

I hope it will be clear that this form of autoethnography has a great deal to offer the reflective theological writer. Very often we will seek to speak out of epiphanic moments of transformation. Frequently these epiphanies will be linked to embodied experiences that are rarely voiced in institutional religious contexts but nevertheless carry great significance for us. Evocative autoethnographic writing can also convey the complexity and ambiguity of our religious selves. Schooled in traditions of Bible reading, preaching and liturgy, we are already imbued with a sense of the purpose and power of evocative language forms. The challenge is to use these anew in expressing accounts of everyday selves and contemporary spiritual life.

Analytic Autoethnography

While many autoethnographers are pursuing paths that take their work further and further away from the traditional forms of social investigation, there are others who believe that the pendulum has now swung too far in the direction of artistic creativity and emotional expression. These critics acknowledge that autoethnography makes a lively, timely and significant contribution to qualitative research. However, they wish to harness its energies to serve a more conventional research agenda – namely the desire to investigate and theorize about the social world.

This view was powerfully expressed in an influential article by Leon Anderson entitled 'Analytic Autoethnography' (2006). Anderson stated that he wished to celebrate 'the value of autoethnographic research within the analytic ethnographic paradigm' (2006, p. 374). It was his belief that the standard ethnographic methods involving journal keeping and note taking have been self-reflexive from their beginnings. Furthermore, insider perspectives have long been recognized and valued within dominant research traditions, provided that the normal critical assessment is made of these and that personal experience is not seen as the guarantor of truth. The position he advocates is that autoethnography be recognized as making a valuable contribution, within proper limits and among other methods, to the processes through which we seek to accumulate data and analyse the world.

This approach might seem modest and sensible. However, Anderson is operating out of what is termed a 'realist paradigm'. He seeks to use autoethnographic material alongside other empirical data 'to gain insight into some broader set of social phenomena than those provided by the data themselves' (2006, p. 387). The processes of generalization, abstraction and theory building that constitute the analytic approach he espouses are anathema to some autoethnographers. They insist on retaining the focus upon particularity and see all social theories as constructed narratives masquerading as factual accounts.

I do not think it is necessary for the reflective theological writer to take up arms in this particular battle. Some of us will tend towards realist epistemologies, and indeed realist theologies, others of us will see the world as constructed and understand our theologies as similarly shaped by human hands. However, this does not mean that these worldviews should never communicate or that we should not see that there are social and political imperatives that require us at times to proceed in one way rather than another. I personally have supervised several doctoral theses in which autoethnography has been effectively combined with other forms of data generation that claim empirical credentials. Often this is the *only* way that the research would have been judged useful and trustworthy in the context it was intended to influence. I was happy to share in this research work despite the fact that I am personally suspicious of realist paradigms.

This may seem like a hopelessly pragmatic approach. However, perhaps the theologian in the world of social research can afford the luxury of not playing by the rules. Our theistic commitments mean any position we subscribe to is likely to be viewed as anomalous within the academic guild. Analytic discourses can be useful instruments for those seeking to promote political changes in the Church and society at large. Nor do I think that we should fear the contamination of theory – although we can view it in various ways ranging from analytic truth to social mythology. I am perfectly happy to append my autoethnographic reflections to articles that are otherwise written in theoretical terms – and have included an example of such practice in this book. In short, I think the reflective theological writer should understand what is at stake in debates between evocative and analytic autoethnographers but not feel the need to be unduly restricted by these considerations in terms of their own writing practices.

Performance Autoethnography

The last form of autoethnography discussed here is 'performance auto-ethnography'. The term 'performance' is not used to imply it takes place in a theatre (although it may do so), but rather that speaking from experience can be a staged act, an intervention, a public and political display. It may be a display that takes place textually or in an educational context. However, even in such cases, its impact is intended to extend beyond the academic environment.

The understanding behind performance ethnography is that the social world is a *performed* world in which people *act out* their lives in accordance with the 'big scripts' of race, economics, gender and so on. However, within the performance of personal lives there is always the chance to improvise, invent and change – or simply forget your lines and thus make involuntary adaptations. This is why the insertion of personal testimony into the social arena is so important. It challenges the idea that there is just one way to be, just one form of the 'good life', and insists that experience is infinitely varied, particular and creative. As Spry writes, 'Performative autoethnography is designed to offer stories alternative to normative, taken for granted assumptions that clog our understanding about the diversity of experience and the systems of power that hold "a single story" in place' (2011, p. 56).

While there is a good deal of common ground between evocative ethnography and performance ethnography, it is the political commitment of the latter approach that is particularly significant. Performances are not simply retellings of personal narratives. Performance autoethnography also mimes dominant narratives in order to undermine them. 'Performers' use many different voices and often their 'texts' are collages (including visual and auditory elements) or bricolages combined of various resources (from childhood memories, letters, extracts from news items, school books, magazines, etc.). These productions may lack the narrative coherence of evocative stories. However, this is a strategic move. The intention is to fracture our understanding of how knowledge works and how performances are enacted.

One of the most influential advocates of performance autoethnography, Norman Denzin, is unashamedly political in his vision for this work. He describes it as 'a way of writing, hearing and listening . . . a return to narrative as a political act . . . It uses the words and stories people tell to imagine new worlds' (2003a, p. 105). However, although Denzin is certainly a militant writer, he is deeply sympathetic to spirituality. He credits liberation theology as one of the sources that have contributed to the participatory politics of resistance that inspires his work. He quotes the author Annie Dillard approvingly in relation to the mysterious and often tragic relation of creation to its creator (2003a, p. 51). He insists that performance autoethnography must be a holistic process that attends to all aspects of life including our relations with the sacred.

> A respectful, radical performance pedagogy must honor these views of spirituality. It works to construct a vision of the person, ecology, and the environment that is compatible with these principles. This pedagogy demands a politics of hope, of loving, of caring nonviolence grounded in inclusive moral and spiritual terms. (2003b, p. 262)

There is a growing interest in this radical form of autoethnography within theological circles. It is one that allows a diversity of voices within a text and insists that the text must be publicly orientated – its place and work is in the world. For the theological reflector this approach encourages us to think beyond the personal and therapeutic aspects of autoethnography and embrace its prophetic and disclosive potential. It also encourages us to see our sacred places as theatres in which worship and ritual may be 'performed' as political acts.

Using Autoethnography

I have argued that autoethnographic writing, in all its forms, is a very creative resource for theological reflection. The term might sound technical but the practice of telling stories that shed light on wider issues or move the reader to empathetic understanding of social questions is one that closely resembles very familiar ways of finding theological meaning in everyday events. Sermons in particular are often constructed in this manner – as we shall explore in the following chapter.

An attention to ethical procedures, how we represent 'the other', is highlighted within autoethnography, and this is particularly important as we seek to bring our stories into public worlds. The method encourages exploration and innovation, and autoethnographic writing is frequently iconoclastic and 'in your face'. It is not a bad thing for theological reflectors to embrace the boldness of this approach in their work. It helps us consider the modes of self-censorship under which we normally construct our stories – and challenges us to transgress many self-imposed restrictions.

I conclude this chapter by borrowing from Denzin's reflections on what constitutes good autoethnographical writing and adapting them for our purposes. This writing should:

- unsettle, criticize and challenge taken-for-granted meanings and socially scripted performances;
- invite ethical and spiritual dialogue while clarifying its own moral positions;
- create resistance and offer utopian visions about how things can be different;
- care and be kind;
- show not tell – using the rule that less is more;
- be good enough to trust: show interpretative sufficiency and representational adequacy, and aspire to authenticity;
- present political, workable, collective and committed viewpoints – which provoke a response!

(Adapted from Denzin 2003a, pp. 123–4)

2

Calls to Preach

In this chapter I use autoethnographic techniques to explore the nature of preaching and in particular the understanding of preaching as a vocational act. This is a work of performance autoethnography and was originally written, like a sermon, to be heard rather than read. As such, it is a highly rhetorical and metaphoric piece employing many of the idiomatic techniques of the preacher in an autoethnographic work.

Mistaken Vocation

'In our church preaching is not a job, it's a calling,' said my minister – kindly. He was trying to be helpful. I had made a mistake in framing my request to be trained as a preacher in terms of willingness to study and pass exams. It turns out that I should first have mentioned the irresistible divine compulsion that was forcing me to enter the pulpit. It had also probably not helped that I had voiced my conviction that I could accomplish the task more proficiently than many of those I listened to Sunday after Sunday.

I was 17, and although young (and arrogant), not entirely stupid. I could sense I had carelessly handled holy things, and I hastily attempted to repair the damage. With all the sincerity of the boy Samuel in the temple I assured the minister that there must have been a voice calling out my name. Thanks to this more appropriate form of application I successfully passed through the various nominating procedures and into my preaching apprenticeship – without really confronting what my 'calling' might be. I wanted to do this thing, was good at it, it felt right. Surely that was 'calling' enough. Thirty years on I no longer find this adequate. Unexpectedly and belatedly I am seeking to work out my call with fear and trembling (to misquote Phil. 2.12–3).

Strangely, a retrospective theology is taking shape which was not the driving force behind my volunteering for service but rather has emerged from it. My developing insights are not systematic or coherent but are passionately formed out of vivid moments in which I experienced calls to preach. In this chapter I present some of these instances as autoethnographic narratives. I have constructed these drawing upon rhetorical devices that are more common in preaching than they are in theology.[1] This way of writing allows me to use the deeply metaphorical language that I find most helpful in addressing what is sacred. These poetic devices serve peculiarly well to enhance perception and thus offer the writer and the reader 'an intimate and [yet] intellectually significant engagement with social and cultural reality' (Gibson 2008, p. 2).

The Dove on the Waters

He had been an RAF dog handler and thus had stood on the other side of the wire from me in those difficult times.[2] We were separated only by the space of the netting and the razor barb. This placed us a lot closer together than we were to people who had never sought out the secluded military bases, never travelled down those narrow, unmarked country lanes where oversized American cars drove on the wrong side of the road. We were both equally distant from people who had never watched the blunt-nosed, black-painted planes flying low over the waving cornfields.

So our first conversations were all reminiscences about places and events that others at the college knew nothing about. There was mutual respect and curiosity. He was already pondering in his heart what standing on the other side of the fence would mean, and meeting me was just one of the many reasons why he painfully changed sides. This was a slow process. I remember the conversations in my study. Late-afternoon shadows, the period before evening prayers, and him telling me about his time on a transport ship. At night, he looked out across the dark, invisible sea. 'I was never sure what it was. I was seeing. Something dark and moving. The sea or the blank screen of my inner eye.' Whatever it was, the ocean outside or within him, he said it felt wrong to be bearing all that violence across its surface. 'Sometimes I imagined I had passage on a slave ship, a death ship, and I could hear

---

1 Practical theologians have long accepted the challenge to create 'thick' descriptions of the subjects they reflect upon (see Geertz 1973). However, the techniques of autoethnography and 'creative analytic practice' extend this process further and allow previously undisclosed elements to become the subject of theological reflection (see Ellis 2004).

2 This chapter is dedicated to the memory of Tim Clay, who died tragically in a climbing accident in 1994.

the moaning of the captives echoed in the ship's deep groaning. There was such pain there, it felt like God.'

We sat in two old armchairs, late-afternoon darkness spilling over the face of the deep, and we were straining to glimpse the spirit brooding over the waters.

'Remember', I said to him as we scanned the waves, 'that she has bright wings.'

Four years later he asked me to preach at his ordination, and I was glad to do so. On that occasion, I did not have to hope or dissemble or bind up the broken promises with my strong words, because actually on that occasion it was *all* really true. The kingdom of God had come very close, and I believed the gospel. On that Saturday evening in Manchester the swords had become ploughshares, and teams were already at work ploughing up the gardens outside ready for the great harvest. Inside the church, between the aisles, the wolf pack lay quietly dozing. The leader cradled a sleeping lamb between his giant paws, while the rest of the softly bleating flock were penned behind the altar rails. The tree of life was pushing up tough, thick shoots right through the floorboards and the new leaves on the branches were for the healing of the nations. And I felt the spirit descending like a dove. She placed an olive branch in my hands and there was such glory in the radiance of her wings. 'See how today all these words have been fulfilled in your sight,' I said, And all the people said, 'Amen.'

The Words of the Prophet

I was standing in the church, and it was full. Completely full. So full there were no seats left, and people were standing at the back and crouching in the aisles. And I was speaking clearly and calmly, and my voice was strong, and it did not waver. As I spoke, there was not a single person listening, believer or unbeliever, man or woman, old or young, who was not moved. We were so many, but we were one body, and it was the words I was saying that were bringing these people together. Many were crying, but so quietly, because they did not wish to miss a single syllable of what was being spoken. I had nearly reached the end of what I had to say, and just for a moment my speech faltered, but I had to regain control somehow – and I did. I went on and said all that had to be said.

Then there was silence. There was the small white coffin lined with silk at the front of the church, and there was silence.

The words were not mine. Although I uttered them, it was not me speaking. She had asked me, and I had offered my voice to my friend.

It was her baby who had been carried into church on his father's shoulder and was now lying still on his smooth bed. All through the service while songs were being sung, while prayers were struggling against the sound of sobbing, I had not allowed myself to take part in the shared grief. I had left my gaze unfocused and had not looked at my friends, had not looked at the little white box, nor at my partner seated beside me or at the cross in front of me. I had a job to do. A serious job to do that required me not to feel but to speak.

Her words were the most beautiful and the most painful I have ever spoken. They joined our agony with that of mothers in Palestine, in the Gulf, in Bosnia. They placed our sweet child in the company of the other holy innocents. But the words did not only express the pain of adults grieving for children they must kiss and walk away from (lost but never lost): it was more than this. Our elegy was for the demolitions going on around us and the deportations and the drug wars. It was for the blackbird whose young had been taken by magpies. It was for the waste of the earth and the lateness of the spring. The whole creation was groaning in those words. And I spoke them clearly and calmly, and I did not falter until I had almost reached the end.

Now I ask myself what was happening, when I stood up at the lectern, gathered myself together, focused at last upon the people around me and began to speak. As I wrestle with this question, I remember a solitary afternoon spent walking the marble floors and meditating under the quiet domes of a great museum. In a dimly lit hall I came across a small clay figure about a foot high. The card told me this figure was entitled 'The Prophet'. Its wide mouth was open in lamentation, and it wore a loosely stitched costume. My stomach lurched when I read the inscription, 'The prophet is clothed in the skins of the dead.' The reason I felt this wrenching in my guts was because I knew what I had read was true.

Sometimes the words are not our own. They come from another place that we must divest ourselves of our very selves to visit. When we speak of it, we must be clothed in the skins of those who are silent. I have not travelled there often. Just a few times.

The Conversion of Saint Paul

I cancelled most of my preaching engagements when my pregnancy was confirmed. The consultant had warned that, given my disastrous reproductive history, I had to take every possible care. So I simply wrote to people and said, 'I am sorry I cannot do this. I have been advised against it.' But there were some commitments I did not feel able to withdraw from. Among these was a 'Chapel Anniversary' that had been booked a full two years beforehand. When I was a child, 'the Anniversary' was the most important weekend of the whole church year, and my memories of these sacred occasions were so intense that pulling out seemed impossible.

The first anniversary I remember was at the Mission. It must have been the year before it closed.

The Mission was our family home. My aunties and uncles and cousins were all around. We were carried as babies to the squat, smoke-stained brick building. It was our allotted portion, and from this safe place on the near bank of the river the sweet chariots would come at last and bear us to the beautiful land.

> If you get there before I do
> Wait for me for I'm coming too.

The Mission was a fantastic place for a little child to dwell – in the meantime. It had a basement hall with rooms off, including a green kitchen that housed a dangerous geyser, a hissing monster whose keeper was my Auntie Irene. One by one she took down from the shelf the large enamel teapots – pale green with chips off the handles and lids – and when each had been filled, the beast lay quiet. Above the basement was the sanctuary. It had a rough wooden plank floor and narrow benches. At the front was a piano and a stage with red velvet curtains. On this anniversary weekend there was a concert. My Auntie Irene, my Auntie Eileen and my Auntie Elsie were the three little maids from school. They had Chinese hats made of stiff wallpaper samples, which tied under their chins with shoelaces. Black woollen plaits hung down their backs. They wore silk dressing gowns with chrysanthemums pinned on the front and pale face powder, eyeliner and lipstick! Even Auntie Elsie.

As each act concluded, the grown-ups became more and more excited. They knew something spectacular was going to happen. Suddenly up from the trap door in the stage came a huge dragon that danced a Chinese dance on its many trousered legs to the accompaniment of chiming triangles. Then a great dinner gong sounded, and the dragon gave a mighty roar before disappearing in a cloud of smoke to the basement below, and we all followed downstairs to consume our feast. From then on, I believed that the dragon lived in the basement, and I kept a sharp lookout for it. Perhaps the battered cupboards and chests of my Sunday school room held a nest of baby dragons? Perhaps they lay huddled together sleeping, gently singeing the old costumes and chorus sheets with their hot baby-dragon breaths? My classroom was secured by 'Jesus friend of little children be a friend to me', but I sensed it also accommodated the faintly discernible traces of beauty, terror and magic. However, these earthly walls soon had to be demolished because the times they were a-changing.

Our new church had a flat roof and a light-filled, functional hall with a sanctuary (cross, communion table and altar rail) at one end and a raised stage at the other. The sanctuary and the stage both had navy blue curtains to pull across and hide them. The rule was that if one set of curtains was open, then the other would be closed. The chairs could be turned round to face either way – or stacked at the side for badminton or dancing. And so now it passed to my parents' generation to mark the birthdays of this new building. They did this by accomplishing a very daring thing. They performed a musical play – but not on the stage. It was in the sanctuary. In this Jesus was born in Alabama and was lynched from a tree. There were no silk dressing gowns or paper hats, the actors all wore black slacks and sweaters. The narrative was sung by my mother's friend Rita, who stood by the side with the microphone and marked each heartbreaking moment in her full, sensuous voice. There was no scenery, but a light behind the cross and the shadow of a tree falling across the blank wall. This stark and terrifying beauty stirred the same awe and exhilaration that the dragon had woken in me. After the play both sets of curtains were drawn, so we could feast decently without being overlooked by any wounded gods. Then we danced. The music was Frank Sinatra, Louis Armstrong and the Beatles. Helen, the minister's daughter, drew me to her and taught me the way to smooch. She was younger than me but taller. I held her close with my head resting on her shoulder, in her golden hair, as we took very small steps. The music of the evening penetrated every part of my body.

So how could I not agree to speak at a Chapel Anniversary? My substance is formed of floating dust from the rock of ages, of hissing steam, of haunting love songs and awful shadows. The veil of my flesh is a velvet curtain. I was born in church and I knew of no other way to fashion a child. This was why I was standing five months pregnant in a cold pulpit, in a cold church, in a cold Lancashire mill town preaching about the conversion of Saint Paul. I did not choose the text myself; it was their choice. And I was trying to explain how the dazzling light both blinds you and gives you sight. And I was trying in my heart to remain faithful to the scalding sweetness that can be encountered in small, smoke-stained, brick buildings standing between rows of terraced houses as well as in new churches with leaking roofs on council estates. I was trying to conduct an electric current that would link these people wearing their winter coats with the naked life within me. This is a necessary connection. Without it all fails.

Your Temple My Dwelling Place

On Sunday mornings it is always a rush to get to church. Now my daughter is in her teens, she has stopped waking up at 6.00 a.m. and singing. She would sleep until lunchtime if she could. Truly, she cannot speak or open her eyes until like a newborn kitten she mews her way blindly to the shower, where she gradually revives. This makes getting out of the house a challenge. But once we sidle in shame-facedly through the side door, settle down on the pew, check the notice sheets, find our places in the hymn book and smile across at each other, I begin to feel blessed. Here I can delight in 'all good gifts around us': my family, my work, my life in this place, this church, these people, the Holy Spirit of God. Although I would not have expected that, after travelling the world, I would settle in this city, it feels good and beautiful to be here as the light shines in through the long, plain Presbyterian windows and we join in a psalm.

There are other mothers sitting at the front with their children. One is a therapist, one a teacher, one a priest, one a politician, one a full-time carer, one returned to study, one sick and longing to go back to work. And, unlike me, these remarkable women are able to produce nativity costumes and cakes to be sold, diagnose childhood illnesses and the ailments of contemporary capitalism – and get to church on time on a Sunday morning! Behind the 'family' pews sit a group of Chinese students gathered together in the central aisle. A man in a kilt takes his vantage point on the balcony. In the body of the church there are retired people who read philosophy, tend allotments, practise Scottish dancing, campaign against globalization, care for grandchildren, cook lunches for students and battle daily with bereavement and the pain of all the world. There are gay and lesbian couples who know this place is not perfect but is better than most, and anyway 'we are here . . . get on with it'. There are men who are kind, and men who are cross. Babies in arms and boys in bands. It is a middle-class church that tries in its own peculiar way to save the world, and it is where I now belong and where I do most of my preaching.

On the Sundays when I lead worship, I am always greeted at the door as if I was some special-sort-of-person, not the breathless, harassed woman who normally turns up late. The vestry is quiet. I make new scribblings on my already-scribbled-upon notes. I fit the portable microphone (I hate it, it hates me, it squeaks) onto the waistband of my skirt. I am fetched to 'bless the choir'(!), and then I follow the person who carries the big black Bible into the church. Somehow as I cross the threshold I become that other, special person. The people look up and expect to be fed and, as I am commanded, it is my job to feed them. I break the bread of life and place it in their hands. But the holy food they need is not brought by me from far away. I name God who is in this place, these people, these lives. 'Look,' I say. 'There is manna on the ground all around us. Do not be afraid to take and eat.' I place the dry ashen wafers in my own mouth to show them that they can do the same. This is how I preach to the people.[3]

All Souls

My mother-in-law, who has dementia, suddenly panicked in the shower. She reached for me, and I had no choice but to step under the jet, fully clothed, and embrace her. I held her once beautiful and still beautiful body, and we were both laughing and crying as the water streamed down upon us. I held in my arms a body, which had known the brokenness of childbirth, had survived the rendering asunder of war, and was rapidly approaching the breaking apart of mind and spirit. Holding her in that moment I knew again the sacredness of the flesh the Word became.

New Year

When I became a Christian, the first few weeks were full of joy and then a kind of resentment settled. All the glamorous ambitions of my teenage years seemed to have been wrecked upon the rock of my new-found faith. After all there was only one possible vocation for me now. I had to deny myself, take up the cross and follow. One day I returned home from school to an empty house. The skies were darkening, a squall was blowing up and the washing was being torn from the line. I rushed out and battled against the wind to gather the

---

3 What follows are extracts from three different sermons.

billowing sheets and awkwardly fold them into the basket. It was hard work, and I remember swearing and thinking this is it. This is what it is like to be a bloody Christian. Struggling with great awkward and unwieldy things that seem determined to get all soiled and spoiled despite my best efforts. And then, even though I was cross, I also thought it was quite funny, and there in the wind and the rain with the muddy sheets I prayed the Covenant Prayer . . . 'I am no longer my own but thine . . . put me to what you will . . . rank me with whom you will . . . may I be employed aside or laid aside for you . . .' And the wind blew and the rain stang, and I was laughing and praying and swearing and carrying in the washing.

Advent

The grain is sown into the earth and then there springs forth first the slim green shoot and then the ear. The heavy harvest swells and rises into bread which is broken to feed the hungry. But what if there are no seeds for sowing? There were no seeds for sowing and yet . . .

Perhaps it was the Psalms of Lament sung all around me that touched my soul like the voice of an angel?

Perhaps it was a cinder from the burning of our houses and vineyards that lodged in my heart and enflamed me?

Perhaps it was my very hunger in those hungry times that caused me to bear fruit where there had been no planting?

Perhaps it was my voice, raised with that of all my people, which brought down bread from heaven?

Perhaps it was the Spirit of God that overwhelmed me and caused there to be a swelling harvest of green beneath my girdle? A child from a virgin field growing, moving beneath my girdle.

The bread rising.

To be broken. To be scattered. To bring life.

The Stairs Where Angels Pass between the Heaven and the Earth

At the end of this chapter I return to a sacred place.

I am nine years old and seated half way up the stairs in our new semi, and my mother is standing at the bottom of the steps. She is looking up at me and – preaching. Her first sermons were practised on me, and the hall was the quietest and best place in our house to do this work.

My mother had a definite call. It was delivered directly from God via the Chair of District,[4] my 'uncle' Bill. 'We need you,' he told her. 'The Church has enough old men like me going back to 1900-and-frozen-to-death. We need young women who can speak directly from their own experience about their faith today.'

And hearing this she responded and began to speak exactly in this way about her life in the new semi with her husband and two small children and the garden that was emerging out of the mud, and how she had encountered God not only in the mission hall and the new church with a flat roof but also *right there* in the midst. And elsewhere, of course, as well. She read, and she could read the signs of the times. Her textbooks were collected sermons by Martin Luther King[5] and Paul Tillich.[6] She preached that we shall overcome, and we shall live in peace some day. And half way up the stairs the foundations were shaken, and I heard the voice of God speaking in the depth of my being.[7]

That is how I was formed as a preacher. I don't think it conforms to the norm.

I think there are two dominant understandings of the preacher's calling. In the first, the solitary male[8] is confronted with an overwhelming sense of the divine imperative. He wrestles with his God, until he finally succumbs and agrees to speak, and illumination comes. This can be sweet or terrifying or both at once, but in whatever form it takes the message is thus received from on high to be faithfully passed on. Ezekiel, Jonah, Saint Paul, Luther; it's basically the same.

The second understanding derives less from the Bible and is rather a product of popular piety. In this the preacher is viewed as an unworldly soul pursuing an unworldly vocation. You can imagine the faded print of the solitary scholar poring over the Holy Scriptures. The everyday room around him is in shadows but a curious light will be imaged radiating from the pages of the book and illuminating his lined and learned face. The print will have a title. This could be 'The Minister's Study', or 'The Scholar Preacher', or 'The Sunday Sermon'. I have seen such prints

---

4 Who in Methodism can play a hugely important role in developing ministries. Actually he was the Chair*man* of the District, but I couldn't bring myself to write this even for the sake of historical accuracy.

5 Martin Luther King, 1981, *Strength to Love*, Philadelphia, PA: Fortress Press.

6 Paul Tillich, 1981, *The Shaking of the Foundations*, Harmondsworth: Pelican.

7 These were also the first books of sermons I read as a curious teenager. I am still rereading them and finding them even more challenging today than I did then.

8 There is something in this paradigm of the lonely man wrestling with God that is not easy to accommodate into more inclusive theologies of vocation. However, this is not to imply that many women do not struggle with their sense of call.

and, although they may no longer hang in the homes of the faithful, they are still imprinted in their minds.

While the first of these images is certainly the more attractive, neither fits well with my own understanding of my calling.

So are there other paradigms in the Bible that help me to understand my vocation? Perhaps. I love the stories of children in the temple. It may be there is something of a Samuel in me after all! But it is not the story of his sleepless night (1 Sam. 3) that I cherish, but the idea of his being raised there in the holy place. Formed and moulded not only through the care of Eli but by the stone pillars, the heavy candlesticks, the arching columns and the small stray birds roosting under the rafters. I love the story of Jesus remaining in Jerusalem because he felt at home in the temple, at ease there in its ancient grandeur. I think there is something very powerful about speaking new words out of old traditions. Igniting dull embers on the cold altar. Of course, sometimes these words will also serve to bring down the walls that once gave shelter, but that too is part of the temple-child's inheritance. I could also mention how important for me have been the stories of Mary and Elizabeth, who are not called to preach the word but to bear the words. To carry them and enflesh them, to be torn open by them – and a sword will pierce your heart also.

My autoethnographic accounts are thus attempts to recontextualize – preaching in its material, communal, ecclesial, political contexts as a process of word (call) made flesh. They image the preacher as being given voice through her body,[9] and as such they celebrate incarnational theologies suppressed in the dominant paradigms of calling. However, the body of the preacher is also a spiritual body in which the mystery of God is encountered dwelling among us in glory. We know this in moments of joy, when all is transfigured, and in moments of the deepest pain, when the Spirit joins with our spirit in a groaning too deep for words. We also know it in everyday life, when we sit half way up the stairs; some way between earth and heaven.

And a last point. I have written this chapter in the same way as I preach. I have shaped and formed and laboured over it in the same way that I think a sermon is crafted. It is a human process but it is also one in which we can recognize, as we may in many other human labours, our participation in the creative work of God. This is my job, and it is my calling.

---

9 Body here refers explicitly to an actual human body, but also recalls the body of the Church and the social body.

3

Betraying Faith

This autoethnographic account was inspired by my experience of participating in a research symposium on religious belonging and secularization theory. I felt very strongly that the judgements made about what people who have committed their lives to a religious or political cause actually experience as faith are massively oversimplified. This episodic 'insider' account deliberately includes much that goes beyond questions of institutional belonging. It is written to 'evoke' the ambivalent nature of faith and recomplexify the issues.

Betraying Faith: selling out, losing your religion, failing to meet expectations, going back on previous commitments, informing on your friends, sleeping with the enemy.

Betraying Faith: revealing signs of belief, demonstrating values through practice, being unable to conceal an allegiance, showing without telling.

Betraying Faith: a belief that undoes the believer, a faith you wish you did not have, convictions that run counter to wellbeing.

Back Then

My best friend Chloe and I knelt with the others by the communion rail and made our promises. It was Easter Sunday morning, and the church was filled with people and daffodils and light. The organ swelled, and it was, 'Thine be the Glory, Risen, Conquering Son'. The minister gave us all books signed on the inside by three people to show that we were members of the church.

Both of us wore white dresses for the special service, but hers was short and lacy and mine was not. We made the promises, as we had practised them, and we believed them. If you meant what you said in your heart, then you would become someone very special and chosen and different. The words we were saying made sense within those high walls with all the brightness of heaven streaming in through the windows. But in the afternoon, still wearing our white dresses, we went paddling in the millpond, then lay down on the grass bank afterwards to talk. There was mutedness in the soft spring air. We felt uncertain that the holiday feeling could last; not sure how we would play our roles in the future – on school-uniform days.

Then Chloe did not go to church with me any more. I had to walk up the hill alone. For a lonely traveller the evening service is the best.

It was winter and already dark. I set off from home carrying my small radio, so that I could hear what the new number-one single was at 7.00 o'clock. I was a few minutes late, because I liked the song, and I stayed outside to listen right to the end rather than entering the lighted building. But in the evening service no one minds very much about such small matters. It is not the regularly devout who journey to this church at night.

In the quiet sanctuary I kept my eyes open as they prayed and looked around me at the people. I had tenderness towards the shy soft-spoken man, who always wore yellow socks. I blessed my former Sunday school teacher, a handsome, deeply doubting man, who held his bowed head in his hands. I was grateful for the evening lady who was playing the piano and glad she was not the cheerful morning organist. Her hands were arthritic, and the piano sounded wistful when she touched it. The preacher we had that night was a man I liked. He had been having a sustained argument with God for many years, and I could see merit on both sides.

I now belonged with these evening service people, sitting in my place on the back row and never in a white dress now. We might look like accidental attenders blown in by the wind. And in a way that would be true. But in fact we were the ones who left our homes to come out at night in answer to an unlikely invitation.

In Another Country

Before I left South Africa I arranged to stay for a couple of weeks with some friends living in a communal house in Johannesburg. I was there when we learnt that yet another comrade had been identified as a government agent.

It was Marie who got the message first. As soon as she heard about Ralph, she knocked on everyone's door, and when we gathered in the kitchen she had already poured grape-black Tassies into teacups. She handed these round along with her packet of Gauloises. I could imagine Ralph ambling noisily in, taking a drink himself and lighting up.

When we had heard what Ralph had done, no one said anything for a while. We just sat there with our drinks. When we did begin to speak, it was just to say 'shit', 'fuck' . . . 'fuck'. . . . 'shit' . . . things like that. Then because the stove was warm, and the wine was strong, and there we all were together, people began sharing little stories about him – but very tentatively at first as if these now had to be doubted. The conversation became warmer and grew fonder. Cecil had got drunk with Ralph at a student conference – it had been a long session, two days and two nights, the best way to get through a weekend in winter on a freezing cold farm somewhere in the Free State. Ralph had slept on Marie's floor for a night during the State of Emergency, when he was moving around 'to avoid detention'. He brought his own bedroll and sleeping bag, but she had lent him a pillow. Sonja remembered meeting him in a hospital corridor, when she was doing her final year placement. His wife had just given birth to a little boy, and he was crying. She lent him small change for the phone.

Thinking about Ralph crying over the birth of his baby led us, of course, to the 'love' question. We often talked about it; it obsessed us – how could it not? Here, for instance, was Ralph whom we now knew to be a traitor, a grand deceiver. This was very serious. Not a game of cheat in which he had played the best hand. People would be imprisoned, forced into exile, could die because of what he had done. But this man loved his family – that had to be genuine? And yet it was to Sonja, his enemy, he had shown the first Polaroid picture of his baby son. He seemed to be devoted to his wife. Despite the floor hopping, partying and late nights in smoke-filled rooms, there was no rumour he had cheated on her. But it was the comrades who had baked the wedding cake, hung the ribbons, played the music, and who were the guests at his wedding.

So was the marriage then also a sham?

Or had they both been double agents from the time they joined the movement?

We had now stopped sharing memories and were imagining them living their new lives in a house in the suburbs with a stoup three sides round. The wine helped. The way we were talking about them, it was as if they had been removed out of our world by a giant hand that had carried them to a place we could never go. It was as if a cyclone had lifted off the roof of their lives and blown them away somewhere fantastical. It was the South African Wizard of Oz.

We sat a long time at the table, but gradually the others left me alone with the last of the Tassies. There were things they needed to do and that I did not need to know about. I sat and thought a long time, then I did the washing up.

I was leaving the country. Leaving these people with whom I had appeared to cast my lot. What lessons had they taught me? That you are closer to your enemies than you are to those who are not involved, who pass by on the other side.

Who is the traitor? The one who plays a part or the one who refuses to do so?

Signed Up

I was a Methodist all my life before I came to Scotland, and although I do like to drink red wine I would never gamble, and I know the words of the hymns and can sing them without opening my book. Also I have been a preacher since I was 18 years old, so this has been a very serious belonging. But the Church of my heart never really took root in the Scottish soil, and as we are settled here and raising a child hard decisions had to be made of a difficult nature. An old, wise friend said to me as we walked through Edinburgh, 'Heather, you have been here for several years, and it is the time to choose now. Your voice is needed in councils of the Kirk.' I recognized his message as an unceremonious calling. I had to put aside my own feelings and do what was necessary without sentiment. So I spoke to the minister, who arranged the transition. It was easy but not painless.

The culture of the Methodist Church Meeting is very like that of a political party. In fact, once I made a mistake, when chairing a local Labour Party branch, and bowed my head to open in prayer. The Kirk Session was very different. The assembled Church of Scotland is more like a court of law than a crusade. There is a cultural difference. And I am English. For all I live here now, and it may be for the rest of my life, I will never be properly Scottish. A citizen perhaps but not indigenous. I can't rise in my soul to a metrical psalm, and I don't have the kind of working knowledge of who-is-who and what-is-what that comes from being raised in a small country. I have a faculty missing that those around me rely on without thinking. Oh well. I get by. And in many ways I like it very much here, and we are only half an hour away from the hills.

So with my ambivalent feelings of being in the place I am supposed to be (am even 'ordained' to be since becoming an Elder), and yet not actually belonging, it was a great surprise to me when I was asked to attend the General Assembly as a Commissioner. I felt very moved and humbled – although I well understood the very practical reasons why I had been asked to undertake this role. I had served on the Kirk's working group on sexuality, and a big vote was coming up on the issue. Those who put me forward wanted to send someone informed, who might be able to speak out if the cause required it. Someone who, at the very least, could be relied upon to vote the correct way. I am utterly trustworthy on matters of that sort.

I had never been inside the Assembly buildings – although many years previously I had travelled up to Scotland to stand on the picket line when Margaret Thatcher paid her famous visit to the Kirk. I walked up the Mound, into the courtyard of New College, past the statue of Knox and up the long stone staircase. I had the badge of my credentials and the card to use for voting. I had a black skirt and was hoping to pass as Presbyterian, because I had been practising. But still I identified more with the people who were handing out leaflets, holding placards and keeping vigil than I did with the other Commissioners walking confidently up the steps. Inside it was both reassuringly familiar – all big church gatherings have something cheerfully generic about them – and utterly strange. Where to go? Which stairs led to what balcony? Whether to sit next to a person I did not know and possibly be wrongly identified through failing to understand the alliances and factions. 'The revised papers are in the Commissioners' pigeonholes.' (Oh my God I did not even know we had pigeonholes – and stuffed with papers.) Feeling here by right and yet a complete outsider.

But it was also something very beautiful.

I fell deeply in love with the Assembly. The serious Commissioners queuing in long lines for the microphones, the Moderator seeking to gauge the mind of the meeting (albeit a Methodist President would have been searching for the heart). The very complicated way you have to use the quaint machine to cast your holy vote. I even began to discern some passion in the body. Fine Scottish voices reading Scripture, singing psalms, joining in the modern hymns sung to haunting old tunes – with an edge of sadness. Good rhetoric, strong and reasoned argument, sharp and direct critique, language made rich by the grace of serious devotion . . . and of course, here as everywhere, the same old conflict.

Although I could say I truly love the whole collected body, I should not forget why I was sent here. To take sides in a conflict.

And this is where it does get very complicated. I know my place, and I am even 'at home' in this bitter striving between Christians. I have been enlisted for a long time, and I know the terrain of battle. How very strange to find that my strongest identity, the thing that brings me closest to belonging and places me at the heart of the Church's governance, is this profane, inglorious struggle.

Doubling

I teach and research at the Centre for Literature, Theology and the Arts at the University of Glasgow. This is a delight, and it pays the bills. I have recently been working on the South African novelist J. M. Coetzee.[1] I am particularly intrigued by the fact that he has developed an alter ego in his later writings. He has produced both novels and short stories about an elderly woman author, Elizabeth Costello, all of which express her struggles with literature. She feels compelled to write, but she is very aware of the failures of her writing and the inability of writing itself to bear witness to the pain of existence.

Coetzee uses Costello to present his own ethical dilemmas and failures in the form of an elaborate literary game. Not everyone likes this. Why would a man 'write as' a woman? Why use literary devices and not just speak out plainly for what you believe? Also, as Elizabeth Costello's own fictions contain a character very like Coetzee, it gets confusing. We don't quite know how to hold the mixed-up authors and characters to account for what they say. And isn't this just too clever-clever and a bit dishonest? I understand these criticisms, but I don't think they grasp what Coetzee is trying/failing to bear testimony to in his fictional work.

I think Coetzee's writing is shaped by the fact that he is a white South African man (see Bethlehem 2005). He was formed as a writer in a situation in which life was complicated. In one of his essays Coetzee discusses the fact that many modern novels are constructed in a multi-vocal, dialogical style.[2] This, he argues, is not a literary affectation but just the type of writing you should expect to emerge out of the highly restricted circumstances prevailing in surveillance cultures – such as those of the Apartheid state.

> By no means all historical situations permit the ultimate semantic authority of the creator to be expressed without mediation in direct, unrefracted, unconditional authorial discourse. When there is no access to one's own personal 'ultimate' word, then every thought, feeling, experience must be refracted through the medium of someone else's discourse, someone else's style, someone else's manner. (Coetzee 1996, p. 223)

---

1 See, for example, Walton 2008.
2 An insight developed out of the generative work of Mikhail Bakhtin on this topic (1981).

This is a motif Coetzee returns to when reflecting upon the work of the Afrikaner poet Breyten Breytenbach, who is best known for his prison memoirs *The True Confessions of an Albino Terrorist* (1985). The title of this work is itself multi-layered and provocative given that the poet, turned ineffective political agent, apparently lied, certainly dissembled and indulged in self-abasing 'confessions' at his trial in order to secure (unsuccessfully) a lighter prison sentence.

Breytenbach's subsequent experiences of interrogation, incarceration and censorship were transformed by him into startling 'mirror poetry' (he was certainly a more effective poet than revolutionary) in which the voice of the poet merges with those of his invisible accusers. The enemy inquisitors are also his brothers and can be imaged either as the Afrikaner authorities or the black South Africans whose cause he has espoused and also betrayed. Coetzee describes how these poems testify to the experience of those in extreme circumstances, who become intimately close to those who abject them. Perhaps not only close. Perhaps some sort of metamorphosis actually takes place as 'the other' is incorporated into the haunted psyche:

> it is not possible to say what position the self holds: the interchange between self and other is, in effect, continuous . . . in the process of suffering the victim takes into himself the degradation of the oppressor, the I becomes double, multiply double: interrogator and revolutionary, criminal and victim, colonizer and colonized, even censor and writer. The black in the mirror is not Other but other/self, 'brother I'.
> (Coetzee 1996, pp. 227–8)

Some critics have spoken of Coetzee as a major shaper of an emerging South African literary tradition that weaves multiple voices and perspectives into unsettling forms of 'sublime' discourse (see, for example, Pechey 1998, pp. 57–74). The role of the sublime is always to deeply disturb through an encounter with something strange, demanding and scary. I view the novel *Elizabeth Costello* (2003) as an important example of this genre. The failing author struggles to respond to the intense suffering of other beings. Their pain presses upon her to the extent that her own identity starts to disintegrate. This penetration by other creatures can also be experienced as an ecstasy, a climax of extreme awareness – which may be just as hard to bear. In the disturbing last pages of *Elizabeth Costello* a strange literary fragment entitled 'Presences of the Infinite' is presented without context or apology. It stands as a description of the awful raptures of imaginative revelation that literature is somehow caught up in:

A dog sitting in a patch of sun licking itself . . . is at one moment a dog and at the next a moment of revelation . . . perhaps in the mind of our Creator (*our Creator*, I say) where we whirl as if in a millrace we interpenetrate and are interpenetrated by fellow creatures by the thousand. But how I ask you can I live with rats and dogs crawling through me day and night . . . scratching me, tugging me, urging me deeper and deeper into revelation – how? (Coetzee 2003, p. 229)

Conflicted

There is a very good part of my job. I get to be where academic debate is actually taking place. Not in texts I mean, but live, like wrestling. I can be present and look and learn. We had two of the most respected experts on religious belonging in the UK in the same room. They liked each other, they enjoyed an argument, they contested their points, they did not agree.

Callum Brown[3] was arguing persuasively that faith was in decline. Those who owned 'no religion' now formed the biggest single group in Scotland. The Kirk was in catastrophic freefall, and the Catholic Church had only been temporarily saved from the same fate by the recent influx of Eastern European migrants. He presented well-sourced figures to support his claims. He meets with friends from the Humanist Society in the pub. There is a growing body of people confident that secularization is now unstoppable.

Linda Woodhead[4] was not claiming that a grand revival of traditional religion was on the cards. However, she saw a situation of transformation and change rather than absolute decline. We need to attune ourselves to contemporary forms of spirituality, she argued; to understand it and interrogate it. Also, we should not believe the body of old truths has stopped breathing. There is still a stubborn and tenacious life

---

3 Author of a number of significant texts on religious decline including *The Death of Christian Britain*, London: Routledge, 2009 and *Religion and the Demographic Revolution: Women and Secularisation in Canada, Ireland, UK and USA since the 1960s*, Woodbridge: Boydell Press, 2012.

4 Woodhead's work has spearheaded sociological interest in changing forms of spiritual affiliation. See for example: Paul Heelas and Linda Woodhead, *The Spiritual Revolution: Why Religion is Giving Way to Spirituality*, Chichester: Wiley-Blackwell, 2004; 'Why So Many Women in Holistic Spirituality?', in Kieran Flanagan and Peter Jupp (eds), *The Sociology of Spirituality*, Aldershot: Ashgate, 2007, pp. 115–25 and 'Gendering Secularization Theory', *Social Compass* 55:2 (2008), pp. 187–93.

here that is capable of regenerating into new forms. She took particular pleasure in the fact that religious adherents have never actually believed what they are officially supposed to believe and even in these chastened times show a delightful heterogeneity, syncretism and inventiveness when it comes to their personal theologies. A fact that it is easy to miss if we only attend to what the religious authorities say about faith.

As usual, I found myself on both sides of the argument as well as not in the argument at all. I can't place myself on the measuring scale of faith.

Faking It

My good friend Redmond decided to take early retirement. His high-stress job as a youth worker in Northern Ireland was taking more and more of his time. He had achieved so much, but the list of needs to be met grew longer instead of shorter and the personal costs were becoming unmanageable. This decision was hard to make, but also something to celebrate as a new life stage and such a good excuse for a reunion of old friends. He invited a group of us to the rambling cottage he had bought on the Antrim coast.

We had a wonderful weekend of clifftop walks and late-night conversations; old photos, gossip, political reminiscence. Despite many years of being dispersed in different cities since our Manchester days, we have all remained very close, but Redmond and I have a special aspect to our relationship that only developed after his return to Ireland. He is an atheist, but working in a hugely sensitive context he considered it important to appear to be integrally part of the community, and this implied religious belonging. He sustained credibility by going quietly but regularly to Mass, sitting at the back of the church and not making a big show of piety. A good strategy. However, it did not furnish him with ready responses to religious questions when these were put to him by the clerics and colleagues he worked with. I became his 'theological coach'.

I tried at first to school him in the theology of Vatican II, so that he could use it to advocate for reasonably progressive positions on community issues. However, he had been too firmly formed in the bosom of the Irish Catholic community for this sort of stuff to resonate with him as anything like a vocabulary of authentic belief. He was hopeless at it. In the end I thought discretion was probably the better part of valour and suggested to him that if anyone ever asked him his religious views he should pause, look thoughtful and say, 'Well, I have a very simple faith . . . ' And stop there. Say absolutely nothing more. I must admit I did not expect quite the spectacular success this strategy proved. He quickly developed a reputation for earthy, common-sense holiness – which I do not think is entirely unjustified. But then he is a close friend.

I was not sure what changes retirement would bring to Redmond's 'simple faith' – not an issue we talked about over our meals or on our walks. However, on the Saturday morning I left the kitchen table where the others were lingering with toast and the newspapers and joined Redmond in the living room. He was watching the television. It was a Requiem Mass for the poet Seamus Heaney, whose work I admire and whose position as a humanitarian patriot Redmond also deeply respects. I sat down to watch it with him. Just the two of us in silence through the piercing sweetness of a Brahms lullaby and the mounting grandeur of the eucharistic celebration. It lasted nearly an hour. It was a holy space. When the Mass was over, we sat together for a while. 'I find', said Redmond, 'that the words of the Catholic faith become more beautiful for me as I get older.'

'It was a grand service,' I agreed.

I could not say what I felt, which is that we had, unexpectedly and unaccountably, worshipped together that morning. He the dissembling atheist and me the often-dissembling believer. That matter had to be respectfully and carefully laid aside.

[B]eliever and unbeliever are both voyagers. In the darkness in which the secret courses of human lives lie hidden . . . [we] are sometimes closer together, sometimes farther apart than appearances indicate. For this reason . . . [we] look searchingly into the eyes of others, seeking a brother or a sister who could be anywhere . . . in the darkness in which we live. (Novak 1965, p. 192)

4

Desiring Things

This work of autoethnography uses experiences of relationships with objects to set theoretical debates concerning the new materialisms in their lived context. The personal narratives are written as a preface to critical reflection in accordance with the 'value added' paradigm of analytic autoethnography. However, it is interesting to note that when a work is constructed with an opening such as this, its impact may extend into the writing that follows. In this piece the personal voice continues well into the theoretical debate, and encounters with ideas are presented in a similar way to the encounters with objects.

A World of Wonderful Things

My daughter was lying pink cheeked and sweetly asleep in bed. Her toys were abandoned on the living-room floor. Blossom, the favourite doll, was sprawled face down on the carpet. Her stiff limbs outstretched and her long golden nylon hair tangled. I bent to pick her up, and it was as if a current ran through me. A small but perceptible force that made me shiver slightly. This doll could not be impersonally handled but commanded respect. She was animated and something of my child's life was bounded up in her. I combed her hair with my fingers, smoothed her dress and sat her in my daughter's little chair, where she could be found and loved again next morning.

It is so poignant each time I return to my parents' house. They are so vividly alive, but my father has been very sick and we can see that he has not recovered strength.[1] Each visit could be the last time we are all together, and we anticipate in our gestures a loss that is palpable but restrained. The very objects in the house manifest this fragile state. Once they were bold and substantial things, sufficient in themselves, confidently approached, used and put away. Now they have a spectral

---

1 Sadly my father did not recover from this illness and died in the summer of 2012.

quality – manifesting for us a past we can only touch through them. I always linger in the kitchen. I lift the blue lid from the sugar bin and breathe in the more-than-50-years of sweetness it has held inside. I take out the spoons shaped like cockle shells, which I so loved as a little girl. The spoons are no longer used. The silver has worn off in places, but they are still pretty. Like a thief of time I slip one into my bag when I leave.

My home now is a modern flat with white walls overlooking a terrace garden. There is a bright, chaotic 1970s vibe blended with, or toned down by, contemporary minimalism. It combines awareness of current trends with idiosyncratic style. What a guest entering would not know is that only the big grey sofa was purchased new at full price. Everything else was found on the street, bought second hand, sold in a sale, or cheap because it was blemished. Things have been repainted, re-covered and arranged to disguise flaws and scratches. I am good at this work and proud of my skills. The achieved whole is immensely satisfying to me, perhaps because I know its secrets. It is my home. As I walk around in the evening, lighting candles, turning down the lights, opening a bottle of wine, I am content. Here we all are sheltered. Here in this place. So blessed.

On the edge of contemporary theory a new materialism is emerging. It restores to us the love of objects and the vitality of things.

When I was a child, to ascribe value to possessions was not a crime. My parents moved into a small new house when I was three years old. For two years we had no carpet in the lounge, and my parents saved for a glorious purple and raspberry creation (it was the 60s!), and we invited all the neighbours round to celebrate the day it was laid down. My father was a sign writer, and the house was full of witty and beautiful adverts made for display around the town. My mother wore full-skirted dresses with rose prints, and scarlet lipstick. She kept her letters in a milksoft leather handbag that smelled of cologne. When Mary Quant came along, she transformed into a slim blonde goddess in black and white and wore false eyelashes that lived, like skinny centipedes, on her dressing table next to the daisy earrings. I had fashion and fun, colour and beauty, and in my hopeful, young, aspiring working-class neighbourhood none of this was a crime.

It was in the early 1970s that the DJ on the Saturday morning show began to warn about pollution and the environmental crisis. I was of an age then when famine and poverty loomed large upon my personal horizon. The seemingly petty material pleasures of my parents' generation appeared as a poor substitute for passionate ideals. The beautiful head of Che Guevara hung on my bedroom wall. When I went to university, I encountered Marxism and liberation theology. I left for Africa immediately after graduation. My faith and life were given over to the struggle, and the love of things had become a kind of crime.

But a fascination endured. I turned to Marx, who so well describes the power of the commodity and wrote, 'A commodity appears at first sight an extremely obvious, trivial thing. But its analysis brings out that it is a very strange thing, abounding in metaphysical subtleties and theological niceties' (Marx 1990 [1867], p. 163). Although the values the commodity represents are, for him, without substance, they have a religious power that is mysterious and compelling, phantasmagorically transforming the everyday. As T. Richards writes, those who seriously seek to comprehend commodity culture enter a 'fantastic realm in which things act, speak, rise, fall, evolve' (1991, p. 11). Walter Benjamin became my preferred companion in this strange land, I think because he loved rather than condemned the objects which, in his messianic materialist perspective, both bespoke and denied transcendence (see Wolin 1994). He loved the arcades and the market stalls, where he rummaged for the infinite among the glittering trinkets and little bits of lace.

And I found other friends who helped me to move beyond the sternness of Marxist critique towards an intuition of the ways in which an engagement with things could enhance politics and practice. Gaston Bachelard, in *The Poetics of Space* (1994), restored to me the world of the house in which the soul is formed. He explores how this world of material intimacy shelters and nourishes the imagination, which is the intimate of action. As I entered his boyhood room, overlooking the fields and deeply scented with the perfume of raisins drying, I found it blessed my own, rather less romantic, memories of childhood in a suburban home.

> The House we were born in is physically inscribed in us . . . We would find our way in the dark to the distant attic . . . The word habit is too worn a word to describe this passionate liaison of our bodies, which do not forget, with an unforgettable house. (Bachelard 1994, pp. 14–15)

Etty Hillesum (1999 [1981]) helped me to understand that combating the ugliness of fascism was not only an effort of will but an aesthetic achievement. Resistance could be sustained through appreciation of sweet-smelling soap and a lilac blouse, the scent of jasmine beneath the eves and a cyclamen carefully placed beside a reading lamp. As her existence became increasingly confined these 'little things' became correspondingly more important – not as possessions but as vehicles for the soul.

I have made a journey from a naïve love of things, through critique to a revised appreciation of the power of things in human life. This could be seen as a journey frequently repeated as we mature. I am sure it is. However, it is also a political and spiritual journey, which is of particular significance at this point in time as we look to the challenges we face politically and environmentally. The dynamics of critique, whether from a Marxist, environmental, or indeed eco-spiritual/theological perspective, inadequately respond to the fact that things matter to people. We have not explored this issue sufficiently, but have sought to maintain our innocence of the truly catastrophic consequences of inappropriate manifestations of desire through forms of analysis that crudely employ terms such as *commodity* and *consumption* without taking seriously the enchanted world in which people and objects interact. As Daniel Miller writes,

> stuff is ubiquitous and problematic. But whatever our environmental fears or concerns we will not be helped by an attitude to stuff that simply opposes ourselves to it as though the more we think of things as alien the more we think ourselves pure. (Miller 2010, p. 5)

I have now come to believe that the development of new forms of materialism that attempt a loving critique of the order of things – Jürgen Habermas describes Benjamin's materialist hermeneutics as redemptive criticism (see Habermas, Brewster and Buchner 1979) – offers the best chance we have to develop an ethical environmental practice. In order to assess the challenges this shift in perspective represents for practical theologians, I now turn to the work of two new materialists, Daniel Miller, an anthropologist at University College London, and Jane Bennett, a philosopher at Johns Hopkins University. I chose these theorists because their work is engaging, polemical, and readily delivers strong ideas that are accessible even in a short chapter such as this.

Daniel Miller and World Making Material

As an anthropologist, Miller has spent many years exploring cultural systems from the West Indies to India as well as maintaining a recurring commitment to research in his own 'back yard' of London, one of the planet's greatest and most complex cities. Looking back over these endeavours, he makes the simple point that 'non-industrial societies are just as much material cultures as we are' (Miller 2010, p. 4), and, indeed, when resources are scarce, the highest degree of social attention and energy must be devoted to the material mechanisms that sustain social interaction. In making this claim, Miller effectively challenges the romance of the primitive and the nostalgia for a purer state of being in which objects were assumed to hold less significance than they do today. Clearly, forms of materialism will vary, but from an anthropological perspective, Miller argues, it is impossible to imagine human culture without the nurturing guardianship performed by things. He takes up and amplifies Pierre Bourdieu's narrative of how among the Kabyle a child is introduced to the order of the house and required to learn that things must be placed high or low, on the left or right. This constructed order represents a domestic induction into a wider cosmology, which maintains the pattern of existence despite the apparent diversity of experience:

> This seems to me to correspond very well to what I call the humility of things. Objects don't shout at you like teachers . . . but they help you gently to learn how to act appropriately . . . objects make people. Before we can make things we are ourselves grown up and matured in the light of things that come to us from previous generations . . . Things, not mind you individual things, but the whole system of things with their internal order, make us the people we are. (Miller 2010, p. 53)

People form webs of meaning through complex interactions with networks of people *and* things – yet so often in our binary culture we assume that healthy relationships with other persons are threatened by an attention to things. This assumption is challenged by a simple but effective piece of research conducted by Miller in an ordinary London street and published as *The Comfort of Things* (2008). Miller and a colleague questioned inhabitants about the objects they lived with. They found that those who enjoyed a rich relationship with objects (commonplace things – a woman kept McDonalds 'Happy Meal' toys; a couple made elaborate Christmas decorations) had a similarly rich relationship with people. Those whose lives were starkly bereft of beloved possessions were similarly starved of meaningful personal relationships.

But his research took Miller beyond reversing the terms of that familiar moral equation stating that there is an inverse relationship between love of people and love of things. He discovered that people *not only* engage with objects as part of a holistic system of meaningful relationships but *also* construct within domestic space microcosmological systems that are often far more meaningful and present to them than the larger social and religious systems in which they may participate at one remove:

> The point is that household material culture may express an order which in each case seems equivalent to what *one might term* a social cosmology, *if this* was the order of things, values and relationships of a society. A very little cosmology perhaps . . . and one that in only a few cases ever develops into an abstract philosophy or system of belief . . . Nevertheless such a cosmology is holistic rather than fragmented and . . . [although] the focus is on the interior space these aesthetics are not isolated from the wider world. (Miller 2008, p. 294, italics original)

Indeed, these micro-material cosmologies sustain identity and help generate the resilience necessary to pattern life creatively and interact meaningfully with others.

Having challenged taken-for-granted assumptions about 'human' and 'thing' relationships by refusing a neat divide between them, Miller continues his deconstruction of our moral economy. He argues that the West accords unwarranted respect to a depth ontology: 'The assumption is the *being* we truly are is located deep inside ourselves and is in direct opposition to the surface' (2010, p. 16). An analysis of how clothes function in a number of specific communities allows Miller to suggest that external (we might call them *surface*) moods, styles, choices relate to questions of real concern to people which are often negotiated at skin level, with implications of greater consequence than we might have supposed. Barriers we may have wanted to keep in place between deep questions and surface (or superficial) matters have already long been breached.

> In the hybrid world that is everyday life, it is often the intimate and sensual realms that are most effective in determining the acceptability and plausibility of the regimes of thought we call rationality and even ontology. Through the realm of clothes we see how, for most people, systems of thinking about the world have to feel right. (Miller 2010, p. 41)

We theologians have an attachment to 'deep' metaphors for human identity. We may thus find it difficult to revalue the superficial and the emotive. However, Miller is asking us to question our hierarchy of values on the basis of the desire people have for things. What is at stake here is a spiritual, ethical and political appreciation of life in the world that fully embraces the palpably material and affective dimensions of life. Miller's Jewish faith informs his desire for a spiritual wholeness achieved by living fully immersed in the ambiguous complexities of the everyday. To wish to escape them is for him a form of hubris with catastrophic consequences. Why, he challenges, have we been active participants in the abjection of things? Perhaps because of our fear of pollution, ambiguity and corruption?

> [D]enigrating material things and pushing them down, is one of the main ways we raise ourselves up onto apparent pedestals divorced from our own materiality and the material reality of the world we live within. I am not sure about a spirituality that is obtained by ideals of purity and separation or that enlightenment is reached by a denial of the material . . . everyday life and the glorious mess of contradiction and ambivalence that is found there. (Miller 2010, p. 156)

Jane Bennett and Vital Matters

Miller's political vision is of a world in which we acknowledge the significance of materialism in order that we find better ways of living in relationship with each other and within our environments. I now turn to the work of Jane Bennett, who shares Miller's conviction that a denial of the importance of materiality has been a key factor in bringing us to the current environmental crisis:

> In the context of, in particular, an American political economy, there seems to be a resonance between the idea of matter as dull stuff/passive resource and a set of gigantically wasteful production and consumption practices that foul our own nest. These practices endanger and immiserate workers, children, animals and plants here and abroad. To the extent that the figure of inert matter sustains this consumptive style another figure might disrupt it. (Bennett 2009, p. 98)

The first step towards disrupting this exploitative system is to acknowledge the enchanting power of the object: not nature, but the thing. From Kant to the romantic poets, from ecofeminism to environmental theology, we have crafted the resources to engage respectfully with the wonder of the natural world. Bennett's concern is that these resources have not developed in relation to the 'other stuff' around us. Instead we have fallen into the habit of 'parsing the world into dull matter and vibrant life' (Bennett 2010, p. vii), and this figure of 'dead or thoroughly instrumentalized matter feeds . . . our earth-destroying fantasies of conquest and consumption' (Bennett 2010, p. viii).

A lot of Bennett's work is figured in respectful disagreement with Marxist perspectives on commodity culture. As I have argued, no one can fault Marx on his prophetic grasp of the mysterious attraction of the commodity. Interestingly, Bennett suggests that Marx's early studies in Epicurean philosophy may have influenced his perspective on the vital power that the object represents. However, Marx and his later followers were so convinced in their diagnosis of the perceptual disorder called 'commodity fetishism', through which '[h]umans become blind to the pain and suffering embedded in the commodity by virtue of an unjust and exploitative system of production, even [at the same time] as commodities – mere things – appear as active agents capable of attracting attention and determining desire' (Bennett 2001, p. 113), that they could offer only the most stringent remedies for this sickness. For a cure they have offered relentless criticism: 'the primary fear motivating their story is that we live in a system where the forces of domination have become resistant to all but the most relentless strains of critical reflection' (Bennett 2001, p. 129).

But what if, asks Bennett, this 'cure' serves merely to aggravate the symptoms we experience and yet brings no relief? What follows if we concede that the wonder and enchantment we experience in relation to things is because they are wonderful and enchanting, because they generate physical, emotional and aesthetic pleasure and actively impress themselves upon us in every aspect of life? Saying yes to this pleasurable encounter is not seduction, and need not imply a reckless abandonment of rational critique but might enliven and sustain resistance: 'part of the energy needed to challenge injustice comes from the reservoir of enchantment – including that derived from commodities. For without enchantment you might lack the impetus to act against the very injustices that you critically discern' (Bennett 2001, p. 128).

In contrast to the anxious spirit of frugality that dominates both political and theological criticisms of the way we live, Bennett advocates the cultivation of a sense of delight in material generativity and plentitude and an affective openness to vital materiality. She ventures that these approaches may be more sustaining of impulses towards justice, sharing and mutuality than life-denying thriftiness. This inclusive, participatory and celebratory attitude towards life in all its fullness is only possible once we abandon our default position that human beings, and possibly other intelligent creatures like dolphins, are the only vital agents ('actants') in the moral universe, and contemplate a new order of things.

> I am trying to take 'things' more seriously than political theorists had been taking them. By 'things', I mean the materialities usually figured as inanimate objects, passive utilities, occasional interruptions, or background context – figured, that is, in all ways that give the creative power to humans . . . Our habit of parsing the world into passive matter (it) and vibrant life (us) is what Jacques Rancière (in another context) called a 'partition of the sensible'. In other words it limits what we are able to sense . . . What would the world look like and feel like were the life/matter binary to fall into disuse, were it to be translated into differences in degree rather than kind? . . . What I try to do when I write is to call myself and others to a different direction, to point to those uneven spaces where nonhumans are actants, where agency is always an assemblage, where matter is not inert, where man is not lord but everything is made of the same quirky stuff . . . I can't predict what politics would emerge from this. My hunch is that the grass would be greener in a world of vital materialities. (Bennett 2009, p. 92)

Vital matter always tends towards a confederacy of agency, a hybridity of subjectivity, a complexity of causality. It promises a new form of non-innocent, participatory politics. The tendency to transform human into machine is countered by an opposing force that anthropomorphizes the agency of matter. For Bennett this is a religious, or at any rate a spiritual, option. While highly critical of both Catholic and evangelical tendencies to place the human at the centre of creation, she is not against a theological anthropomorphism of her own. Borrowing ideas from her friend Hent de Vries and his 'political theology', she compares vital materiality to the stubborn, intangible, imponderable and recalcitrant 'stuff' of existence – or in other words, the absolute.

Questions for Theology

It is obvious that I find the thinking of Miller and Bennett fascinating, but the question remains as to whether it is compatible with theological thinking, which as a Christian theologian I must admit is troubling. While we can identify traces of a confident material cosmology in some elements of the biblical tradition, there are many parts of the New Testament that would conflict with this worldview: overall, the Christian religion is largely resistant to 'stuff'.

However, there are hints within Franciscan and other spiritual traditions that appear to offer some resources for creative new theological thinking in this area. For example, the Franciscan Sister and theologian Ilia Delio celebrates the christocentric reading of the material world – including inanimate objects – that has been developed by Franciscan theologians:

> For Scotus and for Bonaventure, the universe is the external embodiment of the inner Word of God . . . Bonaventure writes that in his transfiguration Christ shares existence with all things: with the stones he shares existence, with the plants he shares life, with animals he shares sensation . . . In his human nature, he stated, 'Christ embraces something of every creature in himself.' (Delio 2003, p. 19)

As is well known, the poet-priest Gerard Manley Hopkins was deeply influenced by Scotus, particularly his notion that each being and object articulates through being itself the divine-self-in-all-things. His kingfisher poem is one of the most famous expressions of this conviction, and in this Hopkins declares that each 'mortal thing' serves God by being itself: 'Crying *What I do is me: for that I came*' (1976a, p. 51). However, the turmoil of Hopkins' later life and his unwilling exile in great industrial cities produced an altered outlook in the poet. In his later work the material order, blighted by trade and mechanization, is no longer viewed as revelatory but as soiled, deceitful and doomed. The fabric of life is 'mortal trash' and 'world's wildfire leaves but ash' (1976b, p. 65). Radical incarnational theology is abandoned in favour of faith in that which lies beyond what exists here on earth. This move is one made by Christian theology over and over again, when it discovers no way of reconciling the ambivalence of material existence with its faith in redemptive providence.

Practical theologians might be thought among those in the guild least likely to abandon the quest to find theological meaning in the common substance of existence, and, as Bonnie Miller-McLemore (2012b) suggests, there are compelling reasons for understanding practical theology as the theology of everyday life (see Chapter 17). However, there are aspects of the way the discipline has developed that currently place us in the front ranks of those who are theologically affronted by the ambivalent mess of stuff.

As Stephen Pattison argues, practical theology is [obsessively] driven by its desire to be useful and make a difference (2013, p. 4). As a busy and frugal discipline with serious work to do, it has very rarely relaxed into reflection upon the affective aesthetic realm or much succumbed to the pleasures of enchantment. As theologians, our concern with the public sphere and the conventions of communicative rationality have been 'complemented' by a corresponding distaste for the domestic and incoherent world of things.

The new materialisms challenge us to reassess this hierarchy of values and rediscover the importance of affectivity, perception and imagination in the theological realm. It will be an uncomfortable and difficult task for practical theologians to enter the ambiguous and problematic world of stuff for, as we have heard above from Miller, there is a loss of purity, a fall involved here. And yet perhaps it will be a *felix culpa*. Personally, I think a glory awaits us in rediscovering the reality of incarnation in an iridescent world of materiality. One of my favourite writers, Elizabeth Smart, presents a vision of enchantment in the material order, which I like very much and which I think speaks of a joy that might empower us in the work to which we have set our hands and our hearts:

Something happened today.
The wet paving stones had a diurnal look.
They presented themselves pathetically, pleading that they last so much longer than life. They greeted me as if we were all dust together at last.
Kinship was established.
This happened coming up Sloane Street, while the traffic lights flashed and black buildings strained upwards waiting to be noticed.
It was a short Sunday love-affair with very little pain.
Afterwards, the dresses in the shop windows leaned towards me like lusty millionaires with generous impulses.
What reward for giving love to a stone.
It was impossible to be poor that whole February day.

41

What do people do at 5.30 in the afternoon, when there's an early amethyst sky and happiness explodes irresponsible and irrepressible over the weary city?

What if perfection strikes loud and shocking on the Tottenham Court Road?

What if even a squashed matchbox can sidle into your sympathies . . .

How to meet the minute except by walking down Tottenham Court Road stuffed with love? . . .

Now is not the time to sit alone in your room, eating plums, reading Kierkegaard, hammering at your sores. (Smart 1991, p. 47)

PART 2

Journalling

5

Approaching Journalling

What is Reflective Journalling?

When we think about journalling, many of us have memories of sporadic attempts to keep a personal diary. Often these efforts are undertaken in adolescence – a time of emerging identity, when self-concern is particularly acute. I still have my teenage diaries and, while I regard them very fondly, they are embarrassing. I would not contemplate sharing their passionate reflections on friendship, or the pages and pages on my hair and appearance, with anyone else.

To be clear, a reflective journal is not a throwback to this kind of chaotic, confessional diary keeping. Although a journal may contain private material, record emotions, chart personal struggles, it also represents a purposeful attempt to achieve deeper understanding and greater self-awareness. Crucially, a reflective journal also charts developments in understanding through specific and measured periods of time. This does not necessarily mean problems are solved or closure achieved. However, it does mean that there is an honest attempt made to gain perspective on an issue of concern without abstracting it from its life context.

Very often journal writing has an immediacy, vividness and informality that may be lacking in other forms of reflective writing; sometimes the urgency of 'getting something down' in the midst of challenging circumstances produces very fine writing indeed. What is written in the heat of a particular moment can alert us to important things that we might miss in more distanced forms of life writing. Furthermore, people who have kept journals for many years often develop a particular voice and style that is very suited to their own character and purposes – and very good to read. However, if you are new to journal writing, if your journalling is to be assessed for learning purposes, undertaken in order to support a reflexive research project, or is intended to produce a public performance of some kind (publication, sermon, artwork or testimony), then it is also very likely that extracts presented from it will be in the form of *edited* work.

In the editing process journalled material will be refined, sections will be reworked, details will be elaborated upon, further material included, and (more importantly) much that it is irrelevant or simply too private to share will be removed. Because people mistakenly identify diary keeping with journalling this reshaping can appear to be an inauthentic, or even a dishonest, process. I think this is an unnecessarily sensitive and unrealistic approach to the ethics of journalling. Often considerable work has to be done to communicate with others what has been hastily recorded as half-formed intuitions or 'notes to self'. The same literary processes of construction are at work in journalled reflection as exist elsewhere in reflective writing. This does not mean, however, that no conventions apply within the editing process.

Principally, a reader encountering journal material would justifiably expect *a record that is chronologically structured around a framework of lived events*. These could be work challenges, intellectual encounters or artistic developments – and sometimes all of these are intertwined. However, time-related as they are, journals often look to the past or anticipate the future. When I edit my own writing for publication, I often allow such invasions from other time zones. I also frequently arrange my work around key points in the Christian year. This gives a shape to events that comes from beyond the actual circumstances themselves. When I work in this way, I usually come to see theological meanings in my journey that would not have been evident without such a structuring device. As my purposes *are theological*, I do not regard this as an illicit move. However, it does serve to alert both the reader and myself to the fact that an interpretative process is in place within the journal pages. This is not merely a straightforward record of things that have happened.

The chronological patterning of journals is thus more nuanced than it may at first appear and is not at all a restrictive convention. In fact it generates the many useful and creative opportunities that exist within the genre. Journals can provide space for problem solving, extended thought experiments, the development of new research agendas and the progressive unfolding of creative projects in poetry, fiction or artwork. It is important, when using journals to develop our thought and practice in these ways, that we make acknowledgement of the sources we are drawing upon for inspiration. This is as important in journalling as it is in an essay. My own journals, not surprisingly, do not contain references or footnotes – although often they contain half-remembered quotes and notes from reading. But when I edit them for publication I attribute these as part of my pact of accountability with my reader.

Clearly how much editing and restructuring of journalled writing is appropriate will depend on the type of reflective journalling that is being undertaken, as we shall explore below. Some reflective processes require the registering of very immediate recollections in as accurate a form as possible. Other types of journal are intended to record developing processes that take place over a considerable period. It is helpful to be clear about the particular requirements of the journal form you are using, if your work is being assessed. Otherwise, just relax and write. It is entirely appropriate to mix and match from several styles of journal keeping, to be personally inventive and to include all sorts of heterogeneous and fanciful material in your journal keeping. It is also very interesting to explore the interaction between your thinking about a theme or issue with the events and circumstances of your everyday life. This highlights points of unexpected integration and alerts you to where disconnections are happening that could be explored further.

Forms of Reflective Journalling

Learning Journals

This type of journal is used in a variety of educational contexts, and its intention is to make learning processes more effective. The theory upon which this practice is based is that ideas that are reflected upon are more profoundly understood and owned by students. One of the leading advocates of this type of journalling, Jennifer Moon, argues that reflective processes are what move learners beyond superficial understandings to deep learning. In this latter stage we can relate new ideas to previous insights, identify patterns, note gaps in our own knowledge, challenge assumptions and creatively employ new critical tools for our own ends. Reflective journal writing can be a very significant part of this developmental process because the learning journal:

- requires that time be given to reflective processes;
- makes learners organize and clarify their thoughts;
- reveals gaps in knowledge and understanding to the writer;
- permits ambiguity and uncertainty to be addressed;
- captures experiences for future consideration;
- allows depth of thought to develop from surface impressions;
- encourages the writer to face fears and hurts;
- attunes the writer to emotions and bodily impressions;
- develops creativity;

- enables solutions to be imagined to difficult problems;
- stimulates play and experimentation;
- trains the writer in rigorous analytic thinking.

(adapted from Moon 2006, p. 31)

Learning journals may be particularly effective when people are encountering ideas that might appear to challenge previously cherished assumptions. They allow students some sort of control and agency within the learning process and create shifts in understanding things that can be personally owned by students rather than imposed from outside (see Picca, Starks and Gunderson 2013).

Within theological contexts learning journals can be used both in relation to content-based courses, where people are often asked to log their responses to lectures, readings and so on, and more often in placement situations in which students encounter varied and challenging circumstances. Identifying what has been learnt and understanding its theological challenges are both important outcomes of this type of journalling work.

Critical Incident Journals

This form of journal is widely used in health and social care, in education and in pastoral training. It differs from a learning journal in that particular incidents and encounters are identified within their life context and selected to form the basis of much deeper and more focused reflection. Usually the critical incident will form the basis of conversation with a supervisor or be reflected upon within a learning group. It is also frequently assessed as part of a professional development programme. In many parts of the world those training for pastoral ministry would be expected to complete a course of Clinical Pastoral Education (CPE). This involves structured reflection, often in a group context, upon pastoral encounters recorded 'verbatim' – that is, in as close to the exact words used as possible. The principles at play are similar to those of critical incident analysis, although structured personal reflection may take place after the incident is initially presented for discussion (on the uses of verbatims see Ward 2005).

The term 'critical incident' is rather misleading. The term is used in planning contexts by emergency services to refer to an event with potentially catastrophic consequences. However, in the context of reflective journalling it can mean *either* an incident typical of many others and therefore important for understanding professional roles and actions, *or* an incident of significance because it raised unexpected challenges. A great deal can be learnt from the examination of apparently mundane and routine situations. A critical incident does not need to be a dramatic event.

Each professional context is likely to have its own particular requirements for the presentation of critical incidents. However, the reflective methods used tend to follow fairly similar stages. A typical format for theological reflection upon a critical incident would be:

- *Description of the incident or experience*: This includes its background causes, any wider contextual influences, your role in events, your feelings in the situation (attend to your emotional responses), what action you took, and who else was involved with this.
- *Analysis of personal response*: Was my action appropriate? What were its consequences? How do I feel about it looking back? What have the responses of others been?
- *Experimental thinking*: Could I have acted differently? What might alternative responses have led to? What can I learn from this event for future planning?
- *Attention to learning*: What have I learnt from this? How has my thinking changed? What new ideas have I developed about my personal role, my professional responsibilities? How has this action changed my beliefs and values, my ethical judgements?
- *Theological reflection*: Where was God in this situation? What faith resources have I brought to dealing with this event? What new theological thinking has emerged from my reflection upon it?
- *Action*: What should I be doing with this knowledge and how can I build upon it? How will these actions be congruent with my new theological vision?

Research Journals

As discussed in Part 1 of this book, on autoethnography, journalling is a very important practice when undertaking research projects. Particularly in ethnographic forms of qualitative research it is important to bring diverse forms of data into conversation, to interrogate how personal preconceptions are being challenged and to record new insights. A journal is also the place to record how certain research strategies have failed to deliver hoped-for outcomes or to work out new ways of proceeding if circumstances change. Journals are sources of data in themselves, and extracts from them are frequently used in theses or publications alongside other forms of material.

Students engaged in all forms of practical theological research are thus encouraged to be actively reflexive in their research processes and to see reflective journalling as a significant part of this discipline. Reflexivity is particularly important in the forms of 'action research' that are becoming increasingly important in the theological context (see Cameron et al. 2010). Action research is attractive for many reasons but principally because of its explorative and open-ended nature, the potential it offers to engage stakeholders in the research process, and also because it is change-directed and value-driven. An action reflection journal undertaken within a theological context would seek to address the following key areas:

- *The background to the intervention*: Why this action at this time? What evidence and research is it based upon? Who has done similar things before? What ethical considerations must be taken into account before beginning? How is this action congruent with faith and values?
- *Planning*: What are the aims? Who are the partners? How do we consult to find out more before beginning this project? Who does the project belong to and in what ways are we mutually accountable?
- *Action*: What have I/we done? What results have there been? Who is affected? Has it gone as planned?
- *Evaluation*: Are the outcomes as hoped? What has been achieved? What has not gone well? What has surprised us? How do other stakeholders feel about the outcomes? What steps need to be taken to test our new understandings more widely? How do we plan effective interventions in the future?
- *Self-assessment*: What have I learnt about myself, my professional role, the people I work alongside?
- *Group-assessment*: What is our new understanding of our corporate identity and social role?
- *Theological reflection*: How does this intervention correspond to our faith and vision? What have we learnt about God in the process of action? What theological resources should we seek to develop for future action?

Creative Journals

Learning journals, critical incident journals and research journals are all now widely used in theological reflection. They have well-understood aims and can be seen to deliver useful outcomes. However, sometimes they can become rather pedestrian. The reliable reflective processes that give students and supervisors confidence can also militate against the development of creative awareness that is so important in theological thinking.

In my own teaching and supervision I have been influenced by the ways in which journalling is employed within arts education in fields ranging from creative writing to fashion design. These forms of journalling are also highly structured and have their own conventions – but within them students are positively encouraged to engage in progressive steps of personal risk taking and thinking outside the box.

In art schools, for example, the sketchbook functions in similar ways to a research journal, charting steps in an artistic project. When setting out to produce work on a particular theme or topic, the student is encouraged to use their sketchbook to record:

- sources from art or design history and contemporary culture that will inspire their own work in this field;
- examples (usually photographs) of contemporary contexts, objects or incidents that also evoke creative thinking on this issue;
- sketches and other images/imaginings displaying their own responses to the theme in the light of these stimuli;
- experiments in diverse media that have helped them shape and embody their ideas further.

Out of this eclectic exploratory phase it is likely that several ideas will emerge as potentially important. A number of these may proceed beyond this initial phase into further creative development. After yet more exploration choices are made as to what is to be honed and shaped into a final outcome.

This type of work encourages imaginative processes and does not shut down promising trajectories prematurely. At its best there is a playful aspect to sketchbook work[1] that is becoming rarer in our increasingly pressured academic environment. The processes outlined above can offer a helpful corrective to more utilitarian forms of reflective thinking. The steps are easily translatable from visual

---

1 That is not to say that this form of education cannot also become as formulaic and restrictive as any other. Context is everything! However, as we borrow methods from other disciplinary sources to stimulate creativity in our own work, we are likely to treasure, at least for a while, the new freedoms they offer.

to language forms. In other words, when researching a theological theme or topic we can:

- locate challenging and inspiring resources from artistic sources – including literature, film, music and so on;
- seek out contemporary narrative accounts that relate to the topic and also resonate deeply with us. These may be found in news media, popular culture or other 'everyday' mediums of communication;
- consider how these resources speak to and resonate with our beliefs and values;
- 'sketch' out, through our own imaginative writing, new responses to these various stimuli;
- intentionally experiment with genre and form (which are the material media of the writing process) to find effective means of expressing new theological thinking;
- identify things that excite us from this research process which we wish to develop further into risky, edgy and performative theological reflection.

Spiritual Journals

I was hesitant about including a special section on spiritual journalling here as all the forms of journal writing mentioned above can be used to support the development of spiritual understanding. Furthermore, we no longer view spirituality as a separate sphere of life divorced from other aspects of our personal journeys. However, we do inherit precious traditions of spiritual journalling from writers whose overriding concern has been to cultivate a growing awareness of God's presence. These are works that can guide and inspire us at those times in which we wish to make religious experience the specific focus of our journal writing. The wartime journals of Etty Hillesum (1999 [1981]) have been a very significant example of this kind of literature for me, and they are a challenging place to begin if you have not encountered this kind of literature before.[2]

Often we focus upon spiritual journalling in the context of a retreat, when progressing through a 'holy' season like Lent or during a period of spiritual direction. In such cases the journal writing is used to foster skills of patient, deep attentiveness. The discipline of receptivity and the painful,

---

2 For a helpful introduction to spiritual journalling practice see also Klug 2002.

slow work of intensifying perception are what are sought through writing that attempts to put into words the brief flash of an epiphany or the almost inaudible prompting of a still small voice. Interestingly in the context of this book, these are precisely the faculties that we seek to cultivate through creative writing. They involve mindful awareness of the small intensities of daily living: the sudden perception of beauty in a flower, an urban skyscape, a human face. They also involve the kind of symbolic sensitivity that is characteristic of all poetic work. The poet and the spiritual seeker alike engage with physical and material phenomena in such a way that they become vehicles for communicating on other levels without losing their commonplace identity. These passages from Etty Hillesum's journals illustrate these processes at work as she speaks of and to God in the most poignant and beautiful writing:

> [F]rom my bed I stared out through the large open window. And it was once more as if life with all its mysteries were close to me, as if I could touch it. I had a feeling that I was resting against the naked breast of life and could feel her gentle regular heart beat . . . And I thought, how strange it is war time. There are concentration camps. (1999 [1981], p. 165)

> But somewhere inside me the jasmine continues to blossom undisturbed, just as profusely and delicately as it ever did. And it spreads its scent round the house in which you dwell, O God. You can see I look after you. I bring you not only my tears and forebodings on this stormy, grey Sunday morning. I even bring you scented jasmine. (1999 [1981], p. 219)

Using Journalling

Journal writing is becoming an increasingly used tool in educational contexts. In a recent curriculum review in my own department we discovered, to our dismay, that students in one particular year group were being required to keep three different journals *at the same time* to meet the demands of three separate courses. This is clearly massive overkill and partly explains why some students are becoming resistant to journal writing. There are others who, haunted by perceived failures in attempts at diary keeping, express fears they will be 'bad' at journalling and lose assessment points because of this. Journal writing for assessment can be resisted for a very different reason. I have encountered students have been keeping journals in their own way for many years. Already highly proficient writers, they are annoyed by suggestions that they change the form of their writing to meet external demands or that they expose their work to critical scrutiny.

While recognizing that there is some substance to these 'resistances', I have found that journal writing, when purposefully embraced, is a hugely helpful process in achieving intellectual clarity and developing creative thinking. However, it is often necessary to free oneself of some of the more common preconceptions about journal writing and view it in a new light. Below are my own attempts to challenge some of the most unhelpful blocks to journal writing.

- You do not need to keep a journal every day or for ever. Many people simply journal once every few days or through specific periods (e.g. holidays, work projects, retreats, times of personal difficulty). This is fine.
- E-journals are good, loose-leafed binders are good. Everything is good. You don't need the gold-edged notebook or the fountain pen – but do use these if you wish, while remembering you may need to retranscribe.
- Don't ignore what is happening in your life generally as you wrestle with an issue. The strength of a journal is that it places your engagement with a challenge in its lived context. Surprising conjunctions occur that are invaluable in progressing your thought further.
- While your course may categorize your journal in a narrow or instrumental way, you don't need to. Learning journal, critical journal, creative journal – whatever. Your journal can be a book of all things, a resource that you will later shape into the form it needs to take.
- So even if your journal has to be done for work or assessment, make it your own place in which you feel comfortable. Include your emotional responses, rant about your irritations, challenge the assumptions of your supervisors and doodle in the margins (literally or metaphorically).
- Re the above: you do not need to show everything you have written. Editing is good for you – and for your reader!
- Experiment and be creative. Try and see the space of a page as an opportunity for discovery. If you don't like the conventional processes of journal writing, try something different that works for you. This is not just OK, it is the way forward.
- Don't be passive, don't be lazy and don't be afraid. Trust the process!

6

The Course Outline: Teaching Theology through Creative Writing

This journal extract was written in a period during which I was seeking to develop my ideas for a new course into a deliverable curriculum. As such it was a reflective aid to the development of a project, allowing me to identify where my inspiration was coming from, where my insecurities lay and what obstacles needed to be overcome. It also allowed me to place my hopes for a piece of professional work in the context of a larger theological frame.

Monday, 15 September

Just one week to the start of term and the first session of my new Master's module 'Theology through Creative Writing'. Been looking forward to teaching this for months but now feel very uncertain about the shape of the course and how it will be delivered. In my mind it carries so much potential that I am having problems configuring it into the scheduled slots on a Monday afternoon in the very 'uncreative' environment of the Upper Seminar Room. There is so much at stake for me in this venture, and it's almost as if I don't want to risk all I have invested by actually teaching the course. So the computer screen is blank apart from the words 'Course Outline', and it is very clear to me now that, although I had to draw up the aims, learning outcomes and sample bibliography for the 'scrutiny and approval' process, I have no idea about how I am actually going to deliver this module. The 'outline' has yet to emerge.

But perhaps I should be more positive?

Although I am not sure exactly how I want to go about this, I know very well how I don't want to proceed. I don't want to start with Saint Augustine's *Confessions* (don't want them in the middle or at the end either). This is not because I don't like Augustine. I am actually very fond of him indeed *despite* the awful legacy and the pretty terrible things he did while he was alive as well! However, whenever the subject of theological thinking as creative writing comes up people reach for *Confessions* as the big, boyish book that legitimizes the endeavour. I don't think this sort of legitimation is what we need. Nevertheless, it is true that *Confessions* contains some amazing passages – like the bit where he hears the child's voice calling in the garden. But what *Confessions* represents could massively overwhelm what I am trying to achieve.

You might read *Confessions* as a kind of parable demonstrating the way in which theology and literature are meant to be positioned in relation to each other. Imagination is supposed to find its fulfilment in a properly sanctified relationship to faith – or be sent away in shame like Augustine's concubine. And while I don't think Augustine actually manages to subdue his passions in writing, the fact that this monumental volume is usually placed on the table whenever theology and creative writing sit down to talk together has a very 'chastening' effect upon nervous new writers. I don't want to be chaste in his way; not yet and not ever. So I need to start somewhere else. Another place entirely.

Not getting very far. Keep thinking about the child calling in the garden. Wonderful image; love it. Would make a great writing exercise to reflect upon it. Perhaps I should go back and read it again.

But can't pursue these thoughts, because of my own child calling to me.

'Mum, if I finish my French before nine, will you come and watch *Desperate Housewives* with me?'

Desperate Housewives/Saint Augustine . . . Duty/Desire . . . Difficult choice.

Tuesday, 16 September

Really resent the way that term starts earlier each year! Although it's supposed to still be the summer vacation, there have been meetings called since the end of August. Today's was on the 'student learning experience' and emphasized all the stuff about student-centred learning, which has become the orthodoxy these days. Walk back past the new Med School. A building designed for groups to work together on co-operative learning tasks. It's lovely. All wood, slate and glass. We don't have the stylish round tables and leather chairs in our department, but I think my new module belongs with many other ventures that represent a sea change in the way we see education. The old world stands in stark contrast with the new. In the past a good postgraduate student was expected to:

- sit alone in the library and read a lot of books;
- ask 'proper' questions (respectful, sensible, answerable) of their sources and their supervisors;
- find out the truth about things and write it down;
- present this neatly packaged into papers that contain reasoned arguments and perhaps the occasional original subclause – but no funny business!
- always use the third person and preferably a passive voice;
- generate useful new knowledge and thus change the world.

Today a good student must:

- still read a lot of books, but can do so in groups or online;
- be attentive to their own lived experience and the questions this raises;
- write in the first person with a strong sense of the contextual claims of their material and the need for accountability in the generation of knowledge;
- craft new narratives, metaphors and symbols that can be shared with others in an ongoing process of creating a new cultural imaginary that has redemptive potential for both individuals and society.

I suppose that, by choosing to locate my own work in an interdisciplinary context, and placing such courses as 'Theology through Creative Writing' on the books, I am signalling that I believe the bright new world is better (more vivid, colourful, creative and transformative) than the (dull, rigid, pedestrian) old world of sure knowledge. But actually I am not a true believer. I have grave doubts about these educational changes – for good reasons.

First, academic rigour can be compromised, and I care about that. Second, I care about politics, and it's too easy to shift attention away from the hard work of discerning strategies for social change towards the more nebulous task of shifting the 'cultural imaginary'. Whatever the cultural imaginary might be, it is clearly a bloody difficult thing to shift! And perhaps most important for me, although I am not proud of myself here, is that I find people who think narrative is redemptive, wholesome and nice very annoying. It is nonsense to regard narrative as natural and pure, innocent of the deceptions and devices that taint philosophical or scientific reasoning. There are scripts – doesn't everybody know that? – that direct the way we 'narrate' our lives and speak about God. Moreover, when narrative is at its most powerful it is art, it is literature, it is fiction, it is not 'true'. So many people talk about narrative as if it were hyper-truth rather than art, and this appears to be a particular problem for theologians as we increasingly look for stories to ground us rather than basing our work upon foundational principles.

No wonder I am having problems in putting this course together. I feel like someone setting out a feast with all sorts of tempting and delicious courses. I am saying 'Come and eat'. But I am also saying 'You need to be very careful because the wine is strong and the sweetness can taste bitter later.' I am saying 'Come and buy your fruits at the "Goblin Market".' Christina Rossetti, like all real poets, understood the temptation of delights that 'taste like honey to the throat/ but poison in the blood' (2001, pp. 2140–52).

Wednesday, 17 September

Met with the Director of Glasgow's Creative Writing Programme this morning to discuss the colloquium we are jointly organizing in January. He is enthusiastic and full of ideas. I am more cautious. Big names require large budgets. These he might possibly be able to access, but I certainly could not. I know he understands the discrepancy between our disciplinary fortunes, and I sense that he also feels an uneasy tension in the alliance. Theology may have fallen on hard times, but she has been once a queen and still makes claim to royalty. Creative writing has popular appeal but, her enemies say, no lineage.

But there's no doubt that despite their 'new-money' status creative writing programmes are flourishing in the contemporary academy. Glasgow's is one of the most successful postgraduate initiatives in the university and the course deserves its great reputation. However, despite this, when I did my own Master's degree in creative writing I travelled all the way from Glasgow to Goldsmiths in London for one day every week for two years. A bit mad, but I needed the space to develop as a writer, and for me this had to be away from my academic home.

It also had to be the right type of course for me. They differ so much. Goldsmiths' is largely based on the writing workshop. However, lots of the others I looked at were basically adapted from old Master's courses in Literature (which had clearly been around for a decade or more to judge by the bibliographies), with a wee workshop added on almost as an afterthought. Because the writing workshop, in which we shared our own work, was at the heart of things, we really bonded as a group. But the course did contain other elements – including a huge emphasis on literary form. What is poetry? What is life writing? What is a novel? I liked this a lot. There are questions, actually theological questions, about form (incarnation) which very few theologians ask and which writers have to wrestle with day in day out. I think these are exciting, and I want to introduce them to my students. It's funny. I know how creative writing is taught. I've read up on pedagogical processes, assessment, etc., and the same goes for theology. But this does not mean I am at all clear how the two can be married together. Like many of those initiated into its rituals, I have come to believe that the writing workshop element has a 'sacred' status – but I also want to discuss theory, ethics, technique, and to present these as inherently theological topics. Oh my God, the poor students! All this in two hours per week.

Thursday, 18 September

Am examining a PhD next week and need to send off my report on it today. The candidate is a practising artist, who has taken works of modern art and placed them next to biblical passages (to which they have little evident connection) with extraordinary results. Striking new meanings emerge. It's really 'creative', and I am very impressed but feel slightly irritated by the fact that he keeps on apologizing for what he is doing. As if he's not sure it's allowed. 'Be brave,' I want to say, and this starts me thinking about how distinctly cowardly I am feeling about this course. I feel miles away from my comfort zone and very exposed. Why is this?

Actually, I have been teaching creative writing in theological contexts for years. But usually I teach all the conventional stuff first, so people are introduced to the competent, professional persona before they encounter the mad woman in the attic. I always start by locating myself in the mainstream: 'These are the methods of theological reflection generated within the tradition, and this is how they can be used.'

Then right at the end of the course I say: 'But imagination is also a means of reflection, a way of knowing and naming God, and so you might like to experiment with creative writing as well.'

Then I give people some easy, non-threatening exercises that most of them quite enjoy but don't ever have to use again, and off we go.

It's a means of getting away with something different in an otherwise conventional setting, but it does represent a marginalization of creative writing. I am guiltily aware of this fact.

And I have committed more crimes. I realize that, even when I have led conferences and retreats specifically on creative writing, I have also gone for safe options. I have introduced spiritual biography (bloody Augustine), spiritual journalling, forms of autoethnography and life writing, but have been really cautious about blending the theological with the fantastical and the fictional. Too dangerous for lots of people – evidently including myself! It's quite another matter, of course, to read 'serious fiction' alongside theological texts. That is much easier to do, and few people raise an eyebrow about this these days. It's when you ask people to write in ways that somewhere deep inside they sense might not be 'straight' that the trouble starts. Come on, Heather. Have the courage of your convictions. Write it slant.

Friday, 19 September

Not a very productive day at work. Did the routine admin stuff necessary for my teaching on Monday but still not a lot of progress with my course outline. I'll have to work over the weekend. Get home to find my daughter ensconced in the living room with her two friends Sophie and Ella. Forgot that I'd rashly agreed they could sleep over tonight. That means the room will be strewn with magazines and smell of nail polish and face cream, as they give each other makeovers. And I'll never get on the computer, because they'll be on YouTube or Facebook or whatever till after midnight. But hey it's nice. I like it really.

Begin to prepare the meal but can still hear them talking in the other room. They are playing the choice game again. It is a favourite on these kinds of easy intimate occasions. What do you like best? Christmas or Birthday? Mountains or Sea? Sweets or Chocolate? Johnny Depp or Orlando Bloom? It's still a choice between goods at this age. Not fire or plague? Drugs or alcohol? Death or despair? Both Sophie and Ella are quite definite. I hear them make quick, clear choices, but my daughter just can't. 'Let me think', 'It all depends', 'I just can't decide'. The only thing she definitely chooses is Johnny Depp. But that's so obvious, it's not a choice really.

I can understand her difficulties. It's the indeterminacy, the ambiguity, the uncertainty that fascinates me in life and draws me to writing. Sometimes I fear my syncretistic tendencies don't fit me that well for the theological guild. I think most theologians prefer things to be one way and not the other. Clearly outlined even! Perhaps this is why there is relatively little theological reflection upon the act of writing itself – a justified suspicion of its veils and traces. Broadly speaking you can divide the assumptions theologians make about their own writing practices into two categories. On the one hand there are those who assume that their words are mirrors of a deeper reality and just about adequate enough to reflect its essential nature. On the other are those who are more concerned that their writing evokes real life and the suffering of the world with sufficient power to provoke a religious response. In both cases the focus lies with a 'reality' beyond writing which demands attention, and the writing practice itself is viewed as of no great significance at all.

I, on the other hand, have always thought it was quite important to write beautifully about God. Well, very important really. Even if the precise meaning of the words can never be exactly decided.

Saturday, 20 September

It is raining. It is windy. I would like to be out walking in the wild wetness, but I have to do the washing and cleaning and make lunch for three teenage girls, when they eventually wake up. This is not how I imagined my life would be. When I was young, I wanted to be a writer. That is, I wanted to be Byron or Shelley actually. Unconstrained, radical, Promethean. But what I have come to understand about writing, from the women I have studied, is that sometimes the most powerful work is produced out of mundane contexts of constraint, obligation and care; situations of responsibility and restraint.

The Guardian once ran a series on 'Writers' Rooms'. It was really interesting. And there was a picture of Virginia Woolf's shed at the bottom of the garden. Nice. But Leonard would insist on keeping the deckchairs and the bowling equipment in it, and there was a school playground just the other side of the hedge. Then there was the Brontes' small, very conventional parlour with its ordinary table and the couch in the corner, where stubborn Emily lay down to die. I felt I learnt a lot just looking at these ordinary spaces.

I once had this student who was really closed and uptight, and I was trying to help her feel a bit freer in her faith. I asked her to write for me about how she sensed the presence of God in her daily life. She said to me, 'I don't think I have the kind of experiences in my daily life that you find God in.' That stopped me dead. I should have been able to find a way to help her explore the sudden sweetness of a domestic epiphany. Shared with her Etty Hillesum's wonderful words about visions in confined spaces (Hillesum 1999 [1981]). Etty's life was crushed to crystal as the Jews in Amsterdam came under increasing persecution. Everything was focused down. The precious bar of lilac soap, the pink blouse, her table lamp, her lover's caressing hands, the worn Bible, the slim volume of Rilke. I guess this process of constriction is the same as the one through which the cloisters, the cells and the deserts generated their erotic theologies.

Enough. Back to the washing, Heather!

Sunday, 21 September

Not raining. A beautiful, fresh morning. To church with my daughter.

It is when she sits close to me in quiet moments that I feel most startled by her.

Coping with nearly a decade of infertility, hospitals, clinics, treatment cycles was what started me writing again. Had stopped entirely when I went to university to study literature! It was desolation and desperation rather than inspiration that led me to it. Or are these all the same? I wrote some of my best pieces in those years, and I know they have communicated powerfully to others. I still find that it is in moments of failure, crippling anxiety or self-doubt that the need to write is strongest. For me it is like prayer I think.

These thoughts raise the old question about whether you can actually teach people to be creative. Of course there are all sorts of techniques you can use to get people to put pen to paper, but does not the creativity take place when people connect to that place of pain within themselves? Does writing (like language) originate in that space of loss, absence and desire? And what about talent? Is it basically a facility for alchemy? The charlatan's knack of turning the unspeakable into words.

And then what capacities should the teacher possess? Clearly, she must herself be a writer, but must she be a 'good writer' or a 'better' writer than her pupils? Perhaps one of the reasons I am daunted by teaching this course is that I worry people will discover that my own work is not very good. I feel inadequate. But this feeling is balanced by the fact that I know very few people have thought or written about this intersection of theology and creative writing (as opposed to the relation between literature and theology, which is a rather different matter). I believe my work is important – if only because of this. Clearly, this mixture of fear and pride must be acknowledged.

It occurs to me that this course outline is itself a piece of creative writing. It requires all the skill and imagination I possess to get it right. Like all creative writing, it puts the writer in a place of both vulnerability and of power. However, there is another element. Really creative writing possesses the shocking quality of an encounter. My course must make space for strange meetings with the familiar unknown. Hélène Cixous said that writing was like a daughter to her (1998, p. 80). The daughter is intimately known but also remains a complete mystery to her mother.

I think that it is intimate mysteries of all kinds that are what my life and faith and writing are about.

I must do this. I will do this . . . By tomorrow morning at the latest.

7

Between Ascension and Pentecost: Towards a Theology of Adoption

Although no formal fieldwork was involved, this is very much a research journal. It charts my encounters within a new area of study and my attempts to craft my own contribution to this field. It is clear that the topic has great relevance to my own family life, and I find the way in which the critical, academic reflection and everyday circumstances interact very helpful. The fact that the work I was doing took place during an important season of the Church's year was also very stimulating. Although quite a 'messy' text, I think it reveals how journalling can bring together diverse sources into unexpected, creative conjunctions.

Thursday, 13 May – Ascension Day

Forgot it was Ascension Day! Remembered only mid afternoon, when I had already missed the Chaplaincy Mass. Before I came to Scotland I regularly went to my local Catholic church to supplement the meagre feasts of my Protestant diet. I go less often here, because the churches are so conservative. As a result, I am definitely less in touch with the liturgical year. Felt a pang of guilt – but only a pang. I have very little investment in this particular feast. I always remember slipping into choral evensong in an Oxford college and having to stop myself from laughing out loud when I glimpsed the stained glass window representing Christ ascending. It was of a cloud with two thin little legs and two big feet sticking out of the bottom. That, I thought, demonstrates the problem we have with this. The Ascension, apart of course from being a holy mystery, is an attempt to resolve difficult questions like how do we move from the period of Christ's ministry, passion and resurrection into a new era? And, most particularly, 'What do we do with the body?' Some resolution of this issue is required to make possible the transition from Easter to Pentecost, but we haven't really resolved our many problems with the absent/present body of Christ. 'Do not touch me' – the intimate mystery in the garden still haunts us.

Today I began reading for the Adoption Symposium, but did not get very far. Became engrossed in thinking about Darlene Weaver's meditations on the theme that 'Christ's body is the most real of all bodies' (2007, pp. 152–3). Her reflections were humane and circumspect, placing this outrageous claim in its proper theological context. However, I was struck again by that alarming tendency in much contemporary Catholic thought (and spreading) to suggest that our human embodied relations are but the shadows of divine reality. I once listened to a devout and tortured gay Christian explaining that for him marriage between men and women was sacred, because the relationship between Christ and the Church was not *like* but *actually* that of bride and bridegroom. This was the divine reality, he believed, that instituted the shadow form of human marriage. This is what made it holy – and simultaneously excluded him from its sacred bonds. I thought, 'How is it that we have come so far from the impulse to name God by drawing upon our experience of joyful nuptial celebrations to a position where we co-ordinate the significance of our mortal lives by mapping them onto ideal celestial forms?' We are forever in the cave and never in the sweet fresh sunshine. I am with Bonhoeffer, who thought there was something faintly distasteful about thinking of God when in the embrace of your lover. Actually, I think it is worse than distasteful, in a world where so many human bodies are abused, tortured, starving and shamed, to imply that God's is the most real body, the pain, struggle and passion displaced to some divine economy in which we share but at one remove. Do not touch me. You can't touch Christ's body. He has gone up in a cloud.

The importance of this matter in theological reflection upon adoption appears to be evident throughout the literature I am encountering. We seem to approach adoption by taking norms for our own practice from those we believe/imagine are operative in the transcendent economy, rather than reflecting upon what our experience of adoption might usefully teach us about God and about human flourishing. Kind of wish it were the other way round.

Friday, 14 May

Today my daughter is working to complete the portfolio she has been putting together for her studies in Art and Design. She is working with a deep involvement and intensity I have never seen in her before. The theme she has developed in her studies and sketches is 'At the Window'. Her final outcome is a self-portrait of her sitting beside a large Glasgow tenement window at night-time. Her features are very clear and distinct, but the reflections in the window are a jumble of silhouettes illuminated by streetlamps and headlights and intermixed with the reflection of objects inside the building. It is very effective, this mixture of clarity and chaos. The night-time and the brightness. The human form distinct, but the world around appearing in surreal and abstract dimensions. The figure seated is clearly deep in thought. This impression is heightened by the reflective images that dominate the centre of the work.

She is painting, and I am working on this paper for the symposium. It is companionable but intense as we both struggle to address issues of self-representation in a manner that does justice both to our own concrete identity and the unknowns within and outside us. Today I have been reading John Wall's work exploring the image of God in the child (2004; 2007). For Wall image and incarnation are linked concepts. The child does not merely resemble the divine but also embodies God. I think my 16-year-old daughter understands, intuitively, that the mere representation of a likeness is not sufficient to convey an image, and she is struggling with other elements in the composition to convey a deeper truth about who she is. A theology of adoption that takes seriously the image of God in the child would, I think, begin to discern that this image cannot be grasped without throwing the contours of the world inside and out into confusion. The image of God as child might be hard to glimpse in a theology of adoption dominated by concerns for what is permissible (how did that word find its way into Christian ethics?), normative or definitive. Recognition of the image of God in the child is always likely to throw other elements of the picture into new and strange configurations. Not least because we would be compelled to consider that the child may wear the face of God in the relation rather than the parent mediating God's love to the child.

Saturday, 15 May

We all got up late today and sat around reading papers, eating bagels with cream cheese and talking intermittently, sharing scraps of news, enjoying the companionable intimacy of family life. This is what I would have missed, I thought, if we were childless. The everyday extraordinariness of it all. After a shower and a strong milky coffee it is time to sit down at the dining table spread with journal articles and get on with things.

Today I earmarked to study social research related to adoption in the UK. One of the most important lessons liberation theology has taught us about theological reflection is always to seek to understand the issue on its own terms before you reflect upon it. I find that I had partially and badly understood a great many things about adoption in the contemporary context. So how interesting it is that in the UK intrafamily adoptions, including adoptions by blood parents, form such a huge part of the overall picture (O'Halloran 2009, pp. 52–76). This is not something I had really factored in. The reasons for this are:

- to make the family structure in hybrid households coherent (a version of the ontological hygiene that Elaine Graham [2002] talks about);
- to ensure rights of decision making about access and so on;
- to gain legal securities;
- to maintain a blood link (*ius sanguinis* in legal terms).

Apart from the intrafamily adoptions a picture emerges of childless heterosexual couples seeking babies (many of whom adopt from abroad using a variety of arrangements); gay and lesbian couples, who are often willing to take older children; couples who volunteer to adopt children with special needs, many of whom in the past would have received institutional care. A complex and rapidly shifting picture, and increasingly shaped by the relatively new dynamic that adopted children now often remain in contact with birth parents, rendering the family leaky and porous. This is interesting – I am enthralled.

I think that when I was struggling with infertility one reason I did not want to think about adoption, had ruled it out in fact, was because the model of the adoptive family I had in mind (in which the parents adopt for purely altruistic reasons) did not seem to map onto my mixed, ambivalent, passionate longings. However, the picture of adoption in the UK confounds my previous view of this 'virtuous' family unit. If we were to make the situation of adoption as it exists the starting point for reflecting on a theology of adoption, then we would come out with something quite different from that emerging in the papers I have been reading. There would need to be a new acknowledgement of ambivalence in human and divine relations. We would have cause to marvel at the heterogeneity and theological complexity of the ties that bind us: ties of blood, culture, care, compassion and desire. We would find cause to celebrate in the loving care of the gay couple who adopt the bullied teenager, the blood father who repents of previous neglect and returns in penitence to renew a covenant with his little girl, the mother of a woman who committed suicide rearing her grandchild in grief and grace and hope. So much, I believe, we could learn of the coming kingdom from experiences such as these. From this perspective, I would be inclined to agree with those who suggest that Christians might see adoption as a mirror for understanding all familial relations . . .

Sunday, 16 May

To church, but my daughter is not with me. She is at home revising for her exams, which start tomorrow. As an Elder and on duty this week I am at the door and greeting the congregation as they arrive. We are a strange and mixed group of people – an eccentric but lovable congregation, and people whom I have learnt to share so much with over the past years. Yes, I think, we are the household of God, and we learn what that means in the day-to-day bearing with each other and embodying forth the love of God that constitutes our communal life. So what then of baptism? That one baptism that so many of the writers I am looking at make the cornerstone of their adoption theology? Well . . . I took my baby to be baptized in the Catholic Church, because her father was Catholic, and I would probably be Catholic too, if the present dispensation were not so oppressive. I took her for baptism despite the fact that I knew (and the priest knew) her conception through IVF was not according to the rules. It was wonderful, our ecumenical celebration – so many people attended that they had to sit on the altar steps and stand at the back of the church. My Auntie Joan, at 70 and a lifelong Methodist, was thrilled at the ceremony.

'They really do it well,' she told me. 'I think we should all have candles and anointing with oil.'

'Yes, and all the Angels and Saints and the Hosts of Heaven looking on and smiling,' I agreed with her. But what do I think now?

Well, of course, I think this event marked once and for ever my daughter's incorporation into the body of the Church. But also I know today she is not with me, and I do not know if, at 16, she will be accompanying me to Sunday worship for much longer. This is also something I wrestle with, which challenges me, and which I cannot resolve with theological formulae. Marked for ever sealed and signed – but not here, not present right now, and I am lonely for her.

It's interesting the way baptism has become such a big issue in contemporary theologies of belonging (see, for example, Bennett 2008).

Many theologians wishing to affirm the place of gay and lesbian Christians within the 'queer' Body of Christ have returned to the font to enforce their title (see, for example, Stuart 1999). And at the same time those who advocate a normative family pattern for natural and adoptive households stand by that same font and make claims about what we learn here about the sort of families God intended to form and what their proper bounds and ties should be. For myself, and as the kind of theologian I seem called to be, I am always interested in the ambiguous boundary points of human life, and baptism is one of these. Yes, it is the point of entry into the Church. Here we share in death and rise renewed to life in Christ. But also yes. Here we say in words and symbols that the birth of blood and water from the mother is not enough. Something is lacking. It is not real birth. Let her be born by the priest and by the Father, then she will be truly a child of God. This is a troubling thought. All these conflicts and unresolved issues as we gather together this Sunday morning as the community of the baptized. As an Elder on duty I stand to read from the Gospel of John the lesson that takes us beyond the blood and water to a unity established before the foundation of the world.

> I in them and you in me, that they may become completely one, so that the world may know that you have sent me and have loved them even as you have loved me. (John 17.23)

Monday, 17 May

I woke in the night. I thought I heard her cry, and I rushed to her room. But she was sleeping. I stood just a moment and watched her as she slept. This now nearly-woman, the most beautiful child there has ever been.

I am an anxious parent. In my own defence I could mention the years of waiting, the miscarriage and the roller coaster of the pregnancy ending with the emergency Caesarean. I could tell of the certainty I felt as they rushed me down the corridor to the operating table that if she died, it would be best to die with her. And also, in my defence, it has recently been a particularly worrying time. She has been sick this year, and we have been afraid. I have held her hair away from her pale face, and I wished to the core of my being that I could bear for her the pain that gripped her body.

So. A theologian such as Oliver O'Donovan (1984) would tell me this beloved daughter was ill conceived. That she is an object of my consuming desire rather than part of God's creative and providential dispensation. I think this is utter nonsense, but you might expect me to say this, bound up and blinded as I am by my own foolish and arrogant desire to possess the child I am denied. Thanks for this sympathetic reflection upon my plight, but I must contend with you.

We are back again to this issue of the child and the image of God. Most of the work I have read on the theology of adoption maintains that adoption should never be undertaken in order that childless parents can receive a child. This is bad. Bad, because God is the really, real parent. Biological parents, in their care for their child, make an imitative response to the love God has for humanity – unless they cannot do so for some unfortunate reason, in which case adoptive parents, as more or less adequate substitutes, come in and do it for them, as representatives again but at one more stage of remove. Note that at each stage in this drama of substitutions the parent stands for God and the child for humanity. If we are to take part in this tableau of mirrors, our parental love must be God-like; an act of gracious self-giving without passion, partiality or desire for self-fulfilment.

But God came to me as child. As the child I ached for. I desired God deeply and God came to me as child. Nothing was unchanged. Every cell, every charged impulse of my soul and body transformed in that birth. I was broken, and I was healed, and I was remade and for ever transfigured in that encounter. I have known such love as cannot be contained beneath the heavens. And I have held it in my arms.

Tuesday, 18 May

My daughter has now sat two exams in two days, and she is tired. Tonight we ordered in a curry. She watches TV while her father and I share a bottle of wine and enjoy the sense of us all taking time out – separate but together.

My daughter and her friends follow a lot of American TV, and it occurs to me, sensitized as I now am to these issues, that all her favourite shows have very prominent adoptive families within them: the *OC*, *90210*, *Friends*, *One Tree Hill*. This was not the case when I was growing up. Nor was it the case that the magazines I read featured such headlines as 'Angelina and Brad to Adopt Again', 'Jennifer Aniston to become a Mother – She Has Already Visited the Orphanage' . . . Of course there were some prominent adoptive families, but today it seems that the family of choice for celebs is expanding to include adopted children from differing ethnic groups and various social contexts. How do we interpret this? Well, perhaps children are no longer viewed as the impediments to the good life they once were (although the increasing number of partners who choose childlessness cautions us against generalizing here). Maybe there is also a fashionable sense that a family can contain and celebrate diversity and represent a model in miniature of our aspirations for human society more generally. However, perhaps we need to subject this phenomenon to more critical scrutiny.

Anthony Giddens (1991, pp. 89–98) and other sociologists have spoken of our contemporary desire for the 'pure relationship'. In the context of a society in which people are seen as creators (artists) of identity, relationships with partners are viewed as a means of enhancing the reflexive project of constructing a successful self. In a pure relationship partnerships may be entered into in order to enhance the identity profile of both members of the couple. According to Giddens pure relationships have these identifying features. They are:

- freely chosen, not anchored in economic or social ties;
- sought for what they can bring the partners involved;
- reflexively organized and constantly scrutinized;
- relationships in which commitment plays a central role;
- focused on intimacy;
- self relationships in which identity is negotiated through linked processes of self-exploration and development of intimacy with the other.

I think the much valorized celebrity family has many of the features of the pure relationship extended to become the 'pure family'. They are created as a means of self-enhancement that involves care, intimacy and commitment (these qualities are present and should not be disparaged). However, they are fragile constructions. The adjective 'pure' is appropriately chosen. What is sought are relationships without taint, stain or flaw which enhance the identity of those who participate within them. I can understand why so many Christian ethicists condemn the modern social configurations that produce such unworldly aberrations. But in the pages I have been reading recently, Christian versions of the pure family abound . . . It is a temptation that falls particularly to the religious, to seek to banish dirt and mess from our human encounters.

Wednesday, 19 May

Of all the church meetings I have attended (too many to count), this must have been the strangest of them all. The Church of Scotland has embarked upon a discernment process in order to decide whether to sanction the calling and ordination of gay and lesbian clergy. The first weird thing about this is that we are forbidden to speak in public about the issues. Strange indeed for a Church that is so peculiarly verbose. Instead, we have to meet as Presbyteries and Kirk Sessions to deliberate on this topic. At our Kirk Session we watch a short DVD presenting opposing perspectives, discuss these together and then, individually, fill in a long ballot sheet indicating where we stand on a range of issues. So is ordaining a gay minister merely wrong, or is it heretical? Is it admissible for a minister to be homosexual/be in a homosexual relationship/enter into a civil partnership or none of the above? Are different (higher) standards required of the clergy from other church leaders including ordained elders? I can't decide whether to answer the questions honestly or engage in tactical voting in the hope of getting a better outcome.

I see this whole procedure as an attempt to deal with a moral panic. Not only my own denomination but the whole Church seems gripped by anxiety concerning our changing familial structures. We might not all take ballots, but we engage in similar reductive, legalistic and ineffective processes when confronting a whole range of perplexing issues. I think the kind of consensus and certainty we achieve through these methods is far from anything I could understand as discerning the mind of Christ. Perhaps it is easy for me to say this. I feel no sense of panic. The family structures of the past I see as no more, and in some ways significantly less, just and sustaining than those we are now creating. The place of children within them is certainly no more commoditized than in periods in the past, when the financial survival of the household was directly related to the economic potential of the offspring produced. The question of whether Christians should offer counter-cultural witness through their marriage and family practices is rather different from whether we valorize the traditions of the past. A genuinely counter-cultural intervention would look very different from this nostalgia for what is lost.

Thursday, 20 May

Today Alison Phipps, Professor of Translation Studies at the University of Glasgow, came to speak to the Departmental Research Seminar. Her theme was translation in theological perspective. However, her paper was actually about how asylum seekers and their befrienders translate their appeals to the authorities into forms that can be heard. This is particularly important for victims of trauma, who find that language betrays them as they make their appeals. There are aspects of experience that defy articulation.

It was a heartbreakingly moving session, because although the debate takes place within the normal academic terms, Alison draws upon her own experience as a befriender. For many years she and her partner have opened their home to be a place of refuge. For the past two years they have had a foster daughter living with them, who is exactly the same age as my daughter. This girl has witnessed many unspeakable events and has been displaced many times in her young life, but has found a loving home at last with Alison. And a deportation order has been issued for her removal. And the family fear that at any time the authorities will come and remove her. The usual occasion for these judicial removals is in the early hours of the morning. Each night the family knows their sleep might be disturbed by a knock on the door.

Alison is an academic and a feminist as well as a Christian. She is aware of the many issues involved in calling the child she has befriended 'daughter'. No formal adoption procedures have taken place or are indeed possible in the context. But somehow no other word 'translates' the relationship this family has formed in a way that is adequate. When she says the word, it is sacred. There is a bond here that I can understand as holy. It is not merely that Alison has made an ethical response to the needs of the child. In this situation of extremis she has heard a voice that speaks out of the confusion and the darkness: 'Mother, behold your child.' The pronouncement was unexpected, but it is compelling. It has translated the experience of care into another dimension and shifted the theological, political and cultural dynamics of this situation onto another level.

Friday, 21 May

Got up very early and travelled to Birmingham for a meeting with colleagues concerned about the future of practical theology in the UK. We are working on issues relating to imagination, representation and cultural memory. My friend Stephen Pattison has prepared a working document. He studied at Cambridge as an undergraduate and the marks of a classical education pepper the language of the paper he presents. He is anxious that contemporary theology is desanguinated (how good a word is that for a lifeless, bloodless form). He believes it needs to be incardinated (given a heart of flesh instead of a heart of stone). The meeting is good and positive, and on the journey home I am still full of the ideas we have discussed. I look out of the window as we pass through the heart of the UK. I lived in Birmingham when I was first married. The buildings of this city are monuments to my own discovery of loving. We pass through Lancaster, where I went to university. The small city looks out over the estuary and towards the wider sea. It was a place where my own horizons opened up and adventurous voyages became possible. Nearby is the place where I was born and spent my early years. It is a place of silver sands, dangerous tides and wild beauty. As night falls we draw into Glasgow. My adopted city. Home now to my family.

I did not expect the journey I have travelled over these last days. I thought I wished to bring my own passionate experiences of mothering into dialogue with the theological literature on adoption. I thought I wished to be self-critical, but I guess I also thought that the debate should be insanguinated. That banishing the desiring relations between parents and children from the debate was dangerous, when blood and water both issue from the wounds of loving. I feel now that I have learnt that many of my preconceptions need to be challenged. I need to admit that I have often felt threatened and judged when people spoke about theology and adoption together – I have to get over that. I need to understand that, just as these landscapes and environments have shaped me blood and bone, there are deep forces at work in our social relationships that are not reducible to biological connections but just as powerful. I need the perspective that can only come from dialogue with others.

I need to get home now and stop thinking about all this. I need some rest.

Saturday, 22 May

Yesterday I felt really positive about all I was beginning to learn in this exploration of adoption. Today as I start to edit my notes and put together the material for the symposium I feel the opposite. I am frustrated by those 'ghost ideas' I have not caught or begun to give form. It seems to me that the things I have not found a way to address are probably more important than the ones I have noted down. This is so hard. I had wanted to raise some issues about how we participate in

God's creative acts. I had wanted to ask what we could learn about this subject from the occluded experiences of motherhood which unite conception, formation and the labours of enfleshment, delivery and birth *and* the continuing relation with the child. What theological conversation should take place between this blood experience and the experience of adoption? I had wanted to speak about – but how can we begin to address? – the dark backcloth against which our debates about child rearing take place. Infertility is a place from which the waste and destruction in the universe can be clearly seen. All those 'misconceptions' women experience are not the result of human greed, sin and folly but seem to be the other side, the mysterious and shadow side, of God's creative and providential love. And then there are all those cries for care that go unheeded. And the awful question of Dostoevsky's Inquisitor. Is the creation of the world justified in the face of even one abused child crying out in fear and abandonment, locked in darkness and receiving no answer? There are places of pain our debates have not yet reached into, and I am not adequate to bring them to the table. But in the light of them all the other questions I am wrestling with begin to appear shallow and of less consequence.

It is a frustrating day, and my partner is working an early shift, leaving my daughter and me with our own appointed tasks. She interrupts me every five minutes, or so it seems. She is bored with exam revision, she is fed up of me being preoccupied with something else. She hovers.

'Would you like some tea?'

'Can we go shopping later?'

'I love you Mummy.'

There I give in. She has me. I open my arms, and all 16 years of her is enfolded in them again.

'You are naughty,' I say.

'So are you,' she says.

I am busy, bad mummy.

No I am not. Blessed Winnicott. I am a good enough mother. I do my best. I am someone who cares and tries, and if it is not perfect mothering (or theology), it will have to do. I'll stop now. I have another life.

Sunday, 23 May – Pentecost

We go to church together. My daughter is still half asleep. Actually, so am I – no good pretending she is the only one who has had to drag herself here this morning.

'What is it today again?' she whispers in the first hymn.

'Pentecost. You know. Wind. Fire. Upper room.' Where did I go wrong? Nowhere. Here she is with me, and here we all are together in this place, where bonds of blood and water are both blessed and this ordinary, lovable congregation affirms its faith. My friend Rachel stands up to read the lesson, proclaiming clearly on behalf of all of us:

For all who are led by the Spirit of God are children of God. For you did not receive a spirit of slavery to fall back into fear, but you have received a spirit of adoption. When we cry, 'Abba! Father!' it is that very Spirit bearing witness with our spirit that we are children of God, and if children, then heirs, heirs of God and joint heirs with Christ – if, in fact, we suffer with him so that we may also be glorified with him. (Rom. 8.14–17)

8

Sad Summer Days

This work demonstrates how journalling can be a resource in times of spiritual struggle. It is also, in some sense, an extended 'critical incident reflection' in which journalling enables me to challenge my personal outlook and theological assumptions. The writing helped me to acknowledge the joy and humour that can be present even in bleak times – and to laugh at myself a little.

Monday, 8 July

Early: A terrible night. I now feel as if I have been washed up on the shores of morning like a survivor from a shipwreck. I am bruised, battered and exhausted, but at this moment I feel quite calm. Or perhaps I am simply too tired to ride the waves of anxiety that swept me through the dark?

I am supposed to get up. This is the rule. You did not sleep. You are exhausted, so you must get up. Not sure whether this is mandated as punishment or cure!

I wander around the flat restless. I can remember that, once upon a time, finding myself alone in a quiet house on a summer's morning I would have been simply delighted and utterly content. Here I am with my cup of tea, the radio (and the leisure to listen longer than I allow myself in term time) and sunshine. There is an intricate pattern of shadows on the living-room wall cast from the wrought iron railings and twining plants outside. I register that it is beautiful, but it does not enter my soul. I do not feel happy. I do not feel at peace.

I am not like this all the time. Not even often. But regularly. I have had these periods of anxiety from early adulthood, but they were briefer then and even sometimes productive in their intensity. But in the past few years these times have become more regular, and I take longer to recover. It is as if at some point on the 'mad journey through' I took too hard a fall. Being a person well adapted to ups and downs I just got up and carried on. Did not notice at the time, but damage was done. There is a hairline fracture that opens wider when times are hard. A crack – but it does not let in light. It lets in dark and stinking water, full of dead things.

I cannot just sit here in the sunshine and hope that peace will gradually fill me. It did once, but it does not now. So, Heather – shower, dress and force yourself to find ease in the only way possible at this moment. Work.

Late: I cannot think how I went for so many years without encountering this writing on 'everyday life' which is so beautiful.[1] I am totally in love with Henri Lefebvre. He is such a Marxist! Dialectics, alienation and the loss of essential being. But between the lines his writing is ecstatic. The motion of life is a headlong dance of desire. Food, touch, taste, the kiss, the caress, the film show, the new dress, the party. And, yes, the tragic too. We traverse 'daily life under the lightning flash of the tragic' (2005 [1981], p. 171). This is wonderful writing.

It is interesting that I have been reading on these pages about what I have known in my life. My 'one song' sung over the years has been the painful joy of the commonplace. This is where I find all that is holy and blessed. I felt this morning that it was beyond my reach. Would never know it again in my sad state. But the reading has brought it back by another route. It got me through. And actually, it has been a good day. Still warm enough in the evening to sit out on our little terrace. So tiny, but it is what makes our flat special. The door from the living room that opens onto the little space of a garden.

Tuesday, 9 July

Early: I know I must not do it. I tell myself, 'You must not hope that because you go to bed happy you will escape the terrors.' I made the old mistake, and they were back so soon. Not even two o'clock, and they dragged me awake again. The counsellor has told me to try and practise mindfulness at times like these. She explained that in order not to return endlessly to those matters that oppress me I should focus upon the moment and simply breathe. Register what is around me in the dark room. Locate myself. Accept the negative emotions, name and recognize them, allow them to be. But breathe and feel. Be in your body and inhabit the moment not the beyond. Let go.

---

1 At this point I had just discovered Henri Lefebvre's three-volume series *A Critique of Everyday Life* (1991b [1947], 2002 [1961], 2005 [1981]) and was embarking on Michel de Certeau's *The Practice of Everyday Life* (1984).

I asked her if she did this mindfulness thing herself, and she said that she was not a particularly anxious person, but she did enjoy a quiet cup of herbal tea when she got home from work! I do not think this really counts.

However, I do concede there is something in this approach, and I even bought a book about it, which I very much like to read. The book is beautifully written, and it has pictures. It exerts a calming influence even if the practice is not delivering much for me at the moment.

Must try and understand what is going on here.

I think the characteristics of the Christian traditions in which I am formed are ones that aren't actually seeking an end to suffering or desire. Certainly not this side of paradise. My formation has been in Methodism – a religion of the heart, emotions, love and longing and the extremes of grace and sin. Its language in hymns and preaching is not moderate. My longstanding adult affair with Catholicism has been similarly sensuous. I like the drama queens and mystics of the faith. I enjoy the heady theatre of liturgy. In religion I like the mountains and the valley gorges with their torrents. These form my spiritual landscape. All of this is a very long way from the light, bright plain of 'simply being and letting go'. Must think more about this one.

Late: This work on everyday life is really taking me into interesting places. I am using it in preparing for a plenary talk to the annual conference of the British and Irish Association of Practical Theology.[2] The conference is on wisdom, and what came straight to my mind when planning the talk was one of my favourite passages of all from Luke 7: the children in the marketplace calling to one another and saying, 'We played the flute for you, and you did not dance; we wailed, and you did not weep.'

They pipe and dance; they mourn and weep, wisdom's children in this bright, noisy, dusty, marketplace. This passage speaks to me so powerfully. Its light and shadows. I have always readily accepted this heady mixture of joy and loss (Luke wants us to recall the sorrowing John and the feasting Jesus), but now I am questioning myself. Can you do this any more? Do you really want to be one of those exasperating children, always weeping, wailing and carrying on? Maybe it is time to grow up now?

---

2 Delivered on 16 July 2013 at York University. A version of this paper now forms Chapter 17 of this work.

It is certainly time to get out now. I have been avoiding people a bit lately, but this is not helpful. My partner and I are going over to visit friends. It will be nice to walk together through the long indeterminate evening. I love Scotland – light till midnight.

Wednesday, 10 July

Not early: This sometimes happens. Last night my mind was raging as if I had a fever. I had to turn and turn in the bed. For hours it was impossible to find any peace, and then, so softly, an almost impossible stillness and beauty descended. Just as though I had been delirious, and then the fever had left me. This was beyond calm. It was like being a child again. No, it went further back. I was an infant. Safer than safe. 'I am quiet now before the Lord, just as a child who is weaned from the breast. Yes, my begging has been stilled' (Ps. 131.2, *Living Bible*). Almost worth going through everything to get here?

No.

So anyway, then I couldn't sleep either because it was so nice just lying there. The soft bed, my partner beside me, birds in the garden. I must have lain like that for at least an hour. Decided to ignore all the rules. Turned off the alarm, fell asleep and now it is nearly lunchtime, and I am writing in bed. Still feel the afterglow.

Later: Very hot. All the plants on the terrace suffering a bit. Need to water some of them twice a day. Don't mind. Love this slow, pottering, playing. I should have been working on the talk, but feeling so dreamy it was impossible. Went for a walk and just enjoyed watching other people out on the streets. A crumbling tenement building near St George's Cross was being refurbished, and on the pavement I found a big, old-fashioned, galvanized metal dustbin. The council uses plastic wheelybins these days, so it was clearly redundant. The bin was half full of rubbish. It brought back another world. My Dad burning garden waste in our metal dustbin at home and the flames sky-high. I couldn't just leave it to be taken away with the rotten floorboards and old carpets. It would serve on my terrace as a planter for the Victoria Plum, which is feeling the heat most badly and needs more depth of soil.

I put most of the rubbish in one of the new plastic bins (there was still an icky layer at the bottom) and set off home. It was actually bloody heavy to carry and so hot. A bus came along and without thinking I got on.

'How much?' I asked the driver.

'Nothing if you promise to get off very soon!' he replied.

Everyone laughed, including me. Mad English woman, hot and dirty, with large smelly dustbin on Glasgow bus. It was very funny.

It was still quite a struggle from the bus stop to our garden, but I felt so proud of myself with this strange trophy. Will get my partner to make holes in the bottom, when he gets back from work. In the meantime I have showered and made tea. Also read over what I have written so far for my talk. Liked it, but realize that it is actually only half written and, frankly, it is also a bit weird. Sometimes with talks they just emerge in the way they are going to be, and I don't have the willpower to normalize them effectively.

Here I am. A woman with an anxiety problem, a wilting plum tree, a smelly dustbin and a wayward talk.

Thursday, 11 July

Early: Not a good night but not the worst. Sometimes in the cycles of anxiety boredom sets in. This is welcome. It allows me to be aware that the familiar record is playing, over and over, but I don't actually need to listen. I can drift in and out of it, and I did manage to get more sleep.

Sitting in the sunny lounge with my tea and the door open to the terrace. I am remembering that I had a bad period of anxiety this time last year and also the year before. Of course, summer is the time when the immediate day-to-day demands recede, leaving more time for reflection. Also two years ago I was exhausted from a difficult year as Head of Department, and a friendship broke down badly causing a lot of emotional fallout. Then last year my Dad was in hospital. He was dying in a dark, closed room with no windows, and outside it was the most beautiful early summer unfolding. On the day of his funeral a rare Red Kite hovered over the church in a clear blue sky. Now, although there appears no immediate provoking cause, I seem to be in danger of experiencing a seasonal disorder. Once again there is this mixture of summer in its sweet perfection and loose ease and this tiresome, tied-up, tedious mess inside me. Will skip summer next year. Try and get study leave somewhere in another hemisphere with a chilly climate.

Later: Realized something important missing for my talk. I need a new dress! Most of my clothes these days are 'vintage' – actually, that is, they are 'charity-shop-second-hand'. I don't mind. I think they are lovely.

I wear wool, cotton, silk, cashmere, full skirts. I enjoy hunting them out and each new find is a little triumph. But despite the fact that I have reached the stage where I don't need, or wish for, a new wardrobe each season, just sometimes I feel this great desire. Well . . .

I was so lucky. A beautiful dress. Pink and black, very fifties, which I had admired when it cost £190, was in the Jaeger sale for £49. YES!

And there were some pink suede pumps in the Hobbs sale that matched.

I am not at all ashamed. On the underground travelling home I open my bags and look at my treasures. My Mum always did this on the bus coming home from town. I was embarrassed then. I am not at all now. When I get home, I put the dress on a hanger, so I can still look at it. It has a presence that gives me pleasure. And I get back to work. The work goes so much better. I sail through the next few pages. Am getting there.

In the bath later I thought of the poem by Molly Peacock, 'Why I am not a Buddhist'. It has some great lines about enjoying food and flesh and fancy things. She is clear that not everything is of equal importance. Of course not. A lovely new lilac suit is in no way comparable to the loveliness of God. Losing a favourite fountain pen is not like losing faith. But, she says, desire is wonderful and 'building a kingdom in a soul' requires desire. There is a downside of course. Desire destroys. It can and does waste and wreck the world. But then, she asks, 'How else but in tatters should a world be?' That is a frightening line. We want the world green and whole, not torn and broken. But there is something in me that loves this tattered world – as it is. Likes the glint of its flashy fragments. I am aware that is a terrible thing to say in the face of all the sorrow and the hunger. I know. I am aware. Also, there is something in me that will let my own-self waste and tear. I will 'let myself go'. Not take due care. To have what? Extreme pleasure in a dress? Yes, perhaps. To possess the kingdom? Yes, this also. For me it is all somehow deeply bound up with that dearly longed-for thing.

Friday, 12 July

Early: Slept better. To relax I imagined myself somewhere else. A place I felt safe. Try not to do this too often, because I know that for me it could become a dangerous habit. But sometimes it is helpful. Was surprised at where I found myself returning. I was walking through hospital corridors. I was in the hospital where my Dad died in Leeds.

Why did imagining myself in a hospital make me feel safe? I think it may be something about things being out of your hands. My anxieties are often bound up with impossible feelings of responsibility. It is a relief not to be in control. But it is perhaps more than that.

I like the institutional. I find it comforting somehow. This is weird. In the hospital, although it was such an awful time, I liked the lino on the floors. I liked the little plaques and notices on the walls. I liked the enclosed garden off the wards. I liked the restaurant with pies and chips and peas or curry and rice. Unlike my brother and sister, who were wonderful, I was not good with machines bleeping or the frequent small crises of breath or heartbeats. I hated tubes being inserted and procedures being carried out. That all scared me very much. So much so I panicked and had to leave sometimes – just get out. But I did like the comfort of ward rounds and temperature taking and blood pressure recording. Charts and graphs. Well, what can I say?

Later: Very unusual to have a PhD viva in the summer, but this happened today. Was the first date both the examiners could manage after the end of term. My student was wonderful. A deeply spiritual and also funny, witty and clever person. She answered all the questions with thoughtfulness and perception. I was very proud of her. So the results were delivered, the forms all signed, and there was a great sense of achievement and completeness to it all. I love this aspect of my work with its diligence, formality and dignity. I am a funny kind of radical. I *think* I have this preference for the dangerous and excessive aspects of spirituality, but actually I am also someone who loves a settled order of things.

But being both 'institutionalized' and on the edge is not really that anomalous. De Certeau was both inside and outside the Church. No one could really say. When he died, the verdict of his Superior was, 'I am not sure if he died a Christian, but I am certain he died a Jesuit.' So often I am content to be held to the breast of the institution. It gives me a space and a place to be. There. My counsellor would be proud of me – listen to her with her 'space to be'! But at other times I like a walk on the wild side. Or actually just a wee stroll and a breath of fresh air – should not be too dramatic about this. When I have these times of anxiety, I am apt to forget that for the most part my life is fairly settled and peaceful. I am not always tossed in the vast ocean or white-water rafting through the valley gorge at all. This is a misperception. More often paddling around the boating pond.

Saturday, 13 July

Early: Slept well. About six hours. That is very good as today I really must get this blessed talk under wraps. When I have a big writing job to do in one day, I have a routine. Start early at home on the kitchen table. Can work there at least till coffee time at 11.00, but after that I need to move on. There are coffee houses I work in. A little circuit of places I like to be. When I get bored or stuck, I move on. It's quite expensive in coffee and cake, but it works for me when the stuff has to be done.

Also I like to pretend to be Simone de Beauvoir sometimes. That is how she worked. In favourite cafés. But I think her way also involved cognac and French cigarettes. And male and female lovers . . . with berets.

Late: I am tired, but the talk is nearly finished, and that is a great relief. I have also packed for the conference. Going down to Leeds tomorrow to stay with my mother for a couple of days and then on to York University on Tuesday morning. My plenary session will be in the early afternoon. I have printed out the current version of my talk, because then if there is a computer disaster (or some other disaster) I won't be naked in the conference chamber. For this reason I have also packed my new dress. It lies lovely at the top of my suitcase. The new shoes, still wrapped in tissue paper, are at the bottom.

So now I lay me down to sleep.

Sunday, 14 July

Early: In the night 'as I lay dying' I thought up a new plan for today. Will not go to church here in Glasgow but rather spend a lazy morning with my partner. Do brunch, read papers, drink coffee and then catch the noon-time train. I will arrive a little earlier than I had previously planned and will take a couple of hours for myself in Leeds. Feel slightly guilty about generating this unaccounted-for 'me' time by neglecting my sacred duties. But hey . . .

Middle of day: This is a very familiar journey. I used to always travel the East Coast route to visit my parents, but when my Dad was sick I needed to make the journey once, or even twice, a week and that way was too expensive. So I started using the old Carlisle to Settle route. I take the fast modern train to Carlisle, and then it is the 'shoppers and ramblers' service through all the little Cumbrian stations and into the rugged end of Yorkshire. The train is staffed by volunteers. 'Enthusiasts', who give an excited commentary on bizarre facts of railway history as we travel along. It is quaint but it is also a beautiful journey on a summer's day. Today the carriage is crowded by people with rosy cheeks and rucksacks. I feel a bit of a freak with my laptop open. I am also a little nervous. I sense this journey is rolling into itself all the other journeys that I made in last year's spring and early summer. It has assumed greater significance because of the plans I made for this afternoon. I am going back to the hospital.

Late: Walked up from the station pulling my suitcase along behind. Passed Leeds Civic Hall with its great golden owls perched on top and neat flowerbeds in front. Leeds Infirmary was on my left. Could enter through the Art Deco original structure with its neat, metal-framed windows, balconies and gently curved sides. Could have done, because I know the networks of stairways and corridors that connect it with the newer 'Jubilee Wing' so well. But I decided to go in the way I did when I was visiting my Dad. So I walked up the hill, past the A&E, and got to the main entrance. The big glass foyer (cold late at night, when you are waiting for a taxi) opens up into the wide entrance hall. The Costa Coffee Shop in the corner is where we sat on rest breaks, when we were keeping vigil. This was the only place open late at night or in the early morning. I have tasted every kind of sandwich they make here so many times. I got to the point where I could not face another Ciabatta or Tuna Melt. 'Just a peppermint tea please.'

Across the large hall are a battery of lifts. I know how the system operates. It is very slow so you must make sure you press at least two buttons and be certain when the doors open the lift is travelling up and not down! My Dad was in a number of different wards here. First, I get the lift to the floor where he was in intensive care. Walk a little way along and then go back and press the button for the stroke ward. Of course, I can't actually get into the wards themselves. You need to press the buzzer to be admitted to these. No, I just keep walking purposefully but without purpose. I am like some spectre in the corridor. I am a seen but unnoticed presence among porters and visitors, the noisy nurses, the medics with stethoscopes and paper cups hurrying from one place to another. Take a long route down to the hall again. Use back stairs instead of the lift. Proud that my body knows the old pathways. Then it is time to go to the last ward. It has been just over a year now. I can do this.

To get to the ward where my Dad died you need to go over a 'bridge' which connects back into the old building. It is a wide thoroughfare;

light with glass sides. Lovely on a sunny day like today. Bleak in the rain. It is my particular ghost road.

I remembered everything. A sharp turn left and the corridor runs down a small slope. They pushed him down here on the trolley, when he was alive, and he never came back. Why? It is only a gentle slope. Surely he could have made it? On my right is the garden. A very lovely garden that my Dad stole plant cuttings from on previous shorter stays. I have taken a few myself, I must admit. For some reason they have started to keep it locked! Shame – it was a great comfort to sit there. It is still possible to rest beside the windows and look into the garden. I did this often, when he was very ill. Just took a few minutes out. Leant my head on the cool glass. I leant my head on the glass again. It was comforting. People came and went. Some gave me that look; the grace of sympathy. 'I do not know what it is, but I am sorry for your trouble.'

I honestly think I could have stayed for hours. Settled in the corner of a day room somewhere. Fallen asleep in a chair. People do this. No one would have noticed. But I wanted to get to six o'clock Mass at the Cathedral. This too was part of my plan and also a retracing of my steps.

The big church is close to the hospital. I went to Mass here, when I could. When it was appropriate to leave him sleeping, or when someone else was taking their time in the quiet room holding his hand. It is funny now – I can see this church is very like the hospital. A bundled-together group of people. Sharing something that is at the same time of ultimate significance and so ordinary it is not worth commenting upon. There is a shared bond but no intimacy. I am not complaining about that. Expressed emotion here would be too much. People are usually seated alone at a little distance from their neighbours. Far away at the front other people are doing things. Even the singing comes from somewhere distant; the choir strangely hidden to the side of the altar place. A general sense of calm in the face of an unendurable drama. When it had all finished, I lit a candle and stood a while before leaving. Feeling empty but also at peace.

Monday, 15 July

Early: It was lovely to get in last night after all my wanderings and be welcomed by my Mum. She was delighted to see me, and, after we had eaten, we spent the rest of the evening curled up on the sofa watching Sunday night TV – which is the best.

This bed is softer than my bed at home. The quilt is thicker. There are more cushions and pillows. I don't always find it easy to adjust, but last night I found it very comforting to just sink in. I slept very well in the house of my mother. It is less easy to work in this bed though. Will get up and face the day.

Late: Some things have come together just in the last couple of days. I have realized that I have a tendency to keep alive old pains, not just because I am obsessive (although I am), but also because they are productive for me. I have used my experiences of infertility and so on to open windows onto the savage side of life. I have kept these windows open, both because I need that view and also because I have felt obligated to present, through my work, this other perspective.

I remember, when I gave a paper to a symposium in Aberdeen, a nice young man who had travelled all the way from his university on the eastern edge of Europe (mountains and pine forests) challenged me about this 'dwelling upon suffering'. He had given his perfectly well-behaved paper the evening before, and it had been favourably received. 'You seem angry,' he said to me. 'Also, you are writing about experiences in your life that took place twenty years ago. I can understand that they were very difficult . . .' He would have been an adolescent boy at that time with bleached, white hair playing beside a lake. 'But I wonder why they are still unresolved for you.' I kept quiet. What could I say? I sensed he had never swum down to the deep places where there is no light.

I know I am most alive in the messy, compelling, tragi-passions of everyday life. I do not seek deliverance from them but rather revelations within them. In fact the thing I probably most fear is the resolution of contraries in a peaceable whole. The stark irresolutions we encounter (they make both beauty and tragedy) are what make us human, and for me these are also the key to understanding God in the light of incarnation. I am clearly still in the marketplace with the children – for religious reasons of course – and they do have such pretty things there.

However, I do also recognize that there is a downside to the way I have lived and thought and related to faith. It has become, at times, dangerous for me, had a bad effect on others and sometimes carried me beyond any conceivable use. As someone who has been proud of her ability to live with paradox and ambiguity, I have to find a way of affirming the significance of a spiritual path that embraces lack and want and desire and at the same time cultivate awareness of the still point of no desire, which is beyond suffering and beyond passion. I can do this, I think, if I see it as a necessary contrary, a creative contrary, a healing other space – rather than an ultimate or a resolution to all ills.

I don't like T. S. Eliot – just prejudice, a personal thing, and of course his early politics. But he does have something to offer here. Particularly in 'Burnt Norton', where he writes of a process in which the mutable and changeless co-exist:

> both a new world
> And the old made explicit . . . (Eliot 1974 [1935], p. 192)

He was talking about the appearance of the still point in the turning world that is simultaneously beyond it (transcending its suffering and incompleteness) but also only comprehensible within an existence in which time and change and loss is 'Woven in the weakness of the changing body' (1974 [1935], p. 192). Only in our human form can we know this. And we know it in a timeless moment. The 'hidden laughter' of children in a garden, he says. The distant sound of pipes and dancing in the public square, say I.

Unlike me he has a preference for detachment, while mine is for passion. But both are necessary.

To be able to hear the piping play, I recognize the need to rest sometimes in the place beyond longing. I think that is what I was instinctively trying to express yesterday through my journeys – though I did not think about it in that way at the time. And it was also something that 'just happened', when I let myself be in the house of my mother.

Tuesday, 16 July

Early: Just because you think you understand something better, it does not mean it is resolved for you. I still awoke in the night to the same old fears – but I am hopeful. I do think I have a renewed vision now of what I am seeking. Managed to get to sleep again around 4.00 a.m.

Woke up to a lovely sunny morning. I have a talk to give today. I am someone who can do this kind of thing – albeit in my own peculiar way. Feel strong and calm and ready.

PART 3

Life Writing

9

Approaching Life Writing

What is Life Writing?

This may seem a rather strange question to ask as everything in this book concerns life writing in some form or another. It is clear that the boundaries between the genres I have employed to structure this text are porous and difficult to sustain. Autoethnography, for example, could be undertaken through journalling; and journals, in turn, offer hospitable means to chronicle the patterns of a life. I have erected distinctions between categories chiefly for the sake of clarity in distinguishing their differing uses in theological practice. It is for this same reason that it is helpful to approach life writing 'as if' it were a distinctive genre that offers, through the well-developed literary traditions of autobiography, the opportunity for focused reflection upon the development of the self. This entails exploring our sense of personhood, identity and purpose. Life writing also raises issues of authenticity and self-awareness that are particularly important as we contemplate our understanding of God. As Michael Novak has written, 'Knowledge of self and knowledge of God mount, one after the other, in an ascending, alternating spiral; and in proportion as we discover who we are, we are made ready to discover who God is' (1965, p. 81).

Because of the close ties between our sense of who we are and our grasp of who God is, life writing has become a key resource in vocational exploration and formation, the development of spiritual awareness, theological research and pastoral care. In all these fields it delivers powerful results. People usually enjoy writing about their lives and find it opens up many opportunities for spiritual reflection. In fact, it has become common within theological texts to describe self-narration as an innate human capacity that is beneficial, therapeutic and perhaps the original and archetypal theological form.[1] However, as explored in

---

1 See Anderson and Foley 1998 for a thoughtful celebration of the power of life narratives in theological and pastoral contexts.

the introductory chapter, narrative is never innocent. Life writing has a long 'life history', and it is important to be aware of the conventions through which it has been structured and the ways in which it has, in turn, structured the development of our understanding of what it means to be a human person.

Many textbooks on autobiography begin with theology. Augustine's *Confessions* is conventionally taken as the starting point for exploring traditions of autobiographical writing, 'both in marking a historical beginning and of setting up a model for other, later texts' (Anderson 2004, p. 18). Many scholars argue that the form of writing Augustine established, as well as the way he tells his tale, continues to inform the way both secular and religious life writing is constructed to the current day (see Newtown 1998, p. 51). This is because his work has been so important that it has been absorbed into our cultural bloodstream and exerts influence whether or not contemporary autobiographers are familiar with the text. Augustine's work does, indeed, make an interesting starting point for exploring life writing. However, this is not simply because of the stature of the text (which can prove intimidating to novice life writers) but also because of the many questions the work raises about the life-writing process.

Some scholars view *Confessions* in a straightforward frame. They see it as a successful attempt to unify and cohere experience in a single narrative that consolidates the author in relation to his own divine Author. 'Spiritual autobiography in the Augustinian mode leads the protagonist from sin to grace like a line of melody seeking resolution' (Bell 1977, p. 116). In this understanding the resolving unity that Augustine seeks is part of his theological worldview. The 'self' with its flaws, faults and inconsistencies is brought to wholeness through the gracious mediation of its Creator. In the process certain aspects of life, many past experiences, relationships and passions, are either expurgated or purged, and what endures is that which is fitting within the redeemed state now entered into. Augustine's life writing is a work of editing and exclusion as well as remembrance.

John-Raphael Staude argues that the movement in *Confessions* from a fallen to a reconciled state establishes the plot structure of subsequent spiritual autobiographies, which are frequently constructed in four parts: before awakening, towards awakening, the life-changing encounter, celebration of the new form of life. 'There are few surprises or changes in this basic story line even in modern re-visitations' (Staude 2005, p. 258). However, he also comments that this pattern of questing and resolution, now well established in Christian literature and beyond, was borrowed by Augustine from the structure of ancient myths and legends. The novelty in his work is the location of the quest in an interior landscape: 'the goal of the quest is not external (such as the Golden Fleece of the Argonauts) nor even the goal of coming home (Ulysses). The goal of Augustine's *itinererium mentis* is to be found within his own heart' (2005, p. 257).

The fact that Augustine employs pagan sources to structure his work is not a criticism. The first Christian icons of Christ were based on images of Apollo, and such cultural borrowings are inevitable in the establishing of new traditions. However, it does demonstrate that theological reflection upon a life story is never a simple matter. As well as drawing from mythology, Augustine has also woven into his account many echoes from Scripture and contemporary philosophical worldviews. These, similarly, do not compromise the telling of experiences recalled in good faith. It is simply that experience is always recounted in modes that rely upon pre-established thought forms and idioms.

The recognition that Augustine's attempts to gain a new form of spiritual coherence cannot liberate him from the heterogeneity that haunts all lives and all writing leads us to consider other fragmenting mechanisms that are apparent throughout the long tradition of spiritual autobiography. Writers seek to demonstrate how their true identity has been found in God, but this happens precisely through a repudiation of many aspects of the self. 'Let me not be my own life,' cries Augustine (1963, p. 290). Furthermore, because it is God rather than the writer who assumes the place of true author of the text/life, a disturbing alterity becomes part of the narrative structure. Larry Sisson calls this tendency 'eccentric', meaning there is a literal 'off centering' at work in spiritual narratives that 'unsettles notions of individual, independent and freely determined authorship' (Sisson 1998, p. 98). Linda Anderson goes further and argues that, while Augustine may be credited with establishing autobiography as the literary mode in which 'the unified, transcendent "I" of the autobiographical tradition' emerges, he also unwillingly testifies to the impossibility of achieving a singular-self. Coherence and chaos are both equally evident within his work (Anderson 2004, p. 27).

These literary considerations are not merely theoretical. They affect how we understand life writing in processes of theological reflection. When I ask participants in writing workshops to describe their lives as a journey, they instinctively adopt many of the devices of myths and fairy stories to image their passage through dark woods, narrow gates, hills and high mountains.[2] They tell stories of quests and treasures,

---

2 The influence of John Bunyan's *Pilgrim's Progress* (1907 [1678]) has been immense. For many centuries it stood next to the Bible as the principal text of Christian devotion throughout the English-speaking world. Like Augustine's *Confessions* it has framed spiritual autobiography to this day.

perils and homecomings. Integrated with these images are favourite biblical themes: lost coins, wandering sheep, prodigal children and so on. In longer narratives people often employ the fourfold structure of awakening to new life described above. They also borrow from contemporary thought forms and idioms, frequently referring to 'finding a true self', 'the real me', 'discovering who I really am', for example, which are all very modern ways of describing personhood.

Like Augustine, contemporary life writers must also struggle with how to express the influence of God upon our life stories; how to reconcile personal choices and actions with God's purposes for us. And, also like Augustine, our work will function to create a healing coherence as we assemble disparate aspects of life into a tale that can be told about a person who is significant and beloved. At the same time, in life writing we may encounter a mystery – if we dare. How can we speak about the intimate darkness in which the human and divine embrace and struggle without the wounding acknowledgement that we are sometimes quite uncertain of either God's name or our own?

Forms of Life Writing

Writing a Calling

Because of its focus upon personal journeys, life writing is often used in vocational training. In counselling courses, for example, participants are often required to construct an autobiographical narrative at the beginning of their studies, which is used to explore personal strengths and areas of possible difficulty that might influence relationships with clients. In the field of values-based practice (which is becoming increasingly important in health, social care and community engagement), an audit of how life experience has contributed to the formation of values is a helpful starting point in the development of strategic actions.

In theological circles the construction of a life narrative to explore a calling has a very long history indeed and now commonly forms an integral part of vocational discernment processes. Similarly, many theological training courses begin with autobiographical reflections that are intended to mark a point where the candidate's life journey has taken a decisive turn. These stories are usually vivid and passionate creations, constructed with great liveliness at a significant moment in which people are setting out to write a new chapter in their lives. Sometimes they also contain striking theological insights, but often people struggle at first with theological reflection and do not go beyond mentioning favourite biblical passages or describing particularly intense spiritual experiences.

As theological awareness increases, and certainly when people are pursuing theological study beyond undergraduate level, a greater degree of sophistication is to be sought in theological reflection. Contemporary theology offers two significant models that are particularly helpful in theological life writing (see Graham, Walton and Ward 2005). Canonical narrative theology develops out of key themes in the work of Karl Barth as interpreted through the contribution of theologians associated with Yale University and, latterly, influenced by the narrative theology of Stanley Hauerwas. This theological model views the story of Jesus, particularly the elements of his passion, as the key to interpreting all other human stories. It is 'God's story', and it provides the framework for interpreting the rest of Scripture, the life of the Church and, indeed, the whole of human history. The task of the reflective writer is to locate his- or herself within the story, and interpreting a 'calling' becomes a question of recognizing your own place in the narrative. This may be done very simply through imagining oneself as an actor in a particular biblical scene as if it were happening now (an ancient spiritual discipline particularly developed within the Ignatian tradition). Alternatively, you may allow some biblical theme, such as waiting in the garden, sharing the Last Supper or walking to Emmaus, to provide the frame for your reflection, drawing you deeper into your own story as well as into the pattern of revelation you have received.

Constructive narrative theology offers an alternative approach. In this there is no effort to place a life story within a biblical framework, but rather to create a new story as elements of experience and aspects of Scripture and tradition are woven together into innovative forms. This weaving process gives new life to our sacred heritage, as it is shaped into diverse patterns within many contexts. It also empowers the weaver, who is able to both challenge and affirm aspects of the faith they have inherited. Interpreting 'calling' thus becomes an active and constructive process of weaving a life story into material in which the divine is vividly, and sometimes startlingly, revealed.

As might be expected, canonical narrative theology is particularly influential in contexts in which great significance is placed upon revelation through Scripture or tradition. Constructive narrative theology has been associated with a more liberal approach to faith. However, there is no reason to feel at all restricted to one model or the other. Both have a great deal to contribute to theological life writing and I happily use either (or even sometimes combine the two) according to need and circumstance.

Writing a Journey

Theological life writing is also a key tool in the development of spiritual awareness as we work with a 'spiritual accompanier' or engage in personal disciplines of self-interrogation. It is natural to desire development in spiritual understanding, and life writing is an established means to mark steps on this journey and record experiences that have proved decisive in shaping faith.

The fourfold stages of the spiritual quest identified in Augustine's writing remain very influential in structuring the stories believers tell about their developing spiritual lives. But there are also those who believe that in the contemporary context our spiritual journeys are rather more complicated than this. In his work on modern spiritual biographies David Leigh argues that Augustine's model no longer serves, and suggests:

> The modern autobiographer is an alienated seeker, struggling with unmediated existence, an autonomous searcher with an unauthorized identity, a self-appropriating thinker struggling with the lack of a stable sense of the self, and an authentic proponent of social change struggling with a paralyzing environment. (2000, p. xiv)

It could be argued that similar challenges to these faced Augustine, who also wrote during a period of massive social change. However, it is no longer the case that we feel the same theological imperative to reconcile the disparate elements of our life stories into one coherent narrative with a happy ending. We are now more likely to concede that faith is formed in situations of ambiguity and constraint and that living with the tensions these represent is a mark of spiritual maturity. Fallings, failings and challenging experiences can be 'reframed' or 'woven' into the whole and do not need to be expurgated or purged from our work.

The recognition that spiritual growth entails embracing 'irresolutions' is supported by influential research on 'faith stages' viewed as developmental phases in human life. The work of James Fowler (1981) established the notion that spiritual understandings are mutable and become more expansive and inclusive as we progress through life. Fowler claims that in the early stages of life faith depends on the external support of friends or family, requires authorizing and objective forms of validation, and often pictures God as an intimate personal friend who looks out for us in difficulty. In these early phases contrasts are very clear and boundaries strong. In later stages (which may not be approached by everyone as they are developmental rather than chronological), we learn to be open to those who are different from us, and to live with ambivalence, complexity and paradox. We become more humble and learn to acknowledge a mystery at the heart of things.

Fowler's work has been subjected to many criticisms[3] and revisions. Nicola Slee, for example, conducted research among women which indicated there were distinctive aspects of spiritual experience that were important to them (such as embodiment, emotional knowledge and connectivity) but had been largely omitted from Fowler's framework (2004). Slee's findings confirmed the broad framework set out in Fowler's stages, but she argued that spiritual life could be cyclical as well as progressive; stages bleed into each other, and periods of spiritual dryness are as important in spiritual development as moments of delight and discovery. In this context spiritual life writing becomes the challenging, but liberating, work of uncensoring the self and allowing wisdom to emerge even out of the fragments of our lives.

Writing a Question

A growing use of life writing lies in the field of theological research. While academic convention formerly silenced the personal voice in the interests of objectivity and rigour, the pendulum is now swinging in the opposite direction. Reflexivity is now understood to be a mark of good academic practice. Furthermore, some significant works of theological inquiry go beyond locating the writer as a 'male, white, middle-class heterosexual', for example, and are now constructed with extended autobiographical and imaginative passages making clear why certain theological questions have emerged as significant for the author (see, for example Taylor 1990 and Althaus-Reid 2000).

In the preface to his book *Participation and Mediation: A Practical Theology for the Liquid Church*, Pete Ward describes his theological method as reflexive: 'it is an acknowledgement that the commitments of the writer are a part of the academic process. In fact they are a vital and creative aspect' (2008, p. 14). He also argues that reflexivity entails making plain the processes of theological formation that have generated particular research agendas within the researcher. He uses the term 'auto/theobiography' to describe this process, and demonstrates

---

3 Mainly on account of assumptions, borrowed from psychological theory, that development can be equated with cognitive skills and move beyond bodily and emotional knowledge; also on the grounds that he universalizes spiritual growth and does not take sufficient account of cultural and gender differences.

how his experiences in ministry have combined with particular theological influences to generate both a life story and a theological quest. Within this book a preliminary exercise in life writing accounts for approximately 20 per cent of the content – but the remaining 80 per cent flows directly from this.

Following from work such as this research, students preparing theological dissertations can be assured that it is perfectly acceptable (and indeed now commonplace) to use life writing to introduce their research questions. The key is to tie the life writing tightly to the topics under discussion and this, like all forms of reflective writing, requires some discipline and skill. How far you can go in extending life writing into the body of the thesis itself depends on your own grasp of the nature and purpose of poetics in theological research, your confidence in your own writing ability, and last but not least your skills in playing the academic game. Almost everything is allowed in an academic context as long as you locate yourself within some recognized tradition of inquiry with its own internal protocols and safeguards. If you wish to work in this way, there will be considerable work to be done in identifying an academic trajectory in which to situate your own writing. However, the work may be well worth the effort as you create a piece of research that displays integrity, engagement and the creativity that theological writing all too often lacks.

Writing as Care

Life writing is an enjoyable act of self-expression which is increasingly valued in our reflexive culture. However, its benefits extend beyond personal and academic development into therapeutic and pastoral contexts. Life writing is increasingly used to encourage people to find (or make) hope and coherence, as they struggle with illness, trauma, change and grief. In the light of the discussion so far it is easy to see why life writing has come to be widely regarded as a healing process, and there is a growing body of literature concerning its use in this way.

In an article exploring spiritual life writing among older people, Staude states:

Spirituality involves connectedness to oneself, others, nature and to a larger meaning. It is associated with creativity, play, wisdom, faith, and a sense of oneness. Writing and reflecting on one's autobiography enhances spiritual growth and can be therapeutic, freeing people from outlived roles and self-imposed images.' (2005, p. 249)

He goes on to argue that theologians and pastoral carers have under-estimated the many benefits of self-narration, which has the potential to be more helpful to many people than traditional forms of counselling and care. Drawing upon the work of the psychologists James Birren and Donna Deutchman, he identifies the following positive outcomes of focused autobiographical writing in a group context:

- a sense of increased personal power;
- recognition of past coping mechanisms and their relevance to current problems;
- reconciliation with the past and resolution of bitterness and conflict;
- a resurgence of interest in past activities, hobbies, commitments and values;
- the development of friendships with other group members;
- a greater sense of meaning in life;
- the ability to face the end of life feeling that one has contributed to the world.

(adapted from Staude 2005, p. 262)

While most research has focused upon life writing in group or institutional contexts, the informal use of life writing can be incorporated into many forms of pastoral encounter with great benefits. If this is the case, it is important that the pastoral carer has also become a life writer and has a direct understanding of the pleasures and perils of this work! In pastoral contexts it is not necessary to tackle the whole of a life story. Life writing can be themed or focused around specific vivid incidents or significant relationships. It can also take many forms, from the construction of short 'witness' testimonies to the creation of works for inclusion in ritual or worship. While such acts can be extremely helpful to people, autobiographical work is not always benign and positive and is certainly not 'risk free'. A traumatized person may find their story is simply beyond telling, and the attempt to place it in a narrative frame would be a violation. As I have argued elsewhere:

There will be many times when helping people tell their stories will lead to healing and peace. However, there will be other moments in which a pastoral response will entail entering alongside another person into the death of meaning and loss of coherence. This does not mean that the pastoral agent has nothing to offer in this situation . . . We may use rituals, symbols or music to allow pain to be communicated rather than constructing stories that promise an illusory reconciliation of tragic circumstances. (Graham, Walton and Ward 2005, p. 73)

Using Life Writing

This chapter has demonstrated how adaptable and capacious life writing can be and the many roles it has to play both in reflection and practice. Most theological approaches to life writing have stressed its sense-making qualities and the ways in which through processes of 'enplotment' we are able to come to a better understanding of ourselves and of the place of God in our lives. While affirming these undoubted benefits, I have been at pains to stress that life writing can also be a way to confront and acknowledge personal fragmentation and loss. It can lead us closer to the dark mystery of God.

In summary I offer the following points for reflection on life writing in a theological context:

- Remember life writing is writing, and be aware of the genre, forms and conventions that you are employing in your text.
- Be aware that the tale you tell about who you are is also a story about who God is. This is *always* the case, even if it is not made explicit in your work.
- Think about the connection you are making between your life story and the stories that are sacred to you. What theological model or principle guides your approach?
- Are you attempting to reconcile the irreconcilable in your text? Sometimes it is better to allow ambiguities and even silences into the writing rather than to strive towards completeness.
- Don't worry about 'childlike' writing. Simple and direct is as good/ better than complex and distant. But children are not innocent, and neither are their stories of themselves or God.
- What is the point of writing your story? Does it aid academic discovery, enable you to address a calling or respond to a spiritual challenge? Might it be a means of avoiding these things through the cosiness of storytelling?
- Jesus taught in parables. These are uncomfortable and unstable stories with equivocal meanings. They bring God close and make God strange. In what way can speaking in parables serve as a model for your own theological writing?

10

Bindweed

This is an extract from a much longer work of life writing in which I try to understand how experiences in my past have shaped me into the kind of theologian I seem called to be. Early relationships, with their many flaws and difficulties, are not cleansed or purged. Anger, selfishness and personal weakness are all evidenced in this writing. However, these are also portrayed as powerfully formative of self-understanding – and in the naming of God.

The poet John Clare loved the common bindweed. The glorious convolvulus with its pure white flowers, more beauteous and fragile than those of the lily.

Of course, the poet was quite mad. Only a madman could fail to recognize his sweet convolvulus as a plant of easy virtue willing to attach herself to anything. She is also malicious. Given to catfights and unprovoked attacks upon her neighbours. She will crowd out those more cultivated than herself. She will steal and smother and strangle. You must root out this plant, because it is neither peaceable nor productive. Convolvulus is a noxious weed.

'What's this?'

'It's convolvulus,' said my grandfather, tearing it down.

'I can't say convolvulus.'

'Tell your mother you can't say convolvulus.'

'I can't say convolvulus, Mummy.'

'Tell your Daddy.'

'I can't say convolvulus, Daddy.'

'Will someone stop that child saying convolvulus, convolvulus, convolvulus . . .'

'Can we pick some convolvulus?'

'No, if you put even the tiniest shoot in your garden it will get a hold.'

'Just the flowers?'

'But they have no stalks to hold them in a vase. See, they need the railings to support them. Look how their green stems wind round and round. The convolvulus has no strength of its own.'

'Why are you so frightened of it then?'

I do not think that things can be ordered, so that everything grows rightly in its proper place.

When I was a student, I fell in love with a man who had a deep sense of holy vocation. He had a very strong effect on those around him. His words seemed to carry special significance, bear hidden meanings, people listened to him. He always appeared to be engaged in some serious inner struggle, even when he was just waiting in the line to buy his cigarettes and newspaper. Perhaps that was why his eyes were always red? Was it from weariness or weeping or gazing too long on invisible things?

These spiritual struggles were not without results; he was the voice of conscience and had separated the sheep from the goats. He could say with confidence what was right and what was wrong. He displayed the marks of his passion, and the air around him carried a crackling charge. But despite all his charisma there was a flaw in him. Sometimes it is necessary for the metal to be mixed with impurities, if it is to survive the cooling process without cracking. In his case the ore was a little too fine.

We both went to the political meetings, spoke in support of motions, voted on amendments and raised our points of order. It was an exquisite mating game. Before he looked at me, I admired him. When he looked and looked away, followed me with his eyes, stood close without speaking to me . . . then I felt my own strength dwindle almost to nothing.

This man became my obsession. I began to dream about how I could help him in his future life. How he would be powerful and pour down fire, and how I should be with him through it all – although it would not be easy. Everyone could see him hold my hand and understand that we were together. I no longer spoke myself at the meetings. His strength silenced me. I loved him to look at me, with his too bright, red-rimmed eyes, as if I was an appealing child. I was even content to hear him say, 'I can't see you tonight, I've got something important to do.'

This love had no simple joy, only immense sensation. I no longer had a mind, I was all body. He had made this change in me. I was sitting in the Junior Common Room in the morning drinking coffee, and many men hovered around wishing to be with me, because I had become nothing more than a deep-throated flower.

But I did not care to attract them. I had no desire apart from him. He was my addiction, but he had another obsession. As well as to the revolution we were making through our magic words (dialectical materialism, transitional demands, to secure for the workers by hand or by brain . . . the means of production, distribution and exchange); as well as to the strikers we stood with in the rain (warming our hands at their brazier and thinking we would stay all day, but nothing happened so we left); as well as to these he had a commitment to the Unborn Child. He said he was absolutely convinced (and always would be) that, when cells began to multiply in the womb, there was human life, and this life must be protected. I was not sure about this at all.

I had been thinking a lot about abortion, because my own mother was pregnant again, and I feared danger. She was all sensation, as I had become through love, because of this new child. She was too distracted to talk and looked as if she had a fever. They had already cut deep into her womb three times. This life was just too fragile, and I was sure it would break. Maybe it could break her? Perhaps it would be born broken?

But my boyfriend said that all was as it should be. The right thing was growing in the right place.

Then my mother started to bleed, and they put her to bed. She felt as if people were poking sharp sticks into every part of her body, and so an ambulance was called.

'I want the baby,' she said.

'But the baby is dead,' they replied; 'we must suck it all away, pluck out every tiny bit, and then you will heal again.'

I was summoned to travel from the university and go to my sad home. To go with my sad father to the hospital with flowers. My mother's skin was translucent. She was drugged and weak. I told her little bits of loving things, and I tried to describe the man who had become the centre of my life. She held on tightly to my hand, trying to feel baby fingers.

I went back to the university. That evening my boyfriend was busy chairing a meeting called to protect the Unborn Child. A woman had come from the national organization to speak. There would be trouble, but that would not worry him; it would confirm the importance of his mission. I was too sick to go. I thought: surely he will knock on my door just as soon as the meeting is finished and stay to mourn with me the death of this unborn baby.

By midnight he had not come, and naked and weeping I crawled into my bed. At that point I did not want to hold this man in my arms. I wanted to kill him. I would have liked to see him crushed and bleeding and broken. I wanted to tell him that he was able to care for things that were invisible and could not be touched, but that he was not able to give the green touch of love where that touch was needed. In the night my mind kept waking me. It woke me with a vision of me pushing this man under a car, hitting him with a stone, plunging skewers into his eyes.

He did not come in the morning either, and I was too weak to seek him out. By the evening I had begun to rage again inside. I showered and dressed with all my nicest clothes and red, red lipstick. He was sitting in the Union Bar, and sweet and sour I went to sit beside him. He finished the important thing that he was saying, and then turned to look at me – with approval, because I was pretty and smart.

'You should have been there last night, it was terrific. And the woman who spoke; she was amazing. I stayed up till three talking with her.'

'My mother.'

'Yes, how is your mother?'

'She is broken.'

He paused. I had not given the right answer.

'She'll be alright. My mother had four miscarriages, and she's alright.'

Now his expression had changed. He was looking at me disappointed, as if I had failed an important test.

Sadly and kindly he explained to me a week later that we were not really compatible. There was something important missing in our relationship. It was not going to survive.

I went down to the Union Bar that evening and saw a student from the year below me standing there. He was one of the ones who had become fascinated by me because of the new scent that hung in the air around me. He was kind, and he was handsome. He had no magic words, no sacred causes or great ideals, but he was a human being, and he would help me.

'Come with me,' I said to him. 'If you don't mind, please stay in my room with me until tomorrow morning.'

We did not sleep. He held me and told me little stories about his school days and pets and sailing in his uncle's boat. And he sang in a band, so he sang to me as well. Sometimes we just lay quietly. He whispered that he had never held someone like me in his arms before. When I was crying, he made a joke, and I had to laugh because he looked so eager, and he had freckles and dimples and open, honest eyes.

We got up early and sat in the kitchen of the student residences. The other women students looked at my young man, as they prepared their breakfasts. They were thinking that I had seduced him for my own desires. I did not care if they thought this. I wanted them to think this. I wanted them to believe that I walked out of the arms of a man who was too pure in his loving and had drawn to myself, for my own pleasure, this lovely companion. I hoped they could see that I was free of my obsession. They could see that I was happy. I did truly feel light and happy. And so they would speak of my shallowness and my easy sexuality. Fine. Good. Let them speak loudly then.

The man with red-rimmed eyes stopped me as I crossed the quad.

'I didn't know you had something else going,' he said. For once he seemed to be really looking at me as if there might be something going on behind my eyes. I wanted to say that he was the only one I could ever love; but I knew it was quite dead. It had been sick from the moment it came into being and was now all over. I just did not speak to this man. I had decided to stay with a clear-eyed honest person who was younger than me until I was healed. He played pinball not politics and his skill and intuition meant he was very good at this indeed. More important, he was happy to take the green life I offered him for all that it was not quite love.

With him I was always glad and calm. My voice returned, and my reason. I liked to sit reading, drinking coffee, looking on while he played pinball with his friends in the common room. I was proud of him. He was funny and bright. But one day I noticed that the way he was looking at me was changing. He had become accustomed to my eyes upon him across the room, and he smiled expecting a look in return that signalled 'we are together despite all these other people, and we are happy'.

Well I was happy, but I was not content, and it was very wrong what I was doing. I was letting him begin to love me, but I was not properly loving him in return. I was the destroyer this time and was holding in my grasp something precious that I would only waste or ruin. Also I was unfaithful, because while he was thinking of nights together in the smoky bar and the kisses later, I was thinking of a long journey all alone. I had begun to make secret plans to leave him. It was time for me to go.

I was travelling to a very cruel land for serious reasons. I wanted to test myself and all the beliefs I had. I wanted to see how people lived, when the fences were destroyed, and the little foxes had broken into the vineyard. I was not going to fall in love or have children. I was not going to build a house to inhabit. I would dwell secure in my own strong soul and take the power of the Spirit for my shelter.

So I had to take a coach to London from where I must also take a plane.

What I did not understand was that I had been tempted into making this journey. It was an old temptation and it was to purity, not to desire.

My good friend Elaine once said to me, 'I have always thought that God was like a huge, lazy, lovely, red-haired woman. Her place is a mess. She leaves her coffee cups unwashed and spots of mould start to form in the dregs and traces. Each cup contains a cosmos to itself. She has this effect on things. She isn't tidy enough to stop them growing.'

She was correct, I think. First there is dust, dirt, even decay. This makes a place for the spores to settle. But I did not know about this generating power at that time in my life. It was not something I understood as I got off the plane in Durban and looked around me at a bright new world.

In this whole continent I did not know one person, and it was a marvellous freedom. Because I was not known, had no roots, I could pretend I was not flesh but air. Here I had a delicious, empty, spiritual purity. Often it was as if there was no me at all and only the serious needs of this serious country.

At first I had lodgings in a long narrow room in a family house. The room was white, and there was a dark little wooden bed, with starched white sheets and a white counterpane at one end and a desk at the other. My Bible was on the bedside table. In the evenings I closed my door and sat in here with the windows open to hear the frogs and the crickets. I worked hard at my desk, taking notes of all I had seen.

I read newspapers and cut out bits to file. I wrote down tables of statistics noting infant mortality, malaria and TB. I studied philosophy and wrote my diary. I liked this serious person I was playing. She had taken her vows and was dedicated like a nun. But then I went to visit. I stayed in another house. There was no place for me there. I had to sleep in the bed of whichever person was away that night or in the space that was left when two people shared one bed. There were no clean sheets. I was sleeping in the hollows other bodies had left in the mattress, in rooms where clothes other people had worn were scattered on the floor and where the cigarettes they had smoked were still in the ashtray.

In this house everyone would gather in the kitchen to drink strong tea, when they got home from the meetings they had been to or the bars they were drinking in. It was the dirtiest kitchen in the world, and it had cockroaches hidden in it. If I walked into this room in the middle of the night, the floor, the table, the walls would be black and rustling with cockroaches, but if I switched on the light in two seconds they would be gone. Back into the cupboards. Back into the drawers. People sat in this kitchen who must not be seen anywhere else. They arrived without notice and were gone again without anyone commenting. Those were things we did not talk about. Everything else but not that. Perhaps they had slipped into one of the beds in this big house and would emerge later in someone's old dressing gown, or perhaps they had slipped away across the border.

One night there was a priest sitting at the table. He brought a five-litre flagon of rough red wine, which we drank from the chipped and stained tea mugs. We talked and laughed, and then he casually took photos from his inside pocket to pass them round. He had with him photographs of people who had been killed in custody. How did he get these, and what was he going to do with them? Don't ask. Just look. I had to gaze on the faces of people who had been hanged and see the way their tongues had swollen and darkened in their mouths as if they had been gagged with the very part of them that was made for speaking. I had to see the dark bloody bruises on their eyelids and imagine how it had been, when the pressure had pushed eyeballs from their sockets. It was as if my vision had been stained. I felt I would never see brightly again. That the negatives of these images would dance across my eyelids each time I closed my eyes.

That old table was our altar.

One hot day I brought home a huge, sweet watermelon and cut it into irregular pieces with the bread knife so everyone could have a slice.

Here we all sat together making sweet potato curry and brandy punch for the Christmas party. We had drunk most of the punch before the party started, and it was the best party ever. That night I did not sleep in a bed at all but on the large sofa in the neglected lounge. Wrapped up next to me in the heavy curtains we had taken down from their rails was a man with long, dark curly hair and deep brown eyes. We had come together in this ugly and painful place, which was more alive than anywhere I had ever been before. But was the excitement I was now caught up in something I could approve of, when so many people were dying? How could there be so much rampant, careless life?

This man was offering me love, and I had to choose whether I would go back to my white room and continue to believe that this was a bleak, pure country or go into his arms and acknowledge this was a place of crimson joy.

In ancient Greece Euripides wrote a play about the tragic love of a wronged woman. 'How unhappy are we women,' said Medea. 'As children we are kept within our walled gardens. No one teaches us the arts of love. What skills we will need to survive in the houses of our husbands. No one tells us of the dangers of love.'

No one tells us of the dangers of love, said Medea. She had grown up in a walled garden and loved with terrible innocence. When this was betrayed, the Lily became a poisonous flower. Because I was not innocent my love could not be terrible like Medea's. It had firm and open petals. There was a faint fresh smell about it like briar roses – but so many thorns. If this man were going to come to me, I would need to make some way through the thorns that had become almost impenetrable since the days of my holy-affair. I would have to prepare myself like a bride.

I slept a lot because this preparation took all my inner energy. It seemed I had never been so tired. Right through the middle of the day I slept, and woke without a headache or the feeling of wasted time. I was lying asleep at the heart of this house in which so much happened. The house was a focus point of power in this enchanted country and in its shelter lay a girl/woman who slept curled-up throughout the day. Although so sleepy I was quite aware of what was happening. I knew that because of what was taking place in me nothing would be the same again. I felt the whole known world was somehow involved in my chrysalis transformation. I was gripped by a terrible nostalgia. The rain would never feel as it had done before on my bare skin. The pavements would be different to walk on. The colours would shift their places in the spectrum. Not only would the world be strange, it would also be dangerous. By surrendering my thorns I was putting myself at risk.

If there came a bang at the door in the night, and the police burst into the house, they would find me where I shouldn't be. They would catch me completely defenceless. Even if they did not enter our room, I knew there were really no places we could hide ourselves away. In the house itself there had to be enemies as well as friends. There was nothing we whispered softly to each other that could not be recorded.

Well, as the defences were useless, I would have to live without them. I could learn to live without them. I could also learn to be dumb blind; to move in a world where I did not see and had learnt not to question, 'Who is that?', 'What is that?', 'What did that person say to you?'

There is one rule. If you do not know, you must not ask.

But if you cannot see or hear, what is left is touch and taste. I touched not only with my outer skin. I touched my friends through those inner nerves that are usually protected. I tasted salt and sweet as I had never tasted them before.

I had not thought you could take a holiday during the war, but we were offered one. We were lent a house that overlooked the ocean. The reflection of light on the waves marked the light walls of our cottage and they were rippled like the sand. The sea roared all the time. After breakfast with strong coffee we would set out to walk along the beach, and although it was the same walk every day, it seemed different, because we found new treasures each time. Our small sea-house was a long way from the main road, and we rarely met any other people. We wrote love messages in the sand and left them there for the waves to wash away. Once we wrote forbidden political slogans in huge letters but quickly rubbed these out again with a stick in case there was an enemy hidden behind the sand dunes. In the evening, our cheeks red from the fresh air and all our limbs heavy, we sat by the fire and looked into the flames. It was not necessary to speak much. Only to try and read what was written in the fire.

11

The Divine Economy of Motherhood

This is a work of themed life writing that takes a number of experiences connected with fertility and motherhood and weaves them together to construct a work of theological reflection upon the experience of parenting. It demonstrates that life writing does not need to be written as a chronological journey. It is helpful and creative to sometimes focus upon specific aspects of our life in order to reflect on these in greater depth. This work also clearly demonstrates the integral relation between our sense of self and sense of God.

Seasonal Factors

It was right at the beginning, about four months in, before I had even begun to think of myself as having a fertility problem. I felt premenstrual early. The tenderness in my breasts and the sharp fleeting pains in my groin. But then my expected period did not come on its (reliable) regular date. I did not hang around. I was straight out to the chemist in my lunch hour, and the test showed positive. I felt quite calm and confident. I was Ms Average Mummy. Things were happening in textbook fashion. It was a Friday, and I carried on at work as if it was a normal day. The walk home alongside the park was lovely. Everything was fresh and green. It was spring, and I was spring. That night we did not go out, even though Friday is the best night of the weekend. All the other people who lived in the house went out, and so we had the place to ourselves. It was quiet. We were happy calmly sitting together. I drank tea, and he had red wine. I started leafing through a book about pregnancy that I had bought weeks ago but not felt able to look at properly before – I've always worried about taking anything for granted. My partner read *The Guardian*, and he kept looking up and smiling at me.

Saturday was a blustery Manchester day. Too cold for a walk, but we spent it companionably in the radical bookshop, where friends moved in and out, and he could look at the political journals, while I browsed the feminist fiction. On Sunday he was on an early shift and left before I awoke. When I did wake up the confident, buoyant feeling of the previous days had left me. 'Well,' I told myself, 'settle down and wait now. This is what it feels like to be pregnant,' but something infinitesimally small seemed to have shifted. As if the barometer needle was now uncertainly hovering over 'Fair' instead of resting there. The pregnancy test I had bought on Friday was the sort that allows you two tries. I went to the bathroom. This time the result was negative, and I had an overwhelming certainty that this verdict was right. There had been an invisible change in the pressure currents.

I was angry. Furious. Much more angry than sad. I had conceived with an open and a willing heart, and so very soon I had become the victim of an unconception. I had been too trusting, too innocent in my confident assumptions. I had been very cruelly deceived. I was so enraged I could not remain in the house. I certainly did not want to go to church, and neither had I any desire to talk to friends. Apart from the park we had no open spaces for brisk walking nearby, and the kind of mental expenditure I needed was not going to be possible in a scary place populated by men in trackies being pulled along by Rottweilers and Pit Bulls. So I went to work. I could not think of anywhere else to go. As it was Sunday, no one else was around. I let myself in with my master key and allowed myself to absorb the quietness of the building. The smell of the library. The dappled light in the chapel. I cannot say I became calm, but I did become concentrated. I went up to my study and wrote an article. Normally I am a slow writer, but I used my energy to carry me through several quick, angry pages. It was good writing. It was about the costs that are not counted, it was about all the waste, all that is spoiled and lost. My words were like the small wisp of smoke that rises when a candle has been snuffed out. I was making theology as an insubstantial memorial to the crushing of my flesh. Writing did help, but it did not take away my anger. I have lived with this tiny piece of shrapnel embedded in my flesh from that moment to this. It did not bleed away when my period started some days later. I can often feel its sharpness, even when I am at rest. Even now that I am a mother.

It is interesting that I conceived again in the autumn.

After the failure of my brief pregnancy, each year brought me back to the same place with no positive results. A barren cycle. I started to find spring disturbing and oppressive. I fully agreed with Eliot's judgement concerning the extreme discomfort the season brings:

April is the cruellest month, breeding
Lilacs out of dead land (1974 [1935], p. 63).

Although, when he said 'lilacs', I think he should rather have written 'buddleias'.

Except that 'breeding buddleias' does not evoke the same sense of cursed melancholy as lilac propagation. Breeding buddleias . . . Cultivating chrysanths . . . Lengthening leeks . . . He would never have written anything so common.

Nevertheless, I remain convinced that he actually meant buddleias. They have long conical heads of shooting purple flowers. They resemble lilacs in feral form. In the 'dead lands' of our streets they send out the first thrusting indications that winter is over. As soon as the days start to lengthen, their vigorous stems start to grow again – not replacing the dead ones but right out of them, among the rotten, blackened flower heads of last year. They grow out of holes in plaster, chimney pots and choked drainpipes. They smother the small front gardens of boarded-up terraces. I hated them. They made the chaos worse. Gardening books warn that you need to be ruthless with these plants. They have to be cut back to ground level each year, or else you end up with this ugly and profane fertility.

Which so oppressed me then. Also, spring just took so bloody long. You think it's there and then it isn't. Winter is holding out. Nothing progresses. You are stuck in an untidy time warp. It is really messy. Brambles, those others of our 'wild' inhabitants, which strangle privet hedges and grow straight out of concrete drives, have great big fat buds on the verge of opening for weeks, and still the hanging tatters of last year's leaves cling on. Then suddenly, after all those weeks of uncomfortable misery, you have a perfect day. Blue skies, white clouds, cherry blossom, bluebells (actually I like bluebells and have forgiven them for returning to live in the city like foxes), bumblebees and baby ducks in the park. It is too sudden and too much. It makes you giddy and gives you a headache. It's too bright and gorgeous.

So, well, I had a problem with the spring. Winter and summer I could do fine, but autumn was the best of all. Gentle, ripening time: 'Season of mists and mellow fruitfulness'.

How good is that? I had a strong sense that if I was ever going to do fruitfulness of any kind, it was going to have to be a mellow sort. An autumn sort. And that autumn was particularly glorious. Not only because of the scarlet and magenta leaves, but also because of the intensity with which I drank in the season. I started IVF on the last day of August, and because it takes much longer than a 'natural' cycle, it defined my passage through the bitterest/sweetest time of year.

At first the bright, fresh mornings gave me hope. This is so beautiful, vibrant, colourful and magnificent that I must acknowledge anything is possible.

Then the wild, windy afternoons gave me courage. This is the defiance of life. It is the expenditure of our energy into the endless darkness of the universe. It is the restless refusal of peace. And the unbearably poignant, still, warm evenings, upon which darkness fell early like velvet, gave me faith. I must admit my form of faith may be a little peculiar. It has to be 'faith in the face of death'. I don't do the other kind. What makes autumn so amazing is the magnificence in mortality. The grace of our giving way. The beauty and the glory of it. Glory to die for. Glory to give life for.

In all these ways the season enabled me to say, 'Yes, I can do this.'

Every day I walked to the hospital at 7.00 a.m. Across the park. Open access at that time – too early for dogs and mountain bikes. Then it was a crowded waiting room with breakfast TV playing loudly and women, anxious about the time, queuing for bloods, scans, injections. A complicated process. If you got in the wrong queue, you could lose 20 minutes and be late for everything for the rest of the day. Afterwards, if I had time, I would cross the road to the art gallery, where the café would just be opening. On rainy days I sat inside, the first customer alone with my coffee, but very often it was sunny, and the tables were still set up in the formal garden. Such a long autumn that year. I sat outside in September, when they gave me drugs to repress my own natural cycle. I sat outside in October, when they gave me drugs to stimulate my ovaries and blood tests and scans to observe how the follicles were ripening. My own harvest festival was in November. All was safely gathered in. By then the tables and chairs had finally been removed, but I sat outside on the broad sweeping steps with my latte in a paper cup, and I was not cold at all. They had harvested the eggs that had ripened, and even now those that had fertilized were growing and dividing. Two days later, and the focused energy of the season, having been offered up to God upon the altar, was returned to me again.

And now I have *almost* lost my terror of the spring. After the miscarriage blue was my favourite colour. Not really a preference, more an obsession. My clothes, my furniture, my pots and vases were blue, and I planted blue flowers in the garden. This is the colour of the Spirit, and it has the power of emptiness and space. Now my favourite colour is green. From mud to moss to uncurling bracken to apple leaf to growing wheat and even straw green. I can do all those colours now because of the changes that she made in me.

Balance of Payments

Within a quarter of a mile of our house, there had been five murders in three years. I am not talking about crosses on some map here. I mean a person had bled to death in the alley next to the bus depot, in front of the off-licence on the corner, next to the railings by the school gate, on the daffodil verge, at the all-night petrol station. There were the invisible outlines of bodies on the streets we walked on every day.

It always happened to someone else. Usually someone involved in whatever it is. But it did make me nervous. Especially because the chaos seemed to come closest when I was feeling the most content. I have a lot of circumstantial evidence to support the theory that you should be most vigilant when you are feeling the least little bit secure.

For instance.

It was a beautiful May evening. I had been working late and left my office at around 10.00 p.m., but there were still people on the pavements, and I was not looking over my shoulder. On my left were the tall silhouettes of the chestnuts and on my right the lights of shops and pubs and restaurants. Despite the traffic I could clearly hear birdsong in the park. Not a nightingale, obviously, but very strong and clear nevertheless – probably a robin. I was happy that I had worked hard and that the world was warm and alive and singing. I let myself say,

'This is beautiful, I am blessed.'

That was a mistake. He swore at me, as he wrenched the bag from my shoulder and slipped through a gap in the railings and into the park. Of course I had my purse in my pocket, I am not that stupid. But there were a packet of red lettuce seeds (lollo rosso), a lipstick (Max Factor) and the mystical writings of Thomas Traherne in the bag. Also I was fond of the bag itself. My mother had given it to me for Christmas, and it was matt leather – purple. I stopped carrying handbags after that. Just used plastic carriers and pockets stuffed with keys, phone, money. If I was going to catch a train or to a meeting, I might risk disguising a bag inside the carrier and taking it out later. Not very elegant but safer.

And then.

We were sitting in the back garden with our coffees after supper. The telegraph pole in the alley was a maypole of wires held taut by the houses around. I said,

'The pattern of the wires is very beautiful against the darkening sky.'

He said,

'Let's open some wine and drink it here together.'

It was Sauvignon Blanc, very cold from the fridge. We were saying how beautiful summer can be in the city. There were a few house martins balancing on the telegraph wires and velvet moths settling on the white flowers. Then I heard the sound of running, and someone threw a bottle against our back wall. It exploded with a sudden stink of petrol, and flames leapt up higher than the first storey of our house. I thought, 'Why us? Why tonight?' as I watched the orange smoke blot out the intricate symmetry of the finely segmented sky.

And another time.

I had been a long while in the bath, which is not so good in a shared house, but the people knew that I liked to do this, and they were kind. I had kept the water warm, and the perfume of the bath oil (mandarin and scented geranium) still lingered in the steam. Nearly time to get out, but the candle was still burning, and I was so relaxed. I did not hear anyone in the alley. It was a complete surprise. The air rifle pellets shattered the frosted glass. It fell everywhere. The warm water was full of icicles. I could not dry myself on the towel which was gleaming with a sudden fall of crystals. I held my clothes in front of me and ran down the corridor. The others came and cleared up all the splinters and fixed cardboard with masking tape to the window frame. I was very cold then, and even when I got dressed, I was still shaking.

So even now I cannot rid myself of the intuition that the happiness in our house (people lying asleep with their bodies spooning their lovers, noisy meals, argumentative political meetings) was not unconnected to the awful things that happened in the streets around it. I have an unsettling conviction that it was because I could hear the bird singing above the noise of the traffic, because I prayed my thanks, that the thief was drawn to follow me. The fact that our back yard was the only one in the neighbourhood in which white flowers bloomed and white wine was being poured seems reason enough to me for a petrol-bomb attack. The perfume and candles obviously prompted someone's attempt to shatter the brittle surface of my world.

I am not a coward in adversity but, because of these experiences, when things seem to be going too well, when I am touching some bliss, then I begin to fear the shadows. So when I was six months pregnant and recklessly allowed myself to buy some tiny socks and three white babygrows, I knew I had purchased more than any human being had the right to own. In the shop I was so happy, but as soon as I left it I felt doomed. When I was struggling in labour, and they were rushing me on the trolley to the operating theatre, I reasoned, quite calmly, that this was because I had painted our bedroom dove grey. There was a fine old silk rug I had found in a junk shop lying sweetly in soft, faded shades of pink upon the floor. I was losing my baby precisely because there was a waiting cradle that had been made especially for her and soft sheets and quilts already turned down.

But that was silly of course, because when I regained consciousness the nurse said:

'It's a girl!'

And I said,

'What's a girl?', because with so much happening I had become rather confused.

And there she was, the little bird, already in my arms, and when they took her away to wash off the blood and dress her, they used one of those tiny white suits, which just goes to show . . .

Almost enough to make you feel ashamed of your fears and yet . . .

I can say quite sensibly that there could not possibly be the awful equilibrium in the universe that I sometimes imagine. There is no fine needle forever quivering in the infinitesimal space between bliss and anguish. I can explain my experiences straightforwardly: you live in the wrong part of the city, you have the wrong sort of body, a melancholy disposition causes you to place these random circumstances in this appalling frame. I can say such things and they are true. I do believe them. But another part of me still whispers insistently that only a fool would believe that there is a right part of the city, another sort of body, a way of telling the tale that is not tragic. It is just that others are more shielded from reality than I have been, and this may be actually their loss and sad misfortune.

Because it does not matter whether it is happening to me or to someone else.

This is not a world of endless generative creations, infinite new births. In all the back alley someone lies bleeding. They are there and part of it. The problem is that, cradling your baby in your arms in her little white suit, it is not pleasant to be haunted by such knowledge.

Loss Adjustment

Jean Rhys lost her baby in Paris (1975 [1939], pp. 116–17). Was it carelessness that had caused this? She was calm, and it seemed as if it was someone else who was crying. There was milky coffee in thick white bowls, fine muslin curtains blowing inwards and the small blooms of intense red flowers beside her white bed. Everyday perfections set alongside her life's empty cradle. They had to bind her, bind her breasts which were tender and her stomach which was swollen. This was to return her unblemished to her previous condition. She got up and left that close-bound world. Somewhere nearby her perfect, white baby lay quiet. She put on her high heels and chorus-girl furs. They seemed pleased that she would walk away unmarked. Red lipstick and rouge. Brandy at the first café.

I was in Paris, when I stopped my milk.

A few weeks before I flew to France, I had been sitting at the kitchen table with my friend Peter. It was Peter who painted the small room where the cot was, just two days before she was born. He found a tiny yellow butterfly on the windowpane and told me this meant I would have a beautiful girl. We were now paying him to paint our hall, because it looked shabby and neglected in contrast to the smart, padded, navy blue and silver pram. But it was slow – there is no urgency in a hall. He liked to talk and read the paper, and I liked him to talk and read the paper. With the money he made he was going to take his seven-year-old son on holiday to stay in tepees in Cornwall. The site was run by Ella Earthworm, and they had been before and both enjoyed it – each night she made a big vegetable stew, and some people played instruments, and everyone sang. He was going to live in a tepee, and I was going to Paris but without my baby. This did not seem so good to me. He was going somewhere nurturing and safe, and I was going somewhere adult and alone. I told him that this was the hardest thing for me to do, and that I was thinking of cancelling my trip.

'Don't be stupid.'

'You don't understand. You're a man.'

'Yes, that's true. A man's brain is like a long corridor with lots of doors. You know the kind of signs they have on them: beer, football, *Guardian* crossword, women in white dresses playing tennis, women in white dresses playing tennis doubles. Yeah . . . right at the end of the corridor is a door marked "Understanding" and you open it, and what do you find? Yeah. Nothing there. Empty space. A sheer precipice – you fall to your death . . . You're right, a man can't understand why it is impossible to leave your daughter with the other person who loves her most in the world, who has looked after her since she was born and is a trained emergency nurse for God's sake!'

I could see the point he was trying to make.

So then I thought: yes, I must go. I will only be away five days, and she will be safe in loving arms. It's a good time to make this break. I will wean my child. Already it is only three feeds a day, and she takes the bottle. So that week I cut the feeds down to two. I fed her at the start of the day and at its quiet ending. The next week I only fed her in the mornings. Then the day came when I had to go, and so it was the last time I fed her.

The taxi took me from the airport and through the suburbs. It slowed down as we passed the church Notre-Dame des Champs. There was the Queen of Harvests not at all abashed by her Christian location, confidently smiling her pagan smile from the stone frieze above the entrance. Not even in disguise with her wheat and her wine, her full-cheeked baby and her flowing breasts. She had turned that cold stone church into a temple. Freaked me out a bit coming across her unexpectedly in the street like that. The conference was held in one of her convents nearby. Not enough holy virgins to fill the honey cells these days so plenty of space for guests. We were in the centre of Paris, but we were also in a small market garden. All the fruits of the fertile earth. The nuns grew potatoes, beans and melons and kept hens. Apricots, pears, cherries and almonds were trained to make the high walls blossom from the inside – from outside you could just see the tips of their branches. The white doves of God flew all around us.

Each morning we had our rolls and chocolate in a room where the French windows opened out onto beds of cabbages and marigolds with intricate tiled paths between them. The room was lined with trellising. Untidy vines were growing inside as well as outside. The mornings were the best times. I tried to sit alone at my table and look out. As I was usually the last to rise, there would often be a time when I was by myself in the garden room, when the other delegates were preparing their papers and reports. I could then imagine what they would be doing at home. He sitting reading the morning paper, and she strapped to his back in her carrier and looking over his shoulder at the world events. Maybe they would be sharing toast. He would cut her a strip, and she would suck it till it was limp and soggy in her clenched hand. There would be conversational murmurings between them. I liked to think of them. But I also liked it that I was alone in the garden room and could drink my lovely chocolate in peace and quietness and then get up and walk slowly along the tiled paths and admire the doves sitting in pairs on the slate roof. Outlined silver white against the morning sky.

Things always got more difficult as the day wore on. My breasts became hard, hot and sore. At lunchtime I would stand in the deep old bath and let cool water from the huge, battered galvanized shower head above fall unevenly over my chest. This is what they recommended in the books. That you take cold showers. I should have known that such advice was not likely to work. I had to express small amounts, because it was too painful not to. It is not easy to dress again, brush your damp hair and pick up your papers and go down and speak about the problems women find in accessing theological education, when all you can think about are your empty arms (have I lost something?) and your painful breasts. I can still remember the bathroom and its grimy frosted glass windows, the smell of disinfectant and rose-scented soap. The water flowing away and mixed with my milk.

Cutting Costs (and Inalienable Assets)

'Something has ceased to come along with me' (Silkin 1965, p. 566), wrote the bearded man who looked like one of the beat generation writers but actually lived in my own hometown in northern England – which is a very long way indeed from San Francisco. He travelled by bus down the congested Otley Road on foggy mornings rather than freewheeling across America's open horizons.

They are the opening lines of his most famous poem. Titled 'Death of a Son', it is about the child with one year, 'Red as a wound', who never laughed or sang or spoke but maintained silence, with something sacred at its core and a 'shining in his quiet' (p. 567). Until his breathing ceased.

And that was the moment when his father imagined the child making a turn, veering away, following another route, requiring his parent to travel on alone. But I am not really convinced about this, that the child ceased to come along with him, because the poet wrote many other works in which his son, 'who died in a mental hospital aged one', reappears. There are glimpses of him in many unexpected places. I think the poet remained bound to his silent companion and the poetry is manufactured out of the silence that this baby, with his red wound, bled into his world.

So personally I have my suspicions concerning surgical accounts of the Oedipal cut, which imply that once the painful wound has been inflicted, parent and child are more or less severed apart – although I am aware that men, in particular, cherish notions of independence and can be more careless, more forgetting, of their charges. For example, my granddad offered to take my six-week-old sister with him to the fish and chip shop. He came back with cod and chips for five, buttered baps, a big bottle of lime cream soda and a Victoria sponge. He left little Mel sleeping peacefully in her pram under the sign that said 'Fresh Whitby Fish'. This is a true story, but it is also true that every family tells the same tales of a child forgotten somewhere. Usually they are being 'taken care of' while the mother is sleeping or busy with other matters. Their absence is only noted when she awakes to her loss.

'Where is my baby?'

But it is not something constant and permanent that women are aware of their offspring at all times. The child does not accompany the mother as an abiding presence – always beside her each time the road turns. No, sometimes they are so far ahead they are invisible. Sometimes they have been too slow and you must wait a long time till they catch up. For weeks they are at your right-hand side, and the next time you look they are left-handed. It is an intimate dialectic of presence and absence. At one moment you are lying in the bath and the clear outline of a tiny foot appears on the tightness of your tummy, and the next the doctors are crowding round you anxious to trace a heartbeat. One day you are breastfeeding and marvelling that this little creature has formed every ounce of its firm flesh from your nourishment. The next day you are crowding into a lecture theatre among a swirl of students who have no notion at all concerning the domestic economy of milk and blood but who are like open-mouthed cuckoos anxious to steal another form of nourishment from you. Walking home next to the park you feel calm but perplexed. Not just 'alone for once' but peculiarly separated,

'I am as solitary as grass. What is it I miss?' (Plath 1990, p. 186).

Then in another moment everything is restored. A communion, more intimate than the womb union, is re-established. We are all home again. It is supper time, and we are together at the big table. Her fingers are tracing my face, and her eyes look into mine. I feed her, and she puts her finger in her bowl and tries to feed me also. I have the smell of her, the touch of her and the love of her, and she has all these things of me. Watching us my friend Peter, who is not at this time painting any part of the house but has just dropped by, says:

'Isn't it nice when they get a bit older and are more responsive?'

'But she has always been responsive!' I counter – too quickly. And everyone laughs at my consternation.

Peter was right actually. He usually is. The communication has grown, is growing. It sustains me. My cup's full and running over. But then every day the precious contents are poured out, and I must become empty again.

Statement of Account

I am very moved by a poem of Sylvia Plath entitled 'Three Women: A Poem for Three Voices; Setting: A Maternity Ward and Round About' (1990). In it three women speak. One rejoices in new motherhood. Another is giving up her baby for adoption – desperate to be free of motherhood and its fearful obligations. The last dreads that she is losing her longed-for child. I used to think the voices were separate and distinct. Now I believe they are deeply intertwined. The voices form a chorus. The work is a triptych revealing differing aspects of the same scene.

What if the theologian is a mother? Must she speak only about sweet milky goodness? Personally I have become so attuned to the disturbed nights that I cannot even begin to imagine what it is like to have a daytime, daylight kind of faith that sleeps right though the darkness. But because maternity is so occluded in our theological reflection it is tempting to emphasize its benign and conventional features and even to place these in contrast to the aspects of paternity whose exaggerated prominence has so damaged western understandings of God.

But I have been formed as a theologian according to a different maternal economy, the features of which still remain largely invisible in theological discourse. This is an economy of risk and loss and unimaginable gains. Of course, I transpose my domestic accounts onto a cosmological canvas. This is what we theologians do. Yes, we work within the boundaries of a religious frame. Yes, we write out of allegiance to the company with whom we travel. But we also work under the daunting licence of the Spirit who has nurtured a strange, unique and compelling life within us.

12

Wild Gardens on the Edge of the World

This work demonstrates some of the framing techniques associated with canonical narrative theology. I have chosen to present a personal story through the lens of a midrash upon a biblical text and via a legend from the Franciscan tradition. However, it also employs many of the features of constructive narrative theology as I attempt to weave both tradition and experience together into a new story. I enjoyed writing this piece, which was originally for performance rather than publication. I think it preserves the sound of my voice in a way that is less evident in more formal academic writing.

First a Wee Story . . .

There wasn't time to pack, when they were expelled from Eden. What to take anyway? The garlands of flowers picked at first light only lasted a day and were bruised and rank by next morning. You can't take the songs of the nightingale that once stirred your innocent sleep. You could not pack the scent of divine sweetness that used to move on the warm evening air. So it was only the clothes that the pair stood up in. Stitched indeed by God's own hand, but rather roughly because of the hurry and the exasperation of the tailor. But still there were pockets, and into them Eve slipped the seed. Much bigger than an apple pip, this was no ordinary Cox's Orange Pippin, and it was smooth and shining. It had not dried out or become shrivelled. She clutched her fingers round it as, bowed low and trembling with fear, she and Adam passed beneath the fiery sword of the Angel and out onto the bright, blank whiteness of the plain.

The first years were very difficult. They moved around a good deal, the boys were born and were very demanding. It was not surprising, Eve often thought, that they were restless and wild given the circumstances. But the girl made up for it. They were more settled by the time she was born, and in the last days of her pregnancy Eve took a stick from the ground and marked out in miniature what she remembered of the contours of Eden. She could not remake the garden of course, but with white pebbles she patterned paths and flowerbeds and in the centre of her labyrinth she planted the seed. Strange, it was moist still and had not grown dull.

It was, of course, a painful birth. But Eve knew better by now how to abandon herself to the dark flood that swept over her and then rise again for breath. The girl grew. She picked the little flowers from the plain and wove fragile necklaces and bangles. She sang as she worked beside her mother, and as Eve closed her eyes to listen she could almost recall the peace of Eden, almost hear again soft footfalls on the paths at evening. As the girl grew, so did the Tree. Eve sometimes wondered if she had made a mistake and had planted just an ordinary fruit tree in her garden. The parent had looked so fine in Eden, but its offspring was rather crooked and bent; white caterpillars swarmed upon its leaves in April, and although she tried to pick off each one the leaves were half eaten and brown at the tips. It did not thrive, but it did survive. The girl grew, the tree lived, and years passed. Eve lost her own moisture and plumpness. She was old now.

One morning she rose from sleep to labour, as was her fate, and she saw with surprise that the tree was hung with flowers. She knew them, knew their dark red hearts, and the fruits that were already forming within. 'Come,' she cried, 'come and look!'; but Adam was already away delving among the thistles (Eden was in Scotland), and her daughter somewhere else, spinning probably. No one came. They found her, when they returned, still beneath her tree, a smile on her face which Adam recognized as the one she had worn long ago, when all the world was blossom. There were petals on her face, her clothes and on the ground all around her. 'How beautiful,' said the girl as she knelt beneath the branches. Adam could not tell whether she was talking about her mother, or the tree spreading out its arms above her and even now standing full laden with fruit.

Now a Legend . . .

What God required of him appeared only very slowly to Francis. At first he was happy enough going more regularly to Mass, fasting longer and confessing with more groans. Then he realized he would have to leave his father's house and the life he had known there. It caused a great scandal but afterwards there were peaceful years spent as a holy beggar repairing the walls and altars of the small deserted chapels in the Umbrian hills. He feared the lepers whose bells he sometimes heard ringing in the lonely countryside, and it was another big step for him to recognize that his life should be spent with them, not on the wooded hills or among the ancient olive groves and vineyards but in the city dumps outside Assisi. With his brothers he made a home in deserted pig sheds that clustered around the small chapel near the city gate. A gradual journey from a fine table, fine clothes and an accommodating faith. From the candles, incense and music of the city churches to this barren, lawless place marked with an ancient stone shrine where the lepers worshipped and the friars bathed their wounds.

Again Francis was happy. It seemed to him that, strangely, there was light and peace here. But then temptation came. What should he really be doing? Perhaps what God required was a pure and shriven heart rather than this haphazard and chaotic life of passionate friendships. Perhaps service could be better given in the calmness of an enclosed cloister or indeed the civilized order of the bishop's palace than in this God-forsaken place? It was the middle of the night, but Francis rose and went out into the sweetness of the fresh air. It was too sweet, even this poverty too rich. The devil was tempting him with the glory of the stars and the gold of the moon. In anguish the saint tore off his monk's habit as if it were no different from the rich silks and furs he had worn in his youth. He strode over to the tangled brambles and threw himself right into the midst of their thorns. And that is when the miracle happened. The brambles became smooth. The matted stalks budded and then flowered. Where barbs had been there was now a glory of roses, roses without thorns. They are still there today. They are still flowering. They have built a great ugly basilica right over the small chapel. The pig sheds are long gone and the graves of the lepers unmarked. But they had to create a garden where the light of heaven still reaches in so that the marvellous roses might bloom.

And an Experience of My Own . . .

When I was young, I lived for a while in South Africa and made many friends among those struggling against Apartheid. I returned home, married, studied and became a lecturer but was glad when an opportunity came to teach for a while in Zimbabwe. Many people I knew were in exile in that country. One in particular, Andre, I was keen to trace.

It did not take long to locate him. I had an old address and worked from there, but it took longer to believe that I had found the right person. When we had last met in South Africa, he was a student activist, a Catholic Marxist, living in a commune in Cape Town and wearing shorts and a leather bracelet on his wrist. Now, so his former neighbour informed me, he was deputy manager of Allied Insurance in Harare. When I eventually found the nerve to phone him at this unlikely corporate location, I expected to receive an angry or puzzled response from a complete stranger. But the slow, amused and arrogant voice was his; unmistakably his, and he arranged to pick me up at the Lonely Donkey next evening,

'Although', he said, 'I don't usually mix in café society.'

This was that strange time in Zimbabwe. Mugabe's brigades had already brought terror to Matabeleland. We knew that, but we were in denial. The streets in Bulawayo are broad enough to turn an oxcart round; a change of direction was still possible. Meanwhile in the bars, beer halls and lounges of Harare's new hotels you could meet with South African exiles (intellectuals and fighters), Cuban military advisers and eccentric fellow travellers like myself. There were other visitors, SADF spies and assassins, and they might be at the next table, sipping Castle lager and listening to our conversations while appearing to talk noisily to each other. I enjoyed the few nights I was able to sit with a cold beer and observe this volatile mix of people. I soon learnt that the serious comrades avoided the places with dim lights and late licences and preferred anonymous burger bars and cheerful pastry shops with checked tablecloths. Andre was cautious about my favourite café, 'the Donkey', with its dusty bottles, tall pepper grinders and small espresso cups. It was near the station and bohemian.

He was wearing a suit and a tie – but not very well. It was not a good suit, and the tie was worse. To me this was a very incongruous thing, to see him wearing these clothes. Particularly as this strange-looking person was talking to me as if we had been briefly interrupted in the middle of a conversation instead of spending the last ten years on different continents.

'So what did I tell you about disinvestment? It's kith and kin. Britain is Apartheid's mother-in-law. How do you think the end of the communist party will affect the solidarity movements? Have you seen Sol? Or is he in Amsterdam? Why are you here?'

He did not listen as I answered. He wasn't really expecting replies. It was just the sort of thing he always said.

'What's happening?'

'What are you doing?'

'Why are you here?'

The way he asked these questions immediately made me feel as if I did not know what was going on, was unsure of my role and should be somewhere else. He had that effect on me. But even so I liked him. I really liked him.

Things got weirder as we drove along. He flung his tie into the back seat, and I noticed that he was not wearing socks with his tan leather shoes.

And where was he taking me? We were heading away from the battered red tin roofs and tangled passion flower and plumbago hedges of the Avenues and into the white highlands. Why live all the way out here?

His house was at the end of a long, impressive drive and had a colonial charm. On the front porch was a large swing, and his two fair-haired little boys were sitting neatly on it eating apples. He kissed them just like Daddy coming home from the office. They wanted to hug him, but he shrugged them off. He was enjoying himself, as if he had a secret joke.

'We'll go in this way,' he said, politely opening the door from the veranda into the living room. Inside was dark and cool. A couple of tired flies were droning around the heavy wooden furniture. The dining table was deeply polished, and six matching chairs were neatly placed around it. On the wall was a picture of a rhino, and a dresser held a substantial array of matching plates, bowls, cups, saucers and, God help me, ornaments.

'So what do you think?'

I was speechless. I did not know what to think. He cracked out laughing.

'Good, isn't it! A typical Rhodie home. Come through . . . Here's the bathroom if you want to wash your hands.'

Smell of disinfectant and a neatly folded pale green towel. Matching soap and flannel. Then a turn in the corridor, a passage leading down and doors off.

'And this is where we live.'

It was altogether different.

I sat in the chaotic kitchen drinking a beer. Carla had come back from work at the hospital and was bathing the boys. But not in the neat guest bathroom. There was another one with a huge stained enamel bath, a big old water tank precariously suspended from the ceiling and grey towels lying on the floor with the discarded T-shirts and underwear.

'So?'

'So what?'

'The house, the furniture, you know . . .'

'I bought the front room.'

'You bought the front room?'

'From a Rhodie guy terrified of black rule. Your problem now. He's gone to live in London.'

'Do you mean London?'

South Africans always say London, when they mean Britain.

'Or Brighton or somewhere. Anyway, he was leaving so I bought the room. Everything. Even the picture and the knives and forks. Had to. Carla and I would never have got it right.'

No, they wouldn't. Carla had looked pretty conventional in her hospital uniform, but she had already swapped that for a T-shirt and Indian print skirt. He could not pick a tie. He forgot the socks to match his smart business shoes. But I had to admit, taken overall, the disguise was pretty impressive.

'So when I have people round from work I take them into the front room and don't let them stray any further than the bathroom. Not that they try to. I keep the wine flowing. We've got crystal glasses. Hey man, we pass for normal. Rednecks not revolutionaries.'

'That's an awful lot of effort just to bring the boss home for dinner.'

'I got the room cheap.'

He looked very pleased with himself and took a swig of beer, waiting for my admiration. We both laughed. But then he looked serious.

'But it's not just that. It's not just about bringing the boys back for a beer. We have to live here. I don't know how long. We've got kids. And it's not safe. It's really not safe.'

After we had eaten (cooked chicken from the take-away, pawpaw and more beer), we stepped out into the other garden at the back of the house. Unlike the front garden the back was wild. Queen of the Night sent its heady perfume out over the overgrown flowerbeds. I picked some to take indoors with me.

'Be careful not to fall in,' said Carla, pointing to the empty shell of the swimming pool. Completely dry and with a layer of rubble in the bottom, 'There are probably snakes.'

In the servant blocks, typically located as far away from the main building as the garden allowed, a noisy family group of more than a dozen people were finishing their own evening meal. They had placed plastic chairs and precarious homemade benches on the cleared earth in front of the grim concrete cells. An old woman raised her hand and offered us a blessing, but otherwise they took little notice of us.

'A gardener and a maid came with the house. But then more and more people turned up. They just live there now.'

I liked the noise, the smell of smoke, the flickering lights in the darkness. I felt at home in this garden with Andre and Carla. Its untidy exuberance was overcoming the cultivated borders of the old country. We sat breathing in the smells and listening to the sounds of dogs and children. We were complicit in our approval of everything around us. But we were also complicit in our awareness of its fragility.

'If they came in the night, and if they came by car, I would hear them turning up the drive,' said Andre.

'Would that help?' I replied.

No answer.

Each of us recited in our minds the silent litany of those the SADF had assassinated, blinded, maimed in Zimbabwe. Car bombs, parcel bombs, shots in the night.

'The children sleep in our bed,' said Carla, 'I don't know if that is better or worse.'

'I guess it's more crowded?' I ventured.

'Too crowded!' said Andre. 'Anyway, if they came in through the front, they would quickly realize they had the wrong place and go away again.'

We all laughed but then fell silent.

'Come and look at the boys,' said Carla.

They were lying one at the head and one at the foot of a double mattress on the floor. On this hot night they lay on top of the sheet, and they were wearing nothing but their underpants. Their golden hair was tousled, and their tanned cheeks sweetly flushed. There is something poignant, no, sacred . . . terrifying . . . about a sleeping child. They were so beautiful.

I followed Carla to another room with a double mattress lying in the corner. She moved a pile of old books and toys from it onto the floor.

'Sorry, I am trying to sort them out.'

When she had left me, I poked through the discarded objects. Among them was an illustrated children's guide to the catechism. Pictures of happy girls and boys, smiling priests dressed in white and a Jesus who looked like Che Guevara. There was also a charming picture book imported from the Soviet Union in which Lenin brought presents to the home of some poor children in winter. Everyone, including Lenin, had very rosy cheeks. I smiled.

I could hear Carla as she went around checking all the doors and windows.

My room was at the front of the house. I was lying naked in the bed with a spray of Queen of the Night in a glass of water beside me. I could smell the perfume. I could hear the distant sound of cars on the highway. I was caught up into paradise. I knew I was not safe.

And Now a Reflection

I told three stories. The first was inspired by some lines in a novel by one of my favourite authors, Elizabeth Smart. She imagines herself compelled to call out to her child as it reaches maturity, 'Go into your garden for your apples are ripe' (1991, p. 112). When I first read these words, their truth struck me hard as a blow. Banished as we are from Eden we nevertheless carry with us the memory of its bliss as well as the seeds we have stolen. I have seen in my own life how again and again I try and mark out a garden's shape in the sand. But this is not just nostalgia for an innocence lost. I am a human child. I want the tree to grow again so that the forbidden fruit can ripen to my reach. It is for this reason there is always a garden to be planted on the whiteness of the plain.

The second story is of Francis – my favourite saint. I have learnt that many saints have similar legends associated with them, the brambles of desire blossoming as roses. I think there is a twist to this one. This saint seeks the spiritual rigour of the wilderness and is terrified of the sweetness of the garden, but the briars lose their thorns and break into bloom before him. I do not think he was pleased, having sought the mortification of the flesh, to find himself in the garden of delight. In my own spiritual life I think I hear laughter when, reaching for dry husks and locusts, I find the honey sweetness of manna on my tongue.

I bring these myths and legends into contact with my life story. I have narrated a real encounter in order to describe the formative experience of being in a place where the garden and the wilderness intermingle and take on new forms. Over and over again I return to the time when I lay unprotected in a wild place with the scent of Queen of the Night invading my dreams.

As I tell these stories I have to acknowledge that I am of the temperament that is always likely to see the innocent garden as a place of deception, its pleasing order contoured by control. I am always very ready to see the wilderness as the site where new forms emerge from chaos. But this dualism is a weakness in me and it is far too simple. Garden and wilderness together engage in a complex and dialectical relation.

It is an insight as old as the Church, repeated by Augustine, Aquinas, Mother Julian, John Milton and sung annually in the ancient hymn of the Easter Vigil, that a happy fault caused our expulsion from Eden and was necessary indeed in that we might encounter God in the flesh, in the incarnation, in the beautiful wildness of this world: 'O happy fault that merited such a redeemer.' But expelled from Eden we do not forget our first home. We carry with us the moist perfume of the garden even in the sharpness of the desert night.

I have come to believe there is great beauty in the wild gardens on the edge of the world. We should not be afraid to venture out and breathe the evening air.

But be careful, dear ones, be careful of the snakes.

Poetics, Theology and Practice

13

Approaching Poetics

Placing Poetics

Part 4 of this book differs in both structure and content from the previous three parts. In each of these a mode of reflective theological writing was introduced and examples given to demonstrate its potential uses. In this part of the text I turn my attention to a broader question, namely the place of poetics within theology.

This is a question that begins with concrete issues concerning writing itself but, as we shall see, quickly challenges us to consider matters with much wider implications. I have thought it important to include this part because there is so little reflection on this topic that is grounded in practice. The reflective theological writer will not be content simply to develop their personal writing skills; it is necessary to have some vision of how the work being pursued engages with other aspects of theological thinking and the wider project of faithful living. However, despite the fact that the questions raised are important, this will be a shorter introductory chapter than the ones found at the beginning of Parts 1 to 3. This is because the substantive discussion takes place within the chapters that follow – each of which focuses upon a specific field in theology and practice. My purpose here is simply to set the scene and begin to introduce some of the key themes that will be debated further.

Poetics as Writing

The term 'poetics' is not commonly found in theological texts. Despite a recent growth in reflexivity there is not (yet) an accompanying awakening of interest in writing as a creative act. Indeed, two dominant authorial strategies in mainstream theological writing serve to restrain such a development. The first (associated with traditions in systematic and philosophical theology) assumes that the point of writing is to communicate true things rationally and objectively with as much clarity as possible. The second (associated with practical, liberative and contextual approaches) assumes that the purpose of writing is to stimulate faithful action. Texts are written with the intention of provoking people to put down the book and do something useful instead. Followers of both approaches happily use literary examples to illustrate their thinking but would tend to see undue attention to writing processes themselves as at best a luxury and at worst a distraction.

Such impatience is understandable. Theology is a serious business and there is important work to do. But I do not think poetics is neglected simply because it seems to lack utility. It is also the case that once we start to ask questions concerning such things as form, structure, metaphor, rhetoric, response, implied readers and constructed authors in a theological context, very challenging issues start to emerge. It could be argued, for example, that behind the cool façade of philosophical theological thinking lie root metaphors and hidden narratives that when exposed unsettle the reasoning process. Similarly, I could make the case that the more activist texts of theology are also, in an important sense, fictive. They are constructed 'as if' their readers and writers were pursuing forms of radical social engagement that are rarely the case. This fiction may be helpful and inspiring but it is fundamentally a rhetorical gesture.

So poetics, even according to its narrowest definition as 'the conventions that structure writing', brings important challenges to theological work. However, 'poetics' is often used to refer to something beyond the literary forms in which we express stories and concepts. It is frequently conceived of in binary relation to another, more dominant, term – poetics thus becomes hypostasized as the oppositional other.

Poetics as Other

Much of my academic work has been in the study of literature and theology. Here there have been a number of attempts to offer models of the relationship between theological conviction and literary creativity. Dating from the middle years of the last century, T. S. Eliot's work has been particularly significant. In his essays and criticism he offers a hierarchical model in which literature is portrayed as hugely beneficial to a Christian society providing it is guided (as a good wife might be by her husband) by the restraining hand of doctrinal theology (1951 [1935], 1939).

These days scholars strive to imagine a more equal relationship – such as this one described by Terence Wright:

> There will always be a tension between conceptual and creative discourse. Systematic theology will continue the necessary attempt to impose clarity and consistency upon language while literature will no doubt maintain its equally necessary task to complicate and enrich the apparent security of theological concepts. (1988, p. 13)

However, even here it is very difficult to break out of hierarchical thinking in which conceptual clarity is the necessity and is complemented (or complicated and enriched) by the contribution of literature.

These examples of attempts to place 'poetic' arts in relation to the higher disciplines of philosophy and theology have an ancient pedigree. They take us back to the development of Greek thought and the archaic fear of the havoc that poets (specifically the dramatists) might wreak within the Republic. Always it is the disruptive potential of poetics that is feared. That it was anticipated poetics would exercise such a baleful influence was because works of human construction were understood as inevitably flawed; imperfect attempts to reproduce or copy things beyond themselves that existed as eternal forms. In contrast, philosophical thinking, expressed in virtuous wisdom, enabled human beings to draw nearer to the spiritual ideal.

Because the poetic has for so many centuries been imagined in contrast to the rational, ethical and spiritual it has come to represent (or embody) a rebellious, anarchic and chaotic force that is passionate, possibly decadent, potentially dangerous and, inevitably, female. Many artists have themselves embraced a romantic understanding of the creative impulse that is founded upon this symbolism. When the term is used, these ancient associations are present, if unexpressed, influencing the way in which contemporary theologians understand (or deny) the poetic in their own writing.

Poetics as Making

There is yet another inheritance from Greek thinking that influences the way in which poetics may function in theological discourse. While in contemporary western culture we often make a distinction between artistic creativity and craft, or between writing a poem and making a table, the term *poesis* derives from the Greek verb 'to make' and links material productivity to poetic construction.

This linguistic link opens up a very interesting theological trajectory. Theologians have been used to denigrating the object world as if this were an obligatory theological response to the perceived dangers of materialism and consumption. Once the concept of making is enlarged to embrace the fabrication of things, alongside the creation of art and indeed the creation of culture, a rather different perspective becomes possible. One that, after Marx, we could understand as revelatory of the essentially productive nature of humans, which comes into being through their material endeavours. In the last chapter of this book I turn to this wider understanding of the term 'poetics' as it has been developed in the work of Henri Lefebvre and Michel de Certeau. Both these writers see poetics as the human genius to create meaningful lives out of the ephemeral and material – out of the stuff we mortal creatures are made of. For these writers a fundamental unity is to be perceived in our making of meaning, our making of relationships, and our making of art and our making of objects. I would go further and insist that a radical incarnational theology can take root in this soil as we contemplate 'God's poetry' as embodied and expressed in material forms.

Poetics as Practice

These wider perspectives on poetics inform all the essays in this final part. If we begin to see poetics, modestly, as incarnate in our own writing practices but look outward from there into our wider social engagement, and beyond that to the way we conceive the human/divine relationship, then it becomes imperative to challenge the notion that poetics is inessential or supplementary – always the other.

In these final chapters I have set myself the challenge to assess how poetics might function in areas to which it might appear, at first, to have little relevance. I am interested in understanding both its productive potential, the 'So what?' question Stephen Pattison identifies as the leitmotif of practical theology (2013, p. 4). I also seek to assess the challenges it might offer to previous assumptions about what good practice entails. If poetics matters, then it should have something significant to say to practical theology, a discipline that is focused upon useful action. It should be able to generate a new perspective upon public theology, a discipline concerned with the Christian 'voice' in questions of social justice. Crucially, poetics should enable us to create pastoral responses to people in pain. Most important of all, poetics should enable us to construct theological wisdom in the midst of everyday life.

14

Poetics and Practical Theology

It must be admitted that poetics and practical theology do not enjoy an easy relationship. Part of the reason for this lies in the very different 'temperaments' that each discipline displays.

Poetics is concerned with the construction of literary texts and the conventions employed by creative writers in the making of these works. It explores literary form, narrative structure, genre, plot and characterization as well as the dynamics of image, metaphor and symbols in the creation of art. When listed thus, these literary devices appear as docile subjects for serious academic study. However, all of them relate to processes of creative transformation through which human language constructs a 'something else', or what the philosopher/poet Hélène Cixous has termed a 'Somewhere Else' (1993, p. 26), beyond the limits of the matter-of-fact, everyday world. Thus the genius of poetics does not lie in identifying norms for stabilizing literary production. Poetics is more interested with the way human imagination constructs narratives by winding its way among and between the factual and the fictive. It explores the capacity of metaphoric utterance to embody the exotic, the beautiful, the tragic, the unknown and the unnameable. It strays beyond the strict bounds of the real to proclaim its own form of truth. The French Thomist philosopher Jacques Maritain reflects that to fulfil its 'spiritual' vocation poetics must venture into places that theology regards as disreputable and dangerous. Poetry, he writes, delights in the senses, delves into the flesh and 'finds its own at every crossroad in the wanderings of the contingent and the singular'. It can be distracted by 'any flash of existence glittering by the way' (1954, pp. 235–6).

The qualities of poetry, which Maritain sees as supremely representative of the creative arts and so vividly describes, have been long distrusted by philosophical theologians conscious of the need for rationality, order and morality in their reflections upon the divine. Although practical theology is the area of theological thinking that is most committed to reflection upon the particular, the embodied and the contingent, it too has been wary of too close an encounter with poetics – but for rather different reasons. Stephen Pattison has often argued that practical theology is a discipline driven by a compulsion to be useful and in which actions always speak louder than elaborate words. 'The most important question in practical theology is, "So what?"' (2013, p. 4). While others have offered longer reflections upon the nature of the subject, Pattison's terse statement gives an accurate character sketch of a field of study concerned to see and think clearly in order to make a difference in the world. Practical theology does not like to linger idly at the crossroads. It does not surrender to the distracting loveliness of life as it flashes by.

We can now begin to understand why poetics does not immediately suggest itself as a diligent co-worker in practical theology's endeavours. In fact the opposite. During the past quarter-century in which practical theology has developed a more confident voice, it has been to the robust and restrained resources of moral philosophy, hermeneutics and the social sciences that it has turned for support. However, recently there have been an increasing number of voices warning against an over-reliance upon epistemological traditions that focus our vision upon what can be conceptually objectified and reasonably analysed, and do not encourage us to quest for traces of the 'somewhere else' of the creative arts.

Among these protesters Pattison himself has reflected upon the embarrassing discomfort felt when practical theology is characterized as a 'soft' subject rather than an empirical discipline; a distress he believes is caused by our desire to align ourselves with scholarly judgements of what counts as knowledge worthy of credibility and respect in the academy (2007, pp. 253–60). Terry Veling has argued that practical theology requires poetics to extend its prophetic vision – the scope of which simply cannot be contained in the realms of the conceptual and instrumental (2005, pp. 195–203). Daniel Louw has warned that processes of rational abstraction can disguise their (western) cultural origins in the cloak of a fictitious universal and thus generate acontextual and inappropriate approaches to pastoral care. He argues that 'aesthetic reasoning' is necessary 'to safeguard a practical theological ecclesiology from becoming so spellbound with a critical analytical method that it ultimately has a very positivistic approach towards human actions' (2001, p. 330). More radically, Nancy Bedford has suggested that praxis-based theologies are in danger of losing momentum as practitioners retreat into safer but less prophetic modes of reflection. In this context, she argues, poetics offers the best hope of safeguarding the insights of liberation theology in vital new forms: 'the use of creativity and imagination . . . a willingness to play with metaphors are ways in which to start discerning how to overcome this time of parenthesis' (2002, p. 162).

Enthusiasm for poetic modes of reflection has been particularly influential within feminist practical theology. Already convinced that a hermeneutics of suspicion should be employed in relation to sacred texts and traditions, women have argued that the dominant discourses of practical theology cannot adequately address the concerns of women unless they stand in a critical relation to the 'Christian tradition in such a way that the ambiguities of life can be endured . . . The brokenness of life in all its aspects cannot be ignored' (Bons-Storm 1998, p. 15). Bonnie Miller-McLemore has argued that feminist practical theology must testify to this ambiguity and brokenness through refusing 'objective' or 'normative' theologies that tame and control dissonant experiences. She advocates a theological process that is transgressive, political and *literary*, and encourages pastoral theologians to employ a 'poetics of resistance' to confront 'the limitations of imposed frameworks . . . to get at the inexpressible without losing a genuine sense of it – much like poetry and prayer' (1998, p. 191). In my own work I have sought to embody experimental forms of pastoral poetics through writing that is metaphoric and reflexive. I view the feminist imperative to re-vision the tradition as a challenge that can be addressed through creative writing practices that attempt, with faithful audacity, to speak about what takes our breath away (Walton 2007a).

Although these interventions demonstrate that the wariness that has characterized the relationship between poetics and practical theology is increasingly viewed as problematic, it would be entirely misleading to suggest that practical theology has been held till now in empirical captivity.[1] In fact there are many areas of its work in which poetics plays an important, if under-acknowledged, role. In preaching, pastoral counselling, theological education and theological reflection the use of poetic resources are widespread. However, when practical theologians employ creative resources, they do not generally view their use as epistemologically significant or reflect upon them in depth. For this reason, I have thought it helpful to focus here upon specific instances in which an encounter with poetics opens new horizons for practical theology as

---

1 The 1999 conference of the International Academy of Practical Theology (Quebec) was on the theme of 'Creativity, Imagination and Criticism: The Expressive Dimension in Practical Theology'. The conference volume of this title features a number of important engagements with poetic and imaginative forms.

a discipline. In doing so it is my intention to highlight ways in which more fruitful encounters between practical theology and poetics might develop in the future.

The Poetics of Church

I begin with what is widely regarded as a 'classic text' in contemporary practical theology. James Hopewell's *Congregation: Stories and Structures* (1988) was his only major work. It was written during his terminal illness, and among its many striking features is the way the author juxtaposes his own search for meaning with an exploration of the manner in which local congregations make sense of their corporate experience. The result is a profound book that moves to and fro between the intricate narrative that friends labour to create around Hopewell's hospital bed and the shared tales that congregations tell of their communal struggles to maintain faith and hope.

Without even beginning to describe the substance of Hopewell's book, it is clear that this is a very unusual, 'poetic' text in which it is impossible to avoid the distinctive narrative voice of the author. However, it is not for this reason it is presented as my first example of a significant encounter with poetics, but rather because of Hopewell's bold announcement of a new insight. 'Christian congregations took me by surprise' (1988, p. 3), he writes, describing a sudden realization that a congregation is best understood as an *artistic creation* brought about by 'persistent imaginative construction of its members' (1982, p. 82). Beyond the structural and organic analyses of congregational life with which he was familiar, Hopewell had glimpsed a glory. Congregations stood revealed as corporate works of delicacy, ingenuity and aesthetic achievement such that even 'a plain church on a pale day catches one in a deep current of narrative interpretation and representation by which people give sense and order to their lives' (1988, p. 5).

Hopewell came upon this insight through painstaking observation of his own ministerial context combined with academic research employing ethnographic methods largely drawn from cultural anthropology. Although Clifford Geertz's insight that cultures can be understood as symbolic systems was influential for Hopewell, it did not seem adequate to describe the complicated narrative work that he observed taking place in local churches. In sermons, pastoral conversations, small talk and gossip, members actively storied their lives in relation to larger narratives of quest, sacrifice and resolution. So significant did this imaginative labour begin to appear for Hopewell that he immersed himself in literary theory and the discourses of poetics to find a new way of understanding congregations.

It is for this endeavour that Hopewell is both best remembered, and most criticized. He enthusiastically embraced the critic Northrop Frye's fourfold typology for categorizing narrative forms. Frye argued that in western culture all stories display predominantly tragic, ironic, romantic or comic features. These forms present differing ways of reconciling divine power and human circumstances, which range from accepting the will of an implacable deity to discerning cosmic harmony in all things. Hopewell found that the tales told by friends around his bedside could be analysed according to Frye's four types, and furthermore that the stories congregations told about themselves and embodied in their practice revealed 'worldviews' that also corresponded to the categories Frye had identified.[2] At the time when Hopewell was writing, Frye's system was already coming to be seen as overly deterministic but, as Hopewell adapted it into an analytical tool for congregations to assess their own worldviews, it yielded useful and persuasive results. Of more enduring significance, however, is the work Hopewell presents on the poetic processes through which congregational identity is constructed. These include: the assumption of 'corporate character', the creation of plots that link past events to future hopes, and the use of symbol and metaphor to convey the vitality of local wisdom. Together these poetic arts sustain narratives with mythic depths that bind congregations into communities of faith.

Hopewell believed that the heart of his book lay in a chapter daringly entitled 'Christ and Eros'. This elusive and fragmentary section, written after Hopewell had learnt 'how I will probably die' (1988, p. 170), represents a celebration in this darkness of the 'erotic' capacities of the rich human imagination and the 'erotically capacious households' that congregations can become when confidently employing their creative resources. He describes Eros as the personification of cultural creativity (1988, p. 165) and seems to be figuratively representing something very

---

2 Hopewell writes:

> Frye portrays . . . a total quest myth that circles from romantic adventure through tragic despair and ironic darkness into a comic dawn . . . Any single work of literature is a recognizable bit of the gigantic circle. No human being sees the whole. Each instead is orientated by a story, toward some direction within the total horizon.
>
> Congregations adopt a similar orientation. Were any of them to be situated in our windowed church building surrounded by the total horizon of the Western world's literary interpretation they would arrange themselves to face a particular point on the circle. Different congregations would face different ways. (1988, p. 67)

similar to poetics as previously defined. The philosophers and theologians recoil from Eros, 'terrible as an enchanter', Hopewell writes. But we should not despise the passion with which human beings desperately plunge into the chaos of life to seize whatever is needed to create meaning. Theology needs to recognize its own dependence upon the 'metaphorical labour' through which 'Eros expresses in part the nature and being of God' (1988, p. 170). Hopewell appears to be reaching towards a view of the congregations as a place of lived encounter between the poetic impulses present in human culture and the animating power of the Christian tradition incarnated in Christ. However, it must be admitted that, while the chapter opens enticing new conceptual space, it does not quite succeed in presenting a picture of how the two archetypal figures of Christ and Eros will embrace. They still stand at some remove from each other at the chapter's end.

Congregation presents a bold vision of the role poetics might play in practical theology's primary task to understand and nurture Christian community. Hopewell does not set poetics apart from other forms of knowledge (*Congregation* employs empirical resources to study congregational life alongside those drawn from literary theory), but he presents imaginative work as essential to grasping the fullness of Christian practice. His work is recognized as foundational to the emerging field of congregational studies but, sadly, his radical poetic vision did not have time to unfold to maturity and is less widely acknowledged.

The Poetics of Practice

Hopewell died in 1984 and was not able therefore to make his own response to another hugely significant publication inspired by the lively life of Christian congregations. Don Browning's *A Fundamental Practical Theology* is elaborated around his study of three churches, including the pioneering study of the 'Wiltshire Church' in which Hopewell also participated (see Dudley 1982). As a researcher his chief interest lay in the hermeneutical processes through which Christians engage in an encounter with their tradition in specific cultural contexts; a process out of which emerged distinctive forms of ethical practice. The 'practical reasoning' Browning identifies at work in each congregation is presented as paradigmatic for understanding the dynamics of practical theology which, he argues, replicates as a discipline the forms of ethical engagement with tradition and experience that can be observed within local Christian communities.

In presenting the interpretative work of congregations (and practical theologians) as practical wisdom, Browning is employing the Aristotelian concept of *phronesis*. This is useful for him, because as a philosophical category it refers to an understanding of ethics as rooted in character and tradition as well as being embodied in thoughtful action. However, Aristotle famously distinguishes between *phronesis* and *poesis*.[3] The first term refers to a capacity to reflect and act well in accordance with a virtuous apprehension of what constitutes the ethical life. In contrast, *poesis*, a word derived from the Greek verb 'to make', is a process of *making* (through crafting an object, artwork or literary composition), which may have pleasant or beneficial results but remains a mimetic activity. *Poesis* produces transient goods that are reproductions of ideal forms. It does not apprehend eternal virtues. This Aristotelian perspective has fundamentally shaped western culture to the extent that creative activity is still seen as fundamentally different from the ethical project of living a good life.

Browning should not be cast as a reductive thinker opposed to poetic insights. He presents hermeneutical processes themselves as forms of imaginative play. Nevertheless, his influential text actively reinscribes Aristotelian thinking into practical theology and effectively minimizes the significance of the poetic processes that so fascinated Hopewell. Recently, however, there have been attempts to come to an understanding of poetics that places it in a more balanced and productive relationship with *phronesis* and affirms the importance of both in the practice of an ethical and creative faith. An example of this approach can be found in the work of John Wall. Wall worked closely with Browning on the 'Religion, Culture and Family Project'[4] and has written extensively on Christian moral practice in family life. It is Wall's thesis that, in a cultural context where moral absolutes are increasingly challenged, a poetic facility is essential for the ethical subject or community. He challenges the hierarchical distinction between ethics and poetics that is repeated in the writings of Augustine, Aquinas, Kant and, more recently, Arendt and Habermas, who also assume a fundamental distinction between moral and creative processes. Wall writes:

Such a distinction between ethics and poetics has had enormous influence over Western moral thought. Augustine's *Confessions* condemns

---

3 The term *poesis* is sometimes used instead of 'poetics' by theorists in this field. As *poesis* is associated so firmly with Aristotelian approaches to the topic I have used 'poetics' as a broader and more accessible term.

4 Funded by the Lily Endowment and charged with addressing the contribution faith communities might make to the revitalization of family life in the United States.

rhetoric and public amusements as morally corrupting for the soul. Thomas Aquinas's *Summa Theologica* repeats Aristotle's distinction almost word for word. Immanuel Kant's second and third critiques draw a sharp line between the objectivity of moral law and the subjectivity of aesthetic taste. (2003, p. 313)

In making the case for a new and more productive relationship between poetics and *phronesis*, Wall draws heavily upon the work of the philosophers Martha Nussbaum and Paul Ricoeur.

Nussbaum, herself deeply influenced by Aristotle, has sought to broaden philosophical understandings of virtuous practice by arguing that literature is 'a vital, perhaps even necessary, instrument for becoming a practically wise person' (Wall 2003, p. 322). For Nussbaum imaginative writing is important because it enables us to observe the complexity of the world in a manner that forbids the reduction of particularity to abstract generalizations. Literature, furthermore, engages the emotions in processes of wise discernment through which we strongly identify with others whose lives are different from our own. The process of reading, for Nussbaum, can be seen as moral formation – particularly so because a person who has creatively engaged with literature will have confronted the tragic aspects of existence and therefore will see ethics not as a triumph of moral will but rather as a struggle with intractable conflicts in difficult circumstances. Nussbaum's work is helpful for Wall because it affirms the significance of poetics when grappling with the deepest moral issues and presents ethical reasoning itself as an open-ended, creative process – a form of art. These insights are deepened through a conversation with the work of Paul Ricoeur.

Ricoeur's hermeneutical writings are widely referenced within practical theology but less attention has been given to the huge significance that metaphor holds within his thinking. Metaphor is a key term for this French philosopher, drawing together the many disparate aspects of his oeuvre. For Ricoeur a metaphor is not simply a figure of speech. It betokens an imaginative capacity to create something new out of the meeting (not synthesis) of different terms. Metaphoric construction is what enables human beings to engage in transformative action in the world as they create new conjunctions that empower them to apprehend existence in fresh ways. Very similar creative processes allow us to fashion seemingly unrelated circumstances into artful narratives that give meaning to personal and social life. Extended further into the field of ethical practice, this imaginative propensity to engage creatively with difference enables human beings to open themselves up to the existence and needs of others – to be challenged at their core by the alterity they encounter. Wall writes of this poetic process:

> This form of moral creativity . . . imagines otherness in order to further imagine self and other ever more radically in common. In the image of our Creator who drew chaos into form and light . . . we are capable of creating moral community amid difference however impossible such a task in fact appears. (2005, p. 60)

Guided by Nussbaum and Ricoeur, Wall constructs an appealing vision of 'poetic *phronesis*', or a poetics that is 'radically involved in moral life' (2003, p. 337). He goes beyond suggesting that poetics is a useful supplement to the traditional concerns of practical theology and argues that, in the 'modern desert' of ethical practice, '[t]he kind of reflexivity involved in poetic *phronesis*' is essential in order to *make* (construct or create) mutually responsible forms of theological/social meaning (2003, p. 338). Wall's defence of poetics makes clear it offers a distinct contribution to the clear thinking and virtuous practice that practical theology values so highly.

The Poetics of Testimony

My final example of a significant encounter between poetics and practical theology is drawn from Rebecca Chopp's work on metaphor, trauma and testimony. Chopp has long displayed an interest in issues relating to language, politics and practice. She was one of the first feminist theologians to address the 'turn to language' in poststructuralist theory.[5] Her interest in poetic practice in the field of practical theology was established with the publication of a reflective and highly personal book, *Saving Work: Feminist Practices of Theological Education*. This work was occasioned by Chopp's observation that theological schools were increasingly training students whose gender, ethnic identity or lifestyle would have excluded them from theological education in the past. Lacking institutional affirmation and personal role models, these 'new' students needed to construct narrative identities to 'survive' and render their presence and concerns visible. The development of 'narrative

---

5 Her book *The Power to Speak: Feminism, Language, God* (1989) is a key work of feminist theology in dialogue with critical theory.

agency', Chopp observed, often emerged through encounters with literature, poetry or autobiography which gave students the 'ability to envision life, be it personal, interpersonal or social in new ways' (1995, p. 43). Indeed, the emergence of narrativity actually seemed to require the use of 'literature and poetry as sources of theological reflection' (1995, p. 109).

Chopp's growing awareness of the significance of poetics in challenging social silence was developed further through an important encounter with a developing genre in literary theory which she termed the poetics of testimony.[6] 'This genre includes poetry, theology and novels and other forms of literature that express unique events or experiences outside the representation of modern rational discourses . . . which rational discourse cannot or will not reveal' (2001, p. 56). While recognizing that some experiences are neglected or denied in dominant discourses, the poetics of testimony is concerned with those aspects of human life that cannot be addressed at all within our usual registers and are currently 'unspeakable'. Experiences of trauma and abuse, ecstasy or pain would fall into this category, and witnessing to their significance requires extraordinary means. Imaginative forms must be created that bear the unbearable into speech. These metaphoric utterances will be fashioned and passed on by those who have been caught up in extreme circumstances and those who bear witness to their suffering. Chopp writes, 'Such discourse is an invention . . . [required] to refigure, refashion and reshape the world' (2001, p. 61).

The poetics of testimony, Chopp insists, has three important implications for theological thinking, and these are particularly significant for practical theology as it considers its relations with poetics. The first is that for Christians the imperative to bear moral witness requires speaking with a 'strange voice', and this must override the wish to construct reasonable accounts of the theological project that are acceptable to others. A practical theology attentive to testimony will be in some senses ruptured and disfigured but, Chopp argues, capable of communicating more in the brokenness of poetic language than it can speak within the protocols of the discourses that currently predominate.

Second, theological discourse plays an important role in sustaining or disturbing the 'social imaginary'. This is a term widely used in contemporary theory to describe the way 'people imagine their social surroundings . . . carried in images, stories and legends . . . the

---

6 Chopp was particularly influenced by the work of Felman and Laub (1992) on trauma and testimony, as will be demonstrated in the next chapter.

social imaginary is that common understanding that makes possible common practices and a widely shared sense of legitimacy' (Taylor 2004, p. 23). Acknowledging deep reliance on Ricoeur's work, Chopp argues that articulating new metaphors (both linguistically and through other means such as ritual and symbolic action) is a vital part of Christian practice. As practical theology is particularly concerned with worship, witness and being alongside those who suffer, it is particularly well placed to engage in the imaginative labours that call into question 'common understanding' and contribute to social change.

Finally, Chopp argues the poetics of testimony is a discourse of alterity. It speaks powerfully out of the realm of the silenced and we encounter it as prophecy; speech that transcends our current context and calls to us with the voice of God. It is not easy to speak of God in public. Practical theologians have wrestled with the challenge to find ways of mediating the Christian message in civil society, and have often felt compelled to translate theological terms into secular phraseology that can function as an approximate coding of their convictions concerning justice and peace. Sadly, in this translation process a great deal is lost – much public theology is barely distinguishable as theology at all. The poetics of testimony is not, however, a discourse that can be tamed. The words are wild and arresting for this is the voice in which the lost and the dead address us. A poetics of testimony will find many echoes and associations with the scriptural and spiritual resources of the Church as these, too, attempt to convey through metaphoric means an account of suffering and salvation that is un-accountable. As any pastor knows, for those who experience extreme suffering, normal language can go only a little way. Quickly we turn to image, symbol and ritual, language formed on the edge of silence, as our resource. A poetics of testimony leads us to understand that what we have learnt in pastoral encounters must become part of our theological labours as we learn to speak of 'the power and spirit of transfiguration' (Chopp 2001, p. 66). As we name the particular agonies of creation, Chopp argues, these are taken up into the absolute of God's transcendence and return to us as a message of hope.

> To say it in traditional terms, transcendence expresses the hope that the memories of suffering will be told and not go unredeemed . . . God as the term of transcendence allows for the remembering of the dead and those who survive, the critique of the present, the creative naming of the future. (2001, pp. 66–7)

I have sought in this chapter to show how poetics can transform our understanding of congregational life, Christian practice and Christian witness in the public sphere. However, these are not distinct areas of concern. All come together in practical theology's quest to name God as the one who calls us to incarnate a witness to passion and resurrection in the poetry of our practice.

15

Poetics and Public Theology

A Personal Problem

For many years now I have lived with an unresolved tension in my faith and life. I am a deeply political person with strongly held convictions that I have no reticence about sharing or acting upon. I am content to use the old-fashioned labels, 'left wing', and 'feminist', to describe these – but recognize that these identifiers must be persistently and pragmatically renegotiated to meet new challenges as they present themselves. I am also a believer, a Christian, and my beliefs are not private opinions. I am a church member, preacher, Elder and theologian, who has participated fully in the councils of her Church. Given that politics and religious faith are the twin poles of my existence, and that I cherish a lively concern for the participation of the Church in public affairs, it might be assumed that public theology would be of particular importance and interest to me.

But this has not been the case. In fact rather the opposite. I have an ambivalence sometimes bordering on antipathy towards much of what appears under the heading of public theology. However, rarely have I articulated what it is that provokes this response. This chapter offers the opportunity for greater reflexivity and the challenge to identify the reasons why I have such huge reservations concerning speaking about God in public.

Personal history is always telling, and it is relevant here. My theological identity first began to take form through my work in the Student Christian Movement in the early 1980s. We were 'the-generation-after' the student radicals who had first encountered and embraced liberation theology (in the late 1960s and 70s) and began to introduce this new thinking to British Christians. I remember devouring the publications they had laboured to produce:[1] slim pamphlets such as *Towards a*

---

1 The first mystery I was initiated into when I began to work for the SCM was how to work the precious printing press upon which some of these works had been laboriously produced.

Theology of Gay Liberation,[2] *The Guerrilla Diaries of Nestor Paz Zamora*[3] and *For the Banished Children of Eve*,[4] were for me bright heralds of a shift in thinking that was not yet to be encountered in the academy or Church. But we were 'the-generation-after' and as such struggled with the legacy of our predecessors. Those who had come before us were wild, sexy and creative. Some had actually built barricades in Paris, participated in student protests in South Africa and chilled out reading poetry with Camillo Torres. Among them were artists, musicians and writers who added their talents to communicating the heady mix of new ideas. The theological energy that they sparked was vital and compelling. The rhetoric passionate and robust. We enthusiastically adopted this discourse and also began to speak of the shared horizon of salvation and liberation, of the God of the oppressed and the poor of the world who were coming out of bondage. But ours also were the days of Reagan/Bush and Thatcher, and the popular movements that had given resonance to the rhetoric (such as that of the Sandinistas in Nicaragua or the Allende government in Chile) appeared to be everywhere in retreat. To be sure, the discourse of liberation conveyed a hope that claimed, and still claims me, but in what sense could it be related to the political circumstances in which we were operating? The first theological article I ever wrote attempted to wrestle with this dilemma. It was titled, 'If God is on the side of the poor – why don't they win?' (Walton 1984, pp. 6–7).

And the Problem with the Church

One of the difficulties about coming after a highly creative epoch is dealing with the messiness left behind. The radical vision that had motivated our comrades and mentors did not easily translate into institutional commitments. We were left to reconstruct an organization that could relate to Christian students and rebuild relationships with church leaders who were disturbed by what they perceived as an irresponsible politicization of the Christian gospel. This was necessary but not glamorous work. Friends who had, like me, been drawn to the Movement precisely because of its radicalism began to express their doubts as to the worth of tarrying with the Church. Why devote energy to sustaining a

---

2 *Movement: The Journal of Radical Ideas and Action*, pamphlet no. 22.

3 *Movement* pamphlet no. 2.

4 *Movement* pamphlet no. 24. This 24-page booklet contains the early work of Rosemary Ruether as well as Mary Condren and Una Kroll.

liberal, bourgeois, social institution that was unlikely ever to embody the liberatory hope they had come to believe was at the heart of the Christian faith? A practical question that shelters a theological one. We had come to grasp with the force of a revelation that there was a connection between political yearnings and divine encounter. At our very best moments we even approached that simple, holy space where Saint Francis, the Anabaptists and others had discerned a world-transforming glory emanating from the marks of Christ's suffering. However, clearly this vision was not only for individual saints and martyrs but for a community, and what if the community that bore the name of Christ did not display the signs of this transfiguration?

In many late-night conversations I found myself acknowledging that quite obviously the Church was not going to become an agent of radical social change and that we should not retain membership on the basis of this unreasonable hope. However, I argued, we belonged because we believed and were nurtured and disciplined in *all* aspects of our lives (including political engagement) by worship, prayer and the sacraments. We believed in God, not the latest cautiously progressive church report on poverty or racism. So here the divide in my life opened up. I was convicted by the sure knowledge that at the heart of faith were claims that were deeply political in essence, that the very discourse of theology was unintelligible unless accountable to the overwhelming reality of human pain and longing. But there was an aporetic distance between these convictions and my expectations of what the lived reality of institutional religious affiliation implied and could deliver. In effect I was implicitly constructing a theology that divided the Church from the world.

On Preferring the Problem to the Solutions

Which was problematic indeed considering liberation theology's insistence on the common world of faith and struggle. For a while I found comfort in contemporary Catholic understandings of a 'discreet' vocation (or a vocation of discretion!) appropriate to the laity, of 'silent witness, social action and political relevance' (Lefebvre 2005, p. 142).[5] This appeared to offer space for much more radical public interventions on an individual basis than could ever be countenanced as a

---

5 This article reflects upon the role of *Lumen gentium* in freeing many Catholics to hold their own political views while leaving public discourse on religion and faith to the clergy.

public representative of the institution. However, this was never going to be an enduringly tenable position for a budding theologian – hardly a discreet or silent calling. I was finding it increasingly difficult to 'pass for normal' in a secular environment.

Of more lasting significance for me was Bonhoeffer's judgement, towards the end of his life, that we had embarked upon times in which the Church was 'incapable of taking the word of reconciliation and redemption to . . . the world' (1973, p. 300). Christian faith must now be practised, he suggested, as a secret (arcane) discipline whose expressions were to be prayer and righteous action.[6] Surprisingly, this bleak judgement sustained my sense that I should proceed boldly as someone called to speak despite being seemingly incapable of saying anything authentically, directly and with integrity about what mattered to me most. Accepting this fact humbly and as a spiritual discipline seemed the paradoxical route to obedient discipleship. What particularly moved me in Bonhoeffer's thinking was the sense I identified of deep love for the language and labours of theology, but an equally compelling view that, due to a combination of the movement of history, the challenge of the times and the judgement of God upon the Church, this had become virtually unspeakable in the public realm. I read his pain in making this judgement and that resonated with my own sense of dislocation. You wrestle with God and you come away limping, facing a restriction on movement that is a painful but a genuine token of encounter. I was also sustained by my conviction that Bonhoeffer was a much more effective pastor, priest, theologian and political actor because he never minimized the ironic contradictions inherent in his own understanding of the demands of the gospel.

A Problem Shared

Although the story I have told above is personal, I know it is by no means uncommon or unusual. Some might even read it as an archetypal 'coming-of-age' narrative in which early idealism is tempered by a more

---

6 He continued by stating that although the day would come when we 'might once again be called so to utter the word of God that the world will be changed by it . . . Till then the Christian cause will be a silent and hidden affair' (Bonhoeffer 1973, p. 300). His position has been variously interpreted. Whereas I take it to be a clear judgement on the Church, others appear to read it as confirming the Church in her role as custodian of the Christian narrative. For discussion, see Harvey 1997.

mature acknowledgement of reality and the limits this imposes. While I have written this account in the first person, I recognize it could also have been constructed as a corporate dilemma. There are a number of theologians currently reflecting upon the problems of speaking about God in public who highlight the specific difficulties faced in making theological interventions in particular cultural and communal contexts.[7] Within their work I see displayed my own dissatisfaction with a number of the assumptions that have guided much public theology in the past, including:

- the liberal hope that there is something inherently progressive in theological discourse per se, when coherently and rationally expressed – which usually means avoiding references to God in any form that could be recognized by the untrained reader;
- the radically orthodox persuasion that the sacred tradition can (somehow) deliver resources for the renewal a deranged and degraded secular culture;
- the postliberal faith in the (incomprehensible) public parable of the story-shaped community.

Advocates of all these approaches offer cogent critiques of the others but, in my opinion, all fail to address the political ambiguity of the Church as bearer of tradition[8] or the equally ambiguous challenges of the way we live now. As for liberation theology, as I have noted, there is a danger that the theological rhetoric of liberation has become so entirely divorced from political analysis that it now represents something very different from the deeply integrated political/theological vision it formerly sought to embody.[9]

When I consider my doubts about all the dominant forms of public theology in the light of the fact that I have spent the last 25 years earning my living as a theologian whose chief concern has been tracing the form God wears in this material world, I often wonder whether the contradictions inherent in my position would have proved overwhelming

---

7 See, for example, Greu 2005 and Whipp 2008.

8 It is possible of course to make a clear divide between the tradition and the Church, but this does not strike me as a cogent option for those concerned with the 'public' role of theology.

9 This is not to devalue significant attempts to understand what liberation theology might be and become in our changed context. See, for example, Althaus-Reid 2008.

if it were not for the emergence of feminist theology[10] as an academic discourse and a motivating force for religious feminists. My career has coincided almost exactly with this development, which has enabled me to reframe, if not resolve, some of the problems that trouble me. Feminist theology has enabled me to adapt and survive, it has occupied me with work to hand, and it has set before me emerging new horizons – as I shall now turn to explore in the second half of this chapter.

Coping Mechanisms

There are many ways in which self-identifying as a feminist theologian has enabled me to negotiate the contradictions I experience in correlating my political and religious convictions. To begin with, although from time to time a number of feminist theologians have raised the issue of the relationship between feminist and systematic theology or cherished the notion of a bold, new systematics reflective of a renewed mutuality in human and divine relationships,[11] the dynamics of the movement have tended to cherish particularity, location and diversity in theological reflection rather than the construction of new grand narratives. For someone who has procured no useful vehicle for transporting her theological convictions to the political realm, it is less problematic to work on specific issues in an episodic and provisional way that emphasizes new ways of being and seeing than it would be to proceed from supposedly self-evident fundamentals – such as the assertion that there is some essential moral coherence between the values of the Christian faith and contemporary forms of participatory democracy (for example). While the early works of pioneering feminist theologians are marked by anxiety concerning the authoritative status of their claims to knowledge,[12] more recently we have come to celebrate the pragmatic, dialogical and narrative features of feminist epistemology.[13] These are in fact highly

---

10 Generally held to have begun with the publication of Valerie Saiving's article 'The Human Situation: A Feminine View' in *The Journal of Religion*, 1960. However, in the UK, 1983 is a key date when SCM Press published Rosemary Radford Ruether, *Sexism and God-Talk: Towards a Feminist Theology* and Elizabeth Schüssler Fiorenza, *In Memory of Her: A Feminist Theological Reconstruction of Christian Origins*.

11 See, for example, Woodhead 1997. Sarah Coakley is currently working on a four-volume work of systematic theology which will set out her feminist reflections upon the nature of God and the place of humanity.

12 Hence the huge significance of the heated debates on the authority of women's experience. See Walton 2007b, pp. 40–1 and 79–83.

13 These working methods are expounded and celebrated in two hugely significant books on feminist philosophy of religion. See Anderson 1998 and Jantzen 1998.

adaptable tools for activists of all persuasions and particularly for those, like myself, uncertain as to their origins and lacking a teleo-logical compass.[14]

Second, it is clear that the ties that bind feminist theologians into an identifiable community are shared political rather than doctrinal allegiances. For some this is a mark of weakness. Susan Parsons in particular has asserted that a preoccupation with 'worldly' progress has blinded feminist theologians to the significance of their sacred calling. As political idealism mutates into postmodern pessimism, she argues, there is an inevitable crisis looming.

> Now the language of empowerment has become a cliché for everything from shoes to electricity and the nostalgia for lost opportunities to make a better world is exploited as a style that has no more credit than a change of clothes. Such is the evidence not of a loss of faith in utopian politics but the very outworking of its logic. (2002, pp. 128–9)

While I accept that Parsons has correctly identified some real tensions among feminists as we seek to ascertain what constitutes a feminist agenda for the twenty-first century, I cannot agree that this should be understood as forcing the recognition that our emancipatory aspirations must now be abandoned as fantasies. To be a feminist, including to be a feminist theologian, implies a will for change, radical change, at every level and a decision to take gender (whether for strategic or essentialist reasons) as the Archimedean point from which we attempt to shift the world. While it is daunting, even awkward and embarrassing, to acknowledge political ideals in an age of cynicism, I have found that it also has many benefits. It does, at the very least, consistently generate the difficult theological questions referred to in the present chapter. More positively it discourages nostalgia, promotes accountability and generates that peculiar form of double vision that is the driving impulse of theology.

To continue with Parsons' critique for a little while longer, as it is an interesting and important one, it is quite unfair to imply that she advocates a wholesale retreat from the political sphere. It is rather that she believes that genuine transformation is generated via divine initiative and that waiting upon God is the most faithful and most radical option for

---

14 See Donna Haraway's essay 'A Cyborg Manifesto: Science, Technology and Socialist Feminism in the late 20th Century', in Haraway 1991, pp. 149–82.

the feminist theologian; a return to orthodoxy is imaged here as a prodigal daughter's return to the family home. But since when has this 'journey back' been a safe option for estranged and abused women? Feminist theology began by addressing this problem, and for those of us who continue to dwell in male-centred religious traditions, it has not been satisfactorily resolved. Personally, I do not regard the self-evident theological heterogeneity encountered within feminist theology as posing more of a problem than orthodoxy and its magisterial defenders. I concede that feminist theologians share no doctrinal consensus, critically identify with a variety of religious traditions, and have very differing understandings of the divine. However, this is not evidence of a lack of theological commitment, nor does it imply that the Spirit shuns our reflections or that our faithless souls will fall into the snares of a despairing secularism. As Marcella Althaus-Reid and Lisa Isherwood have argued:

> One of the many strengths of feminist theologies has always been the ability to include many voices within the debate . . . This is not the same thing at all as having no method and no cohesion, it is, however, about creating space for diverse voices to express what they experience about the divine among and between us. It is about respect and an overwhelming belief that the divine cannot be contained by any one group whoever they may be and however blessed and sanctioned they believe themselves to be. (2007, p. 1)

Theology does not only wear a doctrinal form, and the intensely dialogical nature of feminist theological thinking can be regarded as a positive strength rather than a weakness. My own writing draws heavily upon the work of Jewish, goddess and post-Christian feminists and is enriched by their insights.[15] I have made my choice, and it is in favour of a determined resistance to the current order of things combined with a robust and creative heterogeneity in theology rather than a pessimistic/agnostic approach to politics combined with doctrinal orthodoxy.

Third, there is within feminist circles less reluctance to conceive of an affinity between the political and the spiritual than is observed either in conventional mainstream politics in the UK or among the progressive and left-wing groups I have travelled alongside. Although

---

15 Ursula King writes: 'Women's theological reflections and the dialogue about their experiences move in terms both of commonalities and differences which counteract a falsely constructed unity and an imposed singular worldview that obliterates real differences' (1999, p. 113).

some scholars have registered frustration at the 'isolation' of feminist theology, which is often accused of being slow to engage with the new forms of theoretical thinking (see Woodhead 1999), the forms of estrangement complained about are largely those pertaining to interdisciplinary relationships within the academy. A much more porous membrane exists in the political and cultural arenas. Ritual actions and reverence for the Spirit (variously understood) continue to be significant for many feminist activists.[16] One of my own particular areas of academic research has been exploring the relationship between feminist theology and women's writing (Walton 2007a, 2007b). Feminism is a peculiarly literary movement, and a number of popular women writers demonstrate a deep engagement with feminist theological thinking.[17] While this certainly does not imply fideism it is an indication that there is a lively interest among feminist writers and readers in exploring new images of the divine and women-centred religious traditions ancient and modern. The feminist theologian who places herself within these cultural and political arenas might expect to be questioned about and even called to account for her religious convictions. However, she may experience a sense of surprised relief that it does not prove necessary to change registers in order to communicate her ideas concerning the sacred. She may even find it easier to articulate her theological ideas in feminist public discourse than within her home faith community.

Getting on With It

Feminist theology has helped me to value provisional knowledge, sustained my sense of political agency, educated me to discern God in diversity, and enabled me to play a part in a community curious about and open to the sacred. It has also provided me, as someone in danger of being struck dumb by the theological dilemmas that currently face us, with work to hand. This work is to engage in continual critique. Not the most positive of theological acts perhaps; but while theology continues to be so overwhelmingly male-centred I do not think we should chide ourselves with failure to move from a critical to a constructive mode – and clearly the two are interrelated. Furthermore, criticism need not be undertaken with the sense this implies either a negative

---

16 See, for example, Berry 2009.
17 See, for example, Roberts, Llewellyn and Sawyer 2008 and Owens 2006.

dependence upon the substantive ideas of male thinkers or an ingrained hostility to the work/practices you are critiquing. Luce Irigaray, for example, performs critique as an act of amorous engagement in which a strong, active and desiring female voice laments the blindness and neglect of her male partner (1993, p. 186). It is undertaken out of loving concern for a mutuality in which difference is respected rather than from a desire for separation or blame. The motivation, in other words, is love rather than fear.

This is not to say that critique is not painful as we must engage with the work of those who are close to us both politically and as mentors and friends. To continue to use the first person, I live in Scotland, which is a part of Europe in which public theology has had a more robust and vigorous presence than in many other parts of the continent. The reasons for this are complex but include the size of the nation, the historical relationship between Church and State, the links between social and religious quests for autonomy, the forms of church polity that have emerged here, and the enduring ties between the Church of Scotland and the ancient universities. It is also due to the practice of a number of inspirational figures who have dedicated themselves to practising theology as political service. Among these Duncan Forrester has been a significant voice in articulating persuasive and productive models for undertaking theological work in public.

In his work as Director of the Centre for Theology and Public Issues at the University of Edinburgh, Forrester sought to demonstrate how the Church might effectively engage in the public debate. In doing so, he was keen to emphasize the importance of moving beyond parochialism and accepting the challenges of articulating Christian hope. Public theology, he has asserted, is a serious business: 'It is not the in-house chatter or domestic housekeeping of a sect concerned with its inner life' (2001a, p. 127).

Unfortunately, in phrasing his convictions in this way Forrester employs the gendered conventions by which the public is often differentiated from the feminized environment of both the church and the domestic sphere. This 'slip' is perhaps related to Forrester's deep engagement over many years with a Habermassian model that emphasizes the significance of the public sphere for forms of communicative engagement which, it is envisaged, enable rational and concerned citizens to construct a shared and workable vision of the social good. Forrester is aware of, and sympathetic to, feminist critiques of Habermas that accuse him of privileging certain understandings of rational communication over others and reifying the distinctions between private and public to an extent that the feminine comes to be located effectively in one sphere rather than another (1997, p. 179).

However, such is his attachment to the notion of a productive arena where Christian theologians and church leaders might engage in respectful conversation with others with a view to discerning new social visions that he perseveres with the model while uncomfortably aware of the dangerous binary it reinscribes. And this attachment is understandable. Not only does Forrester stand within an ecumenical, mission-orientated tradition that has sought at significant moments in social life to encourage deep dialogue between Christian representatives and concerned scientists, politicians and artists, but he has also graciously hosted a more radical form of this conversational encounter. Deeply impressed by the challenges of liberation theology, he has sought to include in dialogue those automatically excluded from such Christian social reflection in the past. This includes those who have most interest in reform, including individuals living in poverty, people without secure homes and those convicted by the criminal justice system (2001b, p. 15). He has also wrestled with that most intractable problem of how the Christian theologian can make a contribution to these conversations in a way that can be heard by those who have no interest or stake in religious faith.

Forrester's own convictions locate him broadly within a canonical narrative framework that emphasizes the transformative impact of the Christian story (see Graham, Walton and Ward 2005, pp. 78–108). However, he is well aware that what is offered from the Christian story cannot be the whole script unedited and inappropriately focused to the needs of the moment. Adopting Alasdair MacIntyre's analysis of the contemporary era as one in which authoritative narratives have been effectively shattered (1981), he speaks of offering precious fragments of the Christian tradition that might yet be 'illuminating, instructive or provocative' (Forrester 2003, p. 119) and which can be usefully employed in public debate.

When, as a feminist theologian, I engage in a critique of Forrester's work I name first the continuing impact of the gendering of the public arena and the fact that this contributes to maintaining a space between our communicative action and the unwelcome encroachment of the ambiguous body. I stress that our political practice requires a reappraisal of this enduring division as the practical and symbolic resources of the domestic–embodied–feminine sphere are perhaps our best resource in a reconstructive theological endeavour. A feminist hermeneutics of suspicion also causes me to challenge his optimism that the Christian tradition can straightforwardly serve the cause of social renewal.[18] To be sure, fragments of the Christian narrative can have wonderful liberating potential when they function 'like pieces of glass or gems that catch the light and display its wonderful colours . . . [and] generate a vision that many may share' (Forrester 2003, p. 119). But there are many in Scotland today who have jagged fragments of the Christian tradition lodged within them which are sharp, wounding and bloody. These produce the unhealed wounds of homophobia, gynophobia, domestic abuse, sectarianism and personal guilt, as well as that peculiar form of body-denying common-sense empiricism that so shapes the culture of our nation. I am reminded of the story of the Snow Queen in which the little boy Kay gets the shining fragment of an enchanted mirror lodged in his eye. He is prevented by this from discerning the love and warmth of others and is held captive in an icy kingdom.

My critique of Forrester's work is entirely predictable. It entails the familiar strategy of placing the occluded feminine at the centre of vision and reframing the picture from that perspective. However, such efforts at critique are still too rarely undertaken in my context to be deemed unnecessary. Criticism, as I have argued, remains essential work. Do my reservations concerning the way Forrester has framed his programme of communicative encounter mean that I do not value his contribution or that I would hold myself apart and refuse to be involved in such endeavours? Not at all. He is a great man. He has done very many good and groundbreaking things for which I am profoundly grateful. Furthermore, contemporary feminism does not encourage the forms of political purity that require splendid isolation. Indeed, the most valuable skills Christian feminist theologians have learnt through our long engagement with structures and traditions that are male-centred are deconstructive arts that enable us to both accuse and affirm in a simultaneous and inclusive gesture.

---

18 As Gloria Albrecht has pointed out in her extended critique of Hauerwas, the assumption that the Christian narrative has an essential unity and is not marked by the exclusion of the marginal and dissident is unsustainable:

Hauerwas does not need to acknowledge the difference in the proverbs, prophecies, legends, laws and traditions that fathers pass on to their sons and that mothers whisper to their daughters. Hauerwas seems not to recognise the reality of relationships of domination within the Christian narrative and its tradition, nor the multiplicity of voices, nor the silencing throughout history of many Christians' stories. (1995, pp. 100–1)

A Very Noisy Silence

Having admitted in this essay that I engage in theological work that despite being partial, provisional and critical is also constructive and institutionally engaged, what is to be made of my early reflections upon the problems of speaking about God in public and my sense of this being an impossible task at the present time? Was this simply a rhetorical strategy to engage the reader, when in fact there is very little difference between my own performance as a theologian and that of my colleagues who do not share my reservations? This is not an easy question to answer. In all my work I am haunted by the sense that what is really important to say is challenging me from beyond the limits of my speech. Much of what I write is entirely conventional, but in other fictive and elegiac pieces I am struggling to find forms of expression that are more able to bear the weight that theology does not seem able to carry at the current time. I am trying through them to bear testimony to 'things' about which direct speech seems currently not possible.

Other feminist theologians have expressed their sense that public theology must include within its registers much more than rational discourse if it is to approach the unbearable mystery of human suffering. Writing out of the South African context, Denise Ackermann names the mixed awareness of complicity and pain that inspires her theological work as *lamentation* (Ackerman and Bons-Storm 1998). Rebecca Chopp has sought to imagine a new form of public theology elaborated through the 'poetics of testimony'(2001, 2009), which will give voice to the silenced, transform the social imaginary,[19] and make possible a startling encounter with transcendence. In employing this term Chopp has at the forefront of her concerns the need to reiterate the theological challenges articulated within liberation theology. She writes:

> The poetics of testimony, expressed in a variety of particular and distinct forms, is fundamentally concerned with human and earthly survival and transformation . . . This imperative is also theological, at least for those of us who live Christianity as practices of emancipatory transformation. (2001, p. 57)

As discussed in the previous chapter, Chopp hopes to provoke a significant shift in theological discourse through using poetics, and I am

---

19 Chopp defines the social imaginary as the basic presuppositions, metaphors and rules that frame cultural operations (2001, p. 57).

sympathetic to this move. However, the term 'poetics of testimony' is a borrowed one which when used in its original setting carries an even more ambivalent and disturbing force than can be discerned in Chopp's theological work. The concept is elaborated by the Jewish writers Shoshona Felman and Dori Laub in their important book, *Testimony: Crises of Witnessing in Literature, Psychoanalysis and History* (1992). In this work they explore the impossibility Holocaust survivors and victims of abuse encounter in articulating their experiences. These can only be told partially, elliptically and in a way that renders the world strange both for the hearer and the teller of the story. Felman carries her exploration of crises in witnessing further, to explore the use of poetics by the collaborators as well as by those who would resist oppression. As an example she reflects upon the theorist Paul de Man's fascination with deconstruction. Critics have read de Man's embrace of this reading practice as a way of avoiding the truth of his own complicity with fascism. However, Felman argues, those who have been personally complicit with such historical catastrophes forever read the world as a terrifyingly encrypted code of violence incapable of interpretation. She writes, 'De Man's entire writing effort is a silent trace of the reality of an event' the character of which precludes its own witnessing; this represents 'the very magnitude, the very materiality of what de Man will refer to as the ever threatening impossibility of reading' (1992, p. 140).

Here we see poetics as not only a means of employing differing linguistic gestures to change the idioms of culture. Poetics rather opens up a terrifying revelation. Felman quotes Claude Lanzmann, 'It is like a black sun and you have to struggle against yourself to go on' (in Felman and Laub 1992, p. 252). In this frame, poetics is a broken language spoken by the perpetrators of violence as well as the victims, and it is a form of speech that 'transcends the witness who is its medium, the medium of the realization of the testimony' (p. 3). In this more disruptive and threatening form of poetics I begin to discern the irruption of an unmanageable transcendence, which I have found most disappointingly absent from the public theology I have encountered up till now. It is not a transcendence that passes by us guilty ones but is like a coal that burns our mouths with fire until even we who can't speak will speak. Bonnie Mann, in her book *Women's Liberation and the Sublime*, has described a 'complex, ambiguous, wrenching, relentless, impossible . . . claim by which we are undone, even as we are irrevocably obligated to live by it' (2006, p. 166). I think this is a very compelling description of the theological joy and terror that are provoked by the poetic encounter as well as the political challenges it inevitably produces:

> Our own worlds are torn open at some moment of disruption in which the powerful presence of some Other breaks into the sealed complacency that tends so thoroughly to enthral us. The projects of women's liberation are built in the space between worlds that opens at such moments, in spite of the fact that the meanings that are disclosed through such openings (though they must always be conceptualized) can never *finally* be conceptualized. These are meanings that ultimately have to be lived and struggled over and remade. (2006, pp. 177–8)

16

Poetics and Pastoral Care

The Narrative Turn in Theology

One of the most interesting developments in recent theological thinking has been the extraordinary significance accorded to 'narrative' by conservative, radical and liberal theologians alike. This narrative turn, no doubt born of a postmodern scepticism towards abstract, propositional truth claims, is of particular importance for pastoral theologians and practitioners. It is now frequently claimed that the work of storytelling lies at the heart of the healing encounter between those who suffer and those who seek to meet this suffering with the resources of faith.

However, while storytelling has assumed a position of great importance, there are diverse understandings of the ways in which stories should be told and how they become redemptive for us. In comprehending these differences it is helpful to make a broad distinction between canonical and constructive forms of narrative theology.

Telling God's Story

Canonical narrative theology, as the name suggests, is based in scriptural accounts of the life of Jesus. Although traditions of prayer and discipleship based on the imitation of Christ have an ancient genealogy, it is the work of Karl Barth that has particularly inspired contemporary narrative theologians such as Hans Frei, George Lindbeck, Stanley Hauerwas and, more latterly, scholars connected with radical orthodoxy. Barth regards the story of Jesus as a divinely authorized narrative in which the truth concerning human history is made evident. This story has a scope so great that all human stories can find their meaning within its frame. Canonical narrative theologians imagine the Christian faith as the continuing dynamic outworking of this narrative as believers find their place within the sacred drama. We become

POETICS, THEOLOGY AND PRACTICE

Christian, they argue, as we learn to play our own parts in the story of Christ's passion and resurrection.

Stanley Hauerwas is the theologian who has reflected most deeply upon the ethical and pastoral implications of this particular narrative approach. He has attempted to understand its implications for such pressing medical and moral dilemmas as abortion and euthanasia. However, it is in his book *Naming the Silences* (1990), which reflects upon the suffering and death of children, that his thinking is most powerfully articulated.

In this text, Hauerwas faces the question as to whether the Christian story allows the tragedy of existence to be voiced in a manner that confesses the unjustifiable agony human beings frequently encounter; 'can the story be told without the telling of it domesticating the rage we should feel at death?' (1990, p. 38). His conviction that the utter tragedy of the cross enables this to happen allows him to reaffirm that what matters most of all in living with the unbearable questions of childhood suffering is the fact that these can be comprehended as we sense God's living presence with us in a 'mutual story'. That we have a part to play in this story means that a little child whose life is full of pain is not written out of history but written into God's true story. His or her life becomes important as it is incorporated into the narrative of the community of faith and is thus inscribed into the life of God. There is nothing beyond what the radically inclusive narrative can bear – even the death of a child. 'We believe we share a common story which makes it possible for us to be with one another especially as we die' (1990, p. 148).

The Stories of Our Lives

In canonical narrative theology, meaning is to be found as human narratives are incorporated into God's greater story. However, in constructive forms of narrative theology it is in *the human capacity for storytelling itself*, rather than in a pre-existing grand narrative, that redemptive power is located. In this perspective human beings are seen as story-formed creatures whose lives take shape as they begin to employ the resources of narrative traditions to give shape to their own lives. Paul Ricoeur, whose work on hermeneutics has become a significant resource for narrative theologians, describes a process of 'enplotment' as the means through which human beings give shape to what would otherwise be 'chaotic, obscure and mute' (1991, p. 115).

The operation of plotting synthesizes the heterogeneous aspects of existence and organizes them into an intelligible whole. Living from birth entangled in narratives, we learn to become 'the narrator of our own stories without completely becoming the author of our life' (p. 473).

In another celebration of the constructive power of narrative, the sociologist Arthur Frank (1995) reflects upon the discovery of narrative agency, particularly in situations where illness threatens to deprive people of autonomy and creative potential. Out of his own experience of cancer and heart disease Frank reflects upon the redemptive work performed by those who gain the strength to narrate lives touched by pain to others. In a society that denies human frailty and vulnerability, 'wounded storytellers' witness to others that, while life events are often brutal and unpredictable, a 'story can be told that binds contingent events together in a life that has moral necessity' (p. 176). Frank uses Christian discourse to describe these 'wounded storytellers'. They are suffering servants who bear the marks of pain and embody 'atonement' for others. Through recovering their own voices they are able to bear testimony on behalf of others who are robbed of speech. 'The wounded storyteller is a moral witness reenchanting a disenchanted world' (p. 185).

It is easy to see the pastoral implications of this view of narrative. Making a story that weaves painful circumstances into a wider framework is an act of hope and faith that is of real benefit to the individual, their families and the wider community. Contemporary literature in spiritual and pastoral care encourages pastoral practitioners to see themselves as those who may hear others into speech and assist in the re-patterning of broken and fragmented lives. Towards the end of life storytelling is often portrayed as the most significant action dying people can perform. While others are busy easing painful and distressing symptoms, the chaplain has an evident role to perform in creative listening to the story of a unique human soul.

When Stories Fail

Pastoral agents can certainly gain important theological and practical insights from the work of canonical and constructive narrative theologians. Spiritual caregivers who have the grace to enable people to place their own stories within the embrace of a story that enfolds it are making available the best resources the tradition can offer. Similarly, those who have the creativity to recognize and nurture an emerging self-narrative in the broken speech of a sick or distressed person are witnessing to their faith that God is present and active in each human life and that the particularity of personal existence can be the place of divine encounter.

However, those who have worked closely with those in pain or grief would probably be the first to admit that for some people there may be no comfort to be found in storytelling. Some simply do not find a narrative that can be made to fit the appalling circumstances that confront them. Others have so lost a sense of their own identity that they cannot exercise the creative power necessary to become storytellers. This loss of narrative agency may be a temporary crisis or a more enduring problem. Does it constitute a 'failure' to admit that in some cases we cannot help others to find the healing and relief that narrative is supposed to bring? Or is it rather the case that we need to examine more carefully the extensive claims that are made about narrative in the contemporary literature of pastoral care so that we can learn to recognize what resources we have to offer when storytelling fails?

Trauma and Memory

Recent studies into the effect of trauma have generated significant criticisms of the notion that narrative functions as redemptive practice in cases where the experience of suffering exceeds the conventional means employed to give it voice. In the preface to their edited collection *Tense Past: Cultural Essays in Trauma and Memory* (1996), Paul Antze and Michael Lambek argue that it is not necessarily redemptive to subsume the chaotic/embodied symptoms of trauma into a coherent narrative script. They defy the popular notion that to tell one's story automatically enables healing to take place, and argue that 'there is nothing liberating in narrative per se . . . merely to transfer a story from embodied symptoms into words is not necessarily to exorcise it' (p. xix).

In the same volume Laurence Kirmayer writes of trauma memories that create a kind of un-story in the personal experience of those who have endured intense suffering. These memories are located on the edge of consciousness, 'to be worked around or told in fragments . . . There is no narrative of trauma, no memory – only speaking in signs' (p. 175). What are circulated among us as narratives from such extreme experiences are often attempts by those who have not been subject to such overwhelming circumstances to repair the social fabric by restoring comprehensibility and communication. Those who have experienced trauma themselves are often alien to the coherent accounts of their experiences which others require them to utter.

Having recognized that narrative cannot always restore what has been lost in trauma, what resources do we have to draw upon when we encounter those whose experiences have become unspeakable for them? In answering this question, I think we must cultivate awareness that a crisis in narrative is not merely a personal dilemma for the caregiver, nor does it constitute a pastoral failure. It is rather a window onto problems that unfortunately have not been well aired in theological circles. Theologians have perhaps been too ready to use theodicy to bridge the gaps and fissures in human experience in order to enable us to supply a happy ending to all our stories. The last century's Holocausts challenged philosophers, psychologists, poets and politicians to seek to understand what appeared to be a crisis in human narrative caused by excessive and senseless suffering. Theodor Adorno spoke for an entire generation when he testified that after Auschwitz, letting suffering speak was the condition of all truth – a statement that immediately provokes the response 'How can this happen?' when, as Elaine Scary maintains, 'pain does not simply resist language it actively destroys it' (1985, p. 4).

Many of those who have engaged with this dilemma have argued that when everyday forms of communication fail it is necessary to speak in new ways. What is needed is not narrative but the other resources offered by poetics: images, symbols and metaphors that carry the pain of trauma without committing the blasphemy of trying to represent, comprehend or reconcile the horror in story form. This is what Kirmayer means when he claims there is no narrative of trauma, 'only speaking in signs'.

Elie Wiesel, a Holocaust survivor, whose writing has been important to many Christian theologians, expresses the same sense that on occasions when words fail and stories cannot be told it is our duty to preserve the sacred silence of those who suffer – but in a way that communicates rather than obscures their pain. He puts the issues thus: 'sometimes when no words are possible then silence can become an alternative language. It is possible to have a language of silence. It is about gestures' (Wiesel and Beale, 2000, p. 35).

Speaking in signs, communicating in the language of silence, preserving the gestures of pain. These are difficult and maddeningly imprecise attempts to describe what it means to let suffering speak. However, I believe they are as important to ministers, chaplains and other pastoral agents as they are to the philosophers and poets who have wrestled with these themes. We encounter those whose lives have been torn apart by trauma in our everyday activities as well as in the pages of books. We must find the resources and the gestures needed both to help those who experience trauma to discover their own strange forms of communication and to testify to this brokenness in human life to others.

In doing so the symbols and rituals of our own tradition will be important to us. For some who experience trauma these will have a resonance and a depth that can become a vehicle for communication. However, in other cases the conventional forms of religious symbolism will not suffice. We will have to become skilled in the language of silence and adept at offering new symbols that those who suffer may use to mediate their experience. We will need to develop a new sensibility as to how material objects and physical gestures can embody what words may not. We will begin to learn that there are times when it is not right to supply connections, meanings or resolutions for others. At some points all we will be able to do is preserve the sanctity of their silence. As Shoshona Felman has written, our duty is not to give speech to what is unspeakable so that it can 'talk to us properly', but rather to cultivate our own attentiveness so that it might have the power to address us in its silence (1992, p. 163).

17

Seeking Wisdom in Practical Theology: *Phronesis*, Poetics and Everyday Life

My Text

To what then will I compare the people of this generation, and what are they like? They are like children sitting in the market-place and calling to one another, 'We played the flute for you, and you did not dance; we wailed, and you did not weep.'

For John the Baptist has come eating no bread and drinking no wine, and you say, 'He has a demon'; the Son of Man has come eating and drinking, and you say, 'Look, a glutton and a drunkard, a friend of tax-collectors and sinners!' Nevertheless, wisdom is vindicated by all her children. (Luke 7.31-35)

Prologue

We blink a little at the brightness as we enter the marketplace. Creatures of quiet rooms off long corridors, of libraries and long-pewed churches. We need to shade our eyes as we enter the marketplace.

And then open them wide again for here in town is the Media Circus. Performing now at the edge of the square. Fire eaters, knife jugglers, snake charmers. Taming terror into entertainment for your thrill and delight.

Also here are the traders with the world for sale. The mellow glow of gold standards, the sooty stalls of carbon traders, the clear glass tubes of imagined futures. Behind them, tucked away, are the traffickers. They trade in young men's organs, baby kisses, the slim hips and small breasts of girl children. They like to be discreet. They prefer you to order online.

But we are not here to buy or sell. We are here to be among the many who throng the stalls. Those who travel to the market to buy the ingredients for a meal, shoes for a party, rings for a finger. Those who purchase bread and wine for everyday sacraments. We want to encounter the people seated with friends at the tables. Those who have put down their bags to feed a baby. The ones who are resting on the broad stone steps and watching the pigeons flap and squabble.

We are just not quite sure where we should take our place.

Is it in the crowd? Or somewhere to the side where stand the wise ones and the great debaters of our age? Next to them are the peddlers of religion. Why do they keep looking at us – don't wave! There is a small space somewhere in between. We might fit in there. If we could just get past that group of noisy children.

Seeing the World: Empirical Theology

For the past four years I have served as Secretary to the International Academy of Practical Theology. This work has been important to me. I have tried to listen carefully to the various voices, differing accents, from around the world as they contended the future of our discipline. Much of the fiercest debate has been stimulated by the vigorous research activity of empirical theologians. Dynamic and productive as their movement has been it has not been universally appreciated, and some of the most critical responses to its approach and methods have come from those who understand practical theology as primarily concerned with emancipatory practice. Among these critics feminist practical theologians have been particularly prominent. What principally separates the empiricists from the feminists is the way they think we should apprehend the world and what they believe this implies for theological wisdom. So it seems appropriate to begin this chapter by critically comparing these two movements – both of which are deeply committed to theological reflection on the way we live now.

Empirical theology emerged as a response to an undeniable problem. Johannes van der Ven, whose work I shall use as a reference point (as he is one of the clearest apologists of the movement),[1] describes this dilemma in the following terms. German and Dutch practical theologians, influenced by progressive and socially engaged theologies current in the middle decades of the last century, had adopted a two-stage model to guide their work (1993, p. 2). Stage One entailed a rigorous

---

1 While van der Ven is a clear spokesperson the disadvantage of using his work is that many people engaged in empirical research in practical theology adopt a pragmatic approach and would not self-identify with all aspects of the empirical theology project.

social-scientific interrogation of the lifeworld. Stage Two involved theological reflection upon what appeared to view. This apparently simple model was, however, based upon an assumption of complex interdisciplinary interactions between the social sciences and theology at many levels, from goal setting and research design to data interpretation and construction of normative theories. Empirical theologians, with admirable observational skill, perceived this did not actually take place *in the real world*. Van der Ven notes wryly that practical theological literature implies that interdisciplinary dialogue happens. 'One should realize however that these remarks do not mean that this collaboration takes place' (1998, p. 48). More frequently we have a two-stage process in which social researchers explore an issue and theologians later (sometimes much later) take up this work to engage in secondary reflection upon it.

Empirical theologians are not so much piqued by the fact that social scientists are not generally willing to collaborate in theological endeavours as they are concerned about issues pertaining to ethos within the human sciences and the fact that faith and values are rarely high on research agendas. According to Hans Schilderman, this means the neglect of the challenge to 'interpret the moral and religious forms of meaning that are inevitably embedded in the lifeworld and that constitute our spiritual heritage' (2012, p. 124). This is a serious issue in an increasingly secular age. Furthermore, we are in danger of failing to make adequate pastoral, political and theological responses to the way we live now because we have failed to attend to the forms of spiritual experience that shape contemporary culture. For empirical theologians the solutions are clear. The theologian must become both researcher and reflector. Van der Ven writes that this model 'requires that theology itself becomes empirical. That is that it expands its traditional range of instruments . . . in the direction of empirical methodology' (1993, p. 101).

By empirical methodology, at least in the early years,[2] these new practical theologians meant the quest to generate objective understanding through the use of impartial and reliable instruments that could categorize religious practices and spiritual understandings into reassuring forms of useful knowledge. The benefits accruing from empirical methodology were considerable. Theology could retain a 'scientific

---

2 Qualitative methods are now used by many empirical researchers in practical theology. However, there is a continued preference for critical realism as an epistemological paradigm rather than a thoroughgoing social constructivism.

status' – which was important in many European contexts in which the word 'empirical' continues to signify knowledge that is sound, credible and tested; knowledge that can bear the weight of theoretical development. Furthermore, theologians proceeding along an empirical trajectory could speak in terms respected in the academy and reassuring to funding bodies. This was important particularly in the United States, where charitable foundations have made considerable financial contributions to research projects.

Empirical theology also proved extremely useful to progressive theologians working in Catholic and Barthian contexts, who could present social data as having serious truth claims in a context in which doctrinal theology held a high and assured status. Furthermore, on the basis of their empirical investigations, they could argue for reassessing traditional pastoral values and practices and engage in challenging forms of theological reflection that might otherwise have aroused the condemnation of colleagues. For this and many other reasons it is simply wrong to see empirical theology as the sacrifice of soul to an empirical captivity. Van der Ven makes clear that he views practical theology in pre-Thomistic terms as *sapientia* (wisdom) rather than *scientia* (speculative knowledge), and it is a wisdom that is concerned with understanding and indeed celebrating how people find spiritual meaning, faith, God in the midst of contemporary life (1998, pp. 30–1). This work is done in order that we can do better theology, offer better pastoral care and (as is extremely important to empirical theologians) communicate effectively in a world that no longer comprehends the categories upon which theology is based.

Just as the benefits of new methodological tools are clear, so are the critiques that can be made of the enthusiastic embrace of empiricism as a theological resource. Many practical theologians have doubts about the kind of knowledge of the lifeworld generated through quantitative methods, and these are widely used and very frequently preferred. There is concern that theologians might not be particularly adept at using their new tools and fall into methodological errors. There is also a worry that, operating beyond the disciplinary mechanisms of the social sciences, theologians will 'lag behind' their secular colleagues and adopt outmoded theoretical models into their discourses without subjecting them to rigorous critique – a problem that has certainly afflicted theological reflection in the past!

Many doubts are also expressed by those whose research agendas have been shaped by traditions of socially engaged public theology. In these contexts practical theologians continue to cherish an expansive understanding of the scope of their work and worry that the focus upon 'moral and religious forms of meaning' (see above) represents a limiting agenda that restricts theological vision. In those parts of the world where feminist practical theology is strongest we have also seen a disturbing gender divide emerging in relation to empiricism and emancipatory approaches.[3] While there may be no inherent reasons for this division it is currently sustained by the masculine 'ethos' of the empirical approach which, on the surface at least, appears to abjure the chaos of subjective, affective and emotive thinking.

With a calm common sense, empirical theologians address subjects worthy of attention in good faith. The world is made visible in order that it can be apprehended theologically. Indeed, there is substantial confidence in the theological process. It is theology that determines the research agenda. Theology interprets the results, and even though critical correlation is one of the preferred methods of theological reflection, when empirical theology is functioning according to its own founding paradigms (which is not always the case), the life-world is taken up into a higher theological frame.

There is an assumption about the intelligibility of the world and the innocence of theology that troubles me here.

Seeing the World: Feminist Practical Theology

Feminist practical theologians do not, by and large, feel the same need to critique the failure of the social sciences to attend to faith as they do the failure of the male-centred systems of both theology and the academy to attend to the 'invisible' experience of women. They take for granted the gender-based critiques of knowledge production and assent to feminist epistemological challenges to both research agendas and research processes (see Miller-McLemore 2012a). These challenges include a hermeneutics of suspicion as to how certain topics come to be deemed worthy of serious research attention, and an attentiveness to the invisibility of women's experience within dominant theoretical paradigms. In particular feminists are critical of epistemologies that purport to take a 'God's eye view', or the 'view from nowhere'. They favour, rather, strong objectivity (a form of dialogical reasoning that privileges the understandings forged by those who are most affected

---

3 There are still few women engaged in empirical theological research apart from in the realms of congregational studies.

by issues (see Harding 1991)), standpoint epistemology (see Haraway 1991) and reflexive thinking (see Etherington 2004). In contrast to the ethos of empiricism, feminists celebrate embodiment, emotion and affectivity as instruments for apprehending the world and gaining wise understanding.

Feminist practical theology, which is my own 'academic home', can also justly celebrate numerous achievements. In particular it has drawn attention to the role gender plays in the construction of Christian community (for example Graham 1995, Webster 1995), emphasized the urgent need to respond to inequality, abuse and pastoral neglect (for example Couture 1991, Bons-Storm 1996, Bennett 2002), and championed creative new forms of theological reflection as well as revaluing spirituality (for example Slee 2004, Wolfteich 2002, Berry 2009). Above all it has placed the body, birthing and nurturing, having sex and growing old, lamenting and struggling for justice, at the heart of the theological agenda. The movement might perhaps be criticized for sometimes failing to adequately evidence its claims and appealing instead to the court of 'women's experience'. It continues to show an exasperating lack of interest in questions of normativity, which can make it appear an unreliable ally in the critical environment of the academy. It has also been perceived to be a sectional movement for women only.[4] This criticism, based upon a misunderstanding of the feminist project, justifies male uninterest, further contributing to the gender divide in practical theology. However, recent moves within feminist practical theology to situate its concerns within a wider project of serious theological reflection upon 'the everyday' may go some way to addressing this problem.

By the everyday in this context I refer to the (still very definitely embodied) practices by which the fabric of life is sustained. Bonnie Miller-McLemore, a leading feminist practical theologian, set out an agenda of daily life concerns in her recent *Wiley-Blackwell Companion to Practical Theology* (2012b). This opens with a series of chapters reflecting on everydayness, not as a site of pastoral problems to

---

4 The gender divide in practical theology is very firmly entrenched. I can't count the times when after I have given a talk someone has stood up and said, 'I am a man. What should I do with this?' As if my talk was a sewing machine or an ovulation testing kit – of no practical use to half the planet. But this matter is complicated. Many male practical theologians are quite happy to pay lip service to the important work of female colleagues but fail to read it or engage with it. However, many women practical theologians have taken the same approach to empirical theology. 'That is nice dear. You go and play in your shed with your research instruments while we get on with the important stuff of life.'

be resolved but as the space where embodied practice meets Christian reflection (pp. 6–7). The taken-for-granted activities of daily life have often been regarded as the sphere of women (eating, consuming, caring, etc.), but Miller-McLemore's move is a gesture inclusive of, but beyond, gender to situate the work of practical theology firmly in this productive arena. Arguably this move brings feminist practical theology closer to empirical theology than it was in the past. I think it is becoming increasingly possible to identify much common ground between the two approaches.

Like our empirical colleagues, feminist practical theologians believe we are engaged in a reasonable and intelligible project to see this world more clearly on the understanding that clearer vision will bring wisdom, healing and renewal. Although I have described a preference for quantitative methods among empiricists and reflexive–qualitative methods among feminists, this is also in a process of transition. As the shifting landscape of social research morphs and merges into new forms, research methods are increasingly combined rather than placed in binary opposition. The world of social research is increasingly reflexive throughout and narrative research methods in particular have proved increasingly useful in empirical and feminist theological research.

When it comes to theology, apparent differences also conceal a greater unity than might be supposed. Although many feminist theologians do eschew doctrinal forms of normativity, a strong conviction concerning the goodness of embodiment prevails among us, and this is accompanied by an understanding of a beneficent divine who is deeply implicated in sustaining and healing the material order. It is a positive and generative theological paradigm that holds the commerce of everyday life in high regard. In turn this sustains an impulse to apprehend the lifeworld within a theological perspective and imagine a kind of harmony within it. I think feminist practical theology is just as inclined to see daily life through a theological lens as empirical theology. It is equally wedded to assumptions of the intelligibility of social forms and tends towards a benign understanding of theological practice.

To summarize: both forms of practical theology capaciously receive the insights of lived experience and seek to comprehend them within a higher sacred frame. I think it is very interesting that Don Browning, whose scholarship transformed practical theology in the latter years of the last century, mentored, influenced and collaborated with both empirical theologians and feminist scholars. His vision of practical theology (indeed all theology) as *phronesis* – a wisdom that attends to lived experience, is transformative and change-seeking and *always* interprets the lived context in the light of the values and virtues of sacred tradition – is evident in the endeavours of those engaged in both approaches.

The World Made Strange: Henri Lefebvre and the Critique of Everyday Life

I have hinted my reservations about the assumptions of intelligibility and innocence in key areas of practical theology. It is now time to make these concerns plainer. There is another way of viewing the everyday world which does not perceive it to be straightforwardly comprehensible and would not easily accommodate it within a conventional theological frame.

Michael Gardiner argues that, whereas 'for mainstream interpretative approaches', in the social sciences, cultural studies and, we might add, practical theology, the everyday is the realm of the beloved ordinary, customary and familiar, 'the alternative . . . is to treat it as a domain that is potentially extraordinary' (2000, p. 6). The mundane world can also be the 'privileged site of revelation, mystery and the poetic' (p. 35). I shall begin the pursuit of this alternative perception by drawing upon the work of Henri Lefebvre and Michel de Certeau.

Henri Lefebvre was born in 1901, and by the time of his death 90 years later was widely regarded as one of France's leading intellectuals. An unorthodox and ebullient Marxist, he is celebrated particularly for his work on public space and planning (for example 1991a [1974], 2004 [1992]) and his dazzling three-volume series *A Critique of Everyday Life* (1991b [1947], 2002 [1961], 2005 [1981]).

One of the most significant early influences upon Lefebvre was surrealism and particularly the work of André Breton. Breton, a major spokesperson and apologist for the early surrealist movement, attempted to unmask the madness of the conventionally structured world as revealed through the horror of World War One. Through turning to the strange within the everyday – particularly the unconscious, the dream and the repressed – the surrealists launched their total critique of bourgeois society and the alienation of the human spirit within it. Although he later came to criticize the self-indulgence of surrealism's obsession with the incomprehensible and bizarre, the surrealist gaze influenced all of Lefebvre's later writing.

Through surrealism, as mediated via Breton, Lefebvre was also drawn to read Hegel and embraced an understanding of the dialectic as a restless current of continual motion impelling human life forward through history. Perceptions of a turbulent process in which contradiction is the permanent driver of change are evident throughout his oeuvre. However, his later embrace of Marxism led Lefebvre to locate this movement not in ideal terms but rather as dialectic in material, embodied and everyday living.

It is this dialectical understanding that generated the title of Lefebvre's major work. What Lefebvre refers to as the higher disciplines (including the abstract arts, philosophy and theology) *critique* daily life as an inchoate, chaotic, unformed mess of living, impossible to view clearly and indecipherable to itself; an 'enormous, shapeless, ill-defined mass' (1991b [1947], p. 252). These disciplines assume that to attain full humanity we need to rise above this chaotic scene and gain a vantage point upon it through processes of abstraction. However, in true dialectic spirit this inchoate stuff *critiques* the higher thought forms because they are clearly meaningless, quite obviously absurd, unless related directly to it. So the process of abstraction ironically undermines the very foundations of the abstract arts. In contrast to their presumptions it is the matter of daily life that sustains the human, and the more we seek to codify and tame it the more it resists. This stubborn obduracy escapes the control of ideology and that is what, for Lefebvre, gives daily life its liberative potential.

While his Marxist commitments continually remind Lefebvre of how alienated the lives of the great majority are under capitalism, his perception of the dynamism of the everyday world prevents him from dismissing the massive human achievements that constitute its vibrant riches. While it is important to combat exploitative systems, the critique 'of unfulfilment and alienation should not be reduced to a bleak picture of pain and despair' (2002 [1961], p. 45). Everyday life is shot through with spaces in which 'relations which make the human and every human being take shape and form' (1991b [1947], p. 97). Furthermore, the '"human raw material" in its simplicity and richness – pierces through all alienation and establishes "disalienation"' (1991b [1947], p. 97); a 'veritable profoundness shines through' (2002 [1961], p. 65). This happens in pleasure, desire, play, making, cooking, cinema going, friendship, dancing and so on. You are not a true revolutionary, according to Lefebvre, if you can't discern an ecstatic energy at the heart of things.

However, this electrifying current does not mean that everyday life is wonderful, although it is the site of wonders. In everyday life platitude and profoundness, banality and drama continue to struggle against each other at every level. And for Lefebvre, two things in particular contend with banality to challenge our estrangement from the fullness of life. As a critique of alienation arise the tragic and the festival.

The tragic is that which we seek to banish from the everyday. The alienated world is held in bondage because people cling to custom, order and convention to protect them from the terrors life might otherwise contain. However, the tragic irrupts into our experience, come what may, bringing disaster and loss *and* setting us free from our allegiance to the pathetic comforts of the known world. Lefebvre writes:

> the thinking that does not shy away from the horror of the world, the darkness, but looks it straight in the face . . . passes over into a different kingdom which is the kingdom of darkness . . . Daily life has served as a refuge from the tragic . . . people seek and find security there. [But to] traverse daily life under the flash of the tragic is already to transform . . .
>
> So that the irruption of the tragic in everyday life turns it upside down. (2005 [1981], pp. 171–2)

There is another way of piercing through the banality of the everyday that robs us of our humanity, and that is the festival. The party. For Lefebvre festivals were constructed when those elements that constitute the everyday (intimacy, eating, sharing, memorializing, working with the seasons) come together with explosive force. Festivals are carnivalesque occasions that similarly present to us a world as it might be, for a 'moment'.

Such *moments*[5] are revelatory – like surrealist art, they break through the banality that occludes vision. In tragedy, in festival and in other instances of intensity (both social and personal), conjunctions occur that pierce through taken-for-granted life and allow us to see in new ways. This epiphanic vision is described by Lefebvre in terms not unfamiliar to theologians. Like forms of realized eschatology they unite past and future and enable us to believe in the realization of a possibility. But Lefebvre is adamant in his presentation of tragedy, festival and the significant moment that these don't remove us from the everyday onto some higher plane. They are experienced, he writes, in 'play, love, work, rest, struggle, poetry' – ordinary circumstances that shine with startling effect. 'Sometimes profundity and beauty can be born from . . .

---

5 The concept of 'moments' in which transformatory potential is actualized in lived experience is a key theme in the second volume of Lefebvre's *Critique* (2002 [1961]).

[an] unexpected combination: an encounter . . . they become moments, combinations which marvellously overturn structures' (2002 [1961], p. 66). Moments are profundity and beauty lived.

This brings me finally on my very brief tour of Lefebvre to *poesis*. *Poesis* in Aristotle's thought and elsewhere is often characterized as the, rather inferior, twin of *phronesis* – practical wisdom. It does not carry the same spiritual value as virtuous reasoning. This is because *poesis* is a making (the concept unites art and poetry with manufacture), and making is always a mimetic activity in reference to an ideal.[6] It must inevitably fail to achieve its own aspirations.

For Lefebvre the dialectic materialist, however, *poesis* refers to the supreme, restless, transformative capacity of human beings to reshape their world and create meaning out of the mundane. Looking back on his life's work in the three volumes, he reflects that at first he sought to understand everyday life and analyse it (1991b [1947]). He then sought to understand how we might comprehend the alienation we experience within it (2002 [1961]). At last in old age he was looking for something he termed 'poetic'. A metamorphosis 'through action and works, hence through thought, poetry, love' (2005 [1981], p. 165). As Gardiner writes, for Lefebvre our world making is not a dreary matter of programmed instrumental action in pursuit of clear goals. It is integral to our being in the world and involves 'love, sensuality and the body' (2000, p. 80). This passionate *poesis* is serious art and thus also simple play. It protests, in Lefebvre's strangely theological words, against the 'loss of grace and gracefulness' (2002 [1961], p. 203). He writes that in our playful creativity 'another reality is born, not a separate one, but one which is "lived" in the everyday, alongside the functional . . . It is a domain without limits' (p. 204).

The World Made Strange: Michel de Certeau and the Wonder of Everyday Life

So Lefebvre offers a vision of the everyday in which it is the site of revelation; a realm of mystery shot through with the tragic; a place of profound play secured by the marvellous grace of the poetic. I will come back to the implications of this vision, but I want to thicken it and deepen it before I do so by drawing upon the parallel work of

---

6 It is possible to hold a more positive apprehension of mimesis. See Paul Fiddes who, following Ricoeur, clearly expresses this perspective (2013).

Michel de Certeau. De Certeau was born in 1925 and entered the Society of Jesus as a young man in his mid twenties. He was a brilliant and eclectic scholar whose thought was influenced by many differing intellectual currents. Marxism was one of these. However, it was not the mechanism of the dialectic that was of most significance to de Certeau from this tradition, but rather the Marxist notion that the agents of change are always those who suffer and are marginalized in the current regime. The oppressed are the agents of transformation. For Marx this role falls to the impoverished workers, but for later Marxian thinkers the category is widened to include all those who are insignificant on the margins, abused, mad, mystical and deviant, and who bear in their wounded hands the seeds for the next harvest. De Certeau's oeuvre contains repeated explorations of the significance of the unnoticed and excluded – hence his fascination with the everyday, which is the realm of the invisible, alien and uncounted (see de Certeau 1984, de Certeau, Giard and Mayol 1998). However, it is not only to Marx that he owes this vision of the power of what is repressed.

De Certeau was also profoundly influenced by Lacan's psychoanalytic theory. For Lacan, in order to become human we have to relinquish an originary state of union with the maternal. This originary state is blissful but individuation, subjectivity, cannot exist within it. Our entry into the world of language, identity and selfhood is achieved at the cost of renouncing this deathly paradise. We exist now as human beings through the trauma of our loss. The nameless desire for something we can never recover marks us. We are outcasts and seekers. We are pilgrims who will never arrive at the sacred.

I do not think you have to be a convinced Lacanian or a Marxist to resonate with these powerful ur-myths naming the human condition. De Certeau's genius was to creatively enjoin them to his own understanding of Christianity, an understanding formed in the Ignatian tradition. This is a tradition that is on the road. Jesuits are a restless, travelling community. It is also one in which the spiritual life involves attention to emotion, affect, the senses, and is imaged as a creative work. Ignatius advised his spiritual seekers to imaginatively enter into the life of Christ in the following manner: 'to smell and to taste with the senses of smell and taste the infinite gentleness and sweetness of the divinity . . . to touch with the sense of touch – as, for instance, to embrace and kiss' the places made holy by the divine presence, 'always taking care to draw profit from this' (see Ivens 1998, pp. 96–8). This is a profoundly embodied way of encountering God, and de Certeau was particularly influenced by Maurice Giuliani's contemporary reinterpretation of the

Ignatian exercises in which wondering attention, prayerful openness to everyday life itself, was intended to form the spiritual habitus of the seeker (see Sheldrake 2003, p. 333).

This wondering attention must be focused upon what de Certeau calls the particular. Attention to the particular is not easy. All our epistemological categories, de Certeau argues, are attuned to the abstracted generality, but 'ordinary culture puts our arsenal of scientific procedures and epistemological categories on trial' (de Certeau, Giard and Mayol 1998, p. 256). In a gesture similar to Lefebvre's, he argues that everyday life *seems* to be a formless and inchoate world which can only be seen at all through the lenses of our various epistemological regimes. But, contests de Certeau, our analytical models are 'too little elaborated to allow us to think through the inventive proliferation of everyday practices . . . there remains so much to understand about the . . . "obscure heroes" of the ephemeral, those walking in the city, inhabitants of neighbourhoods, readers and dreamers' (de Certeau, Giard and Mayol 1998, p. 256). He was filled with 'wonder' at the creativity of obscure women in kitchens and the humble and tenacious challenge their unnoted existence posed to dominant theories of social life.

The sense of astonished admiration that de Certeau gains from attending to the practices of everyday life generates his analysis of the resistance it offers to the control of the system – all systems, any systems. We have been through many years of political pessimism in which the influential theories of scholars like Jean Baudrillard and Zygmunt Bauman have led us to be rather sceptical about human powers of resistance to the overwhelming totalitarianism of consumer capitalism. However, de Certeau was not so pessimistic. We do not notice the resistance, he says, just as we fail to understand life in the particular, because our untrained (or perhaps too trained) eyes cannot perceive its hidden ferment in the everyday and also, crucially, because it cuts its fabric from the same stuff the system is woven out of.

De Certeau offers a clear, historical example of the resistance that is fabricated from the resources of the system. When the conquistadors came to Latin America, bringing their religion and way of life, it appeared to wipe out and obliterate the wisdom of the indigenous peoples. These had no choice but to employ the language, symbols and rituals of the invaders, and they did so – having no choice. But they transformed them in use, making them signify differently for them from how they did for their oppressors. So, writes de Certeau, the strength of their difference lay in the manner of their consumption. And thus it is for us today. We may think that people who watch popular television programmes, for example, are passive consumers of a product designed to ensure their conformity to a system. We fail to see the work that consumers do (which is invisible to us) to re-imagine what they receive. We need to ask what the consumers make with the product. If we do so, we may discover that the 'making in question is a production, a *poesis* – but a hidden one, because it is scattered over areas defined and occupied by systems of production' (1984, p. xii). Through their creative work, 'users make (*bricolent*) innumerable and infinitesimal transformations of and within the dominant cultural economy' (1984, pp. xiii–xiv).

In fact, for de Certeau, the whole of everyday life is not a passive realm of consumption but a making (sometimes a making do) with the resources to hand, which are the resources the system provides. They are admittedly limited and restrictive but, nevertheless, as we use space, create conviviality, talk to children, even earn our livings, we are continually engaged in active forms of self- and social production. De Certeau sometimes describes this productive work as reading. Readers do not simply receive a text. They also imaginatively reinscribe it. The people we too easily dismiss as passive consumers he would characterize as also being active readers, 'unrecognized producers, poets of their own acts, silent discoverers of their own paths in the jungle of functional rationality' (p. xviii). Their creations he compares to the strange but haunting artworks of autistic children – or, we might say, to the surrealist art that makes the world strange and gives a new focus to the everyday.

De Certeau thus presents everyday life as scattered with marvels and retaining space for a *poesis* of microinvention in which we resist with 'sweet obstinacy' (Certeau, Giard and Mayol 1998, p. 213). This may appear an outrageously optimistic vision but it is one born from de Certeau's perception of the sufferings of the excluded, from the traumas of our wounded humanity and the mystical intensity of patient attention to particularity. It is only through these that we gain the wisdom to see beyond the confining boundaries of our current epistemological categories and marvel at the poetic revelation of the everyday. In a similar manner to Lefebvre, de Certeau would certainly argue that we cannot see ourselves as believing people, as Christians, unless we do transgress these boundaries. 'Boundaries are the place of Christian work and their displacements are the result of this work' (de Certeau in Sheldrake 2003, p. 32).

Practical Theology and the Everyday

I love the passage from Luke's Gospel that sounded the keynote for this chapter. I enjoy contemplating how in their contrasting modes of fasting and celebrating both John the Baptist and Jesus embody Sophia who has made her holy dwelling among us.

If I were to characterize the wisdom I encounter in the poetic approach of Lefebvre and de Certeau and contrast it with the practical wisdom of empirical theology and feminist practical theology, then I would have to say it does not walk a middle road but tends towards extremes and is full of exaggerated excess. A denunciation of the evils of the system is combined with a careless, joyous confidence that these evils cannot prevail against what is counted as humble and of little worth. As such, it has deep resonances with aspects of the Christian tradition. However, it stands in stark contrast to many very worthy discourses in theology which are seeking to comprehend the everyday world as a place of wholesome coherence and embodied rationality where ordinary practice can innocently meet with theological reflection in a non-problematic union.

It is of course a polemical and rhetorical gesture to position *poesis* in relation to *phronesis* in the ways I have been doing throughout this chapter. As I have argued previously, the two engage in fruitful dialogue within practical theology at many levels. Nevertheless, while poetics remains so poorly understood and so badly neglected, it is worth making the gesture and attempting to reclaim for our discipline the extraordinary energy of the poetics of everyday life, which Lefebvre and de Certeau so powerfully describe.

We have much to gain if we can do so. The first thing I think we can receive from the theorists of the everyday is what has been termed in relation to surrealism (but it fits very well here too) 'a hermeneutics of wonder' (Gardiner 2000, p. 35). We can be, even as grown-up theologians, children playing in the marketplace and holding in our perceptive gaze all those intensities of tragedy and festival that the grown-ups engaged in commerce there might fail to discern.

A second gift we might receive as wise children is a way of seeing those things that are currently invisible to our favoured epistemological approaches. Lefebvre has talked about the revelatory power of moments and de Certeau of the challenge of particularity. Both are advocating a process of attentive engagement with things we may have perceived as being of little worth, which are hard to study and impossible to pin down in texts and tables. But can we afford the expense of this mystical perception? Is what it reveals worth noticing? Can we justify in this world, where so much needs attention, reform, adjustment, devoting our energies to the resistance represented by ephemeral pleasures and small passions? Can we afford to go to the dance hall with Lefebvre? Walk with de Certeau for hours down streets that lead nowhere? Can we afford not to?

From children playing in the marketplace we might also receive a theological challenge. I have characterized both empirical theology and feminist practical theology as tending to take up the everyday and interpret it within a higher theological frame. This is possible because the everyday exhibits a sacred face that has a sure and certain place in the redemptive economy. But the children weeping and piping alert us to the need to watch what is happening all around us and stoop down to see it more closely.

I have just finished some work on theology and materiality in which I have reflected on incarnational theology in the Eastern traditions. Orthodoxy has a very high view of material existence as in the process of being taken up into the harmonious life of the divine. Through the divine liturgy of Saint John Chrystostom, Orthodox Christians address a God who is celebrated as both active to sanctify creation – and present in the elements that are sanctified: 'You are the one who offers and is offered, who receives and is distributed, Christ our God and to you we offer glory.' For contemporary Orthodox theologians such as Schmemann, the material world can be viewed, the world can be seen, as the material of 'one all-embracing Eucharist' in the process of consecration and reconciliation (1965, p. 16).

This incarnational theology is truly very inspiring – but there are other ways of understanding the incarnation which have rather differing emphases. I am particularly influenced by Franciscan traditions, which reflect less upon the material in the process of transport towards deification and rather more upon the incarnation as a radical kenosis that does not so much raise up as gaze down, touching the very depth of matter as it splits, fissures and proliferates and finds in the stone, the street, the dance, the dress the very flesh of God. This view is less interested in incorporation and harmony than in sharing in the passion, the wounding and the glory of this living. This everyday life. This living God.

Bibliography

Ackermann, Denise and Bons-Storm, Riet (eds), 1998, *Liberating Faith Practices: Feminist Practical Theologies in Context*, Leuven: Peeters.

Albrecht, Gloria, 1995, *The Character of our Communities*, Nashville, TN: Abingdon Press.

Alter, Robert, 2000, *Canon and Creativity: Modern Writing and the Authority of Scripture*, New Haven, CT and London: Yale University Press.

Althaus-Reid, Marcella, 2000, *Indecent Theology: Theological Perversions in Sex, Gender and Politics*, London: Routledge.

Althaus-Reid, Marcella (ed.), 2008, *Liberation Theology and Sexuality*, London: SCM Press.

Althaus-Reid, Marcella and Isherwood, Lisa, 2007, *Controversies in Feminist Theology*, London: SCM Press.

Anderson, Herbert and Foley, Ed, 1998, *Mighty Stories: Dangerous Rituals: Weaving Together the Human and Divine*, San Francisco: Jossey-Bass.

Anderson, Leon, 2006, 'Analytic Autoethnography', *Journal of Contemporary Ethnography* 35:4, pp. 373–95.

Anderson, Linda, 2004, *Autobiography*, London and New York: Routledge.

Anderson, Pamela Sue, 1998, *A Feminist Philosophy of Religion*, Oxford: Blackwell.

Antze, Paul and Lambek, Michael (eds), 1996, *Tense Past: Critical Essays in Trauma and Memory*, London: Routledge.

Augustine, 1963, *The Confessions of St Augustine*, trans. Rex Warner, New York: Mentor.

Bachelard, Gaston, 1994, *The Poetics of Space*, trans. Maria Jolas, Boston: Beacon.

Bakhtin, Mikhail, 1981, *The Dialogic Imagination: Four Essays*, trans. Caryl Emerson and Michael Holquist, Austin: University of Texas Press.

Baudrillard, Jean, 1994, *Simulcra and Simulation*, Ann Arbor: University of Michigan Press.

Bedford, Nancy, 2002, 'Little Moves against Destructiveness', in M. Volf and D. Bass (eds), *Practicing Theology: Beliefs and Practices in Christian Life*, Grand Rapids, MI: Eerdmans, pp. 157–81.

Bell, Daniel, 2001, *Liberation Theology and the End of History: The Refusal to Cease Suffering*, London: Routledge.

Bell, Robert, 'Metamorphoses of Spiritual Autobiography', *English Literary History* 44:1, pp. 108–26.

Bennett, Jane, 2001, *The Enchantment of Modern Life*, Princeton, NJ: Princeton University Press.

— 2009, 'Agency, Nature and Emergent Properties: An Interview with Jane Bennett', *Contemporary Political Theory* 8:1, pp. 90–105.

— 2010, *Vibrant Matter: A Political Ecology of Things*, Durham, NC: Duke University Press.

Bennett, Jana M., 2008, *Water is Thicker than Blood: An Augustinian Theology of Marriage and Singleness*, Oxford: Oxford University Press.

Bennett, Zoe, 2002, *Introducing Feminist Perspectives on Pastoral Theology*, Sheffield: Sheffield Academic Press.

Berry, Jan, 2009, *Ritual Making Women: Shaping Rites for Changing Lives*, London: Equinox.

Bethlehem, I., 2005, 'Materiality and the Madness of Reading: J. M. Coetzee's Elizabeth Costello as a Post-Apartheid Text', *Journal of Literary Studies* 21: 3–4, pp. 235–54.

Bolton, Gillie, 2005, *Reflective Practice: Writing and Professional Development*, London: Sage.

Bonhoeffer, Dietrich, 1973, *Letters and Papers from Prison*, London: SCM Press.

Bons-Storm, Riet, 1996, *The Incredible Woman: Listening to Women's Silences in Pastoral Care and Counseling*, Nashville, TN: Abingdon Press.

— 1998, 'Putting the Little Ones into the Dialogue: A Feminist Practical Theology', in D. Ackermann and R. Bons-Storm (eds), *Liberating Faith Practices: Feminist Practical Theologies in Context*, Leuven: Peeters, pp. 9–26.

Breytenbach, Breyten, 1985, *True Confessions of an Albino Terrorist*, New York: Farrar, Strauss & Giroux.

Brown, Callum, 2009, *The Death of Christian Britain: Understanding Secularisation 1800–2000*, London: Routledge.

— 2012, *Religion and the Demographic Revolution: Women and Secularisation in Canada, Ireland, UK and USA since the 1960s*, Woodbridge: Boydell Press.

Browning, Don, 1991, *A Fundamental Practical Theology: Descriptive and Strategic Proposals*, Minneapolis, MN: Fortress Press.

Bunyan, John, 1907 [1678], *Grace Abounding and the Pilgrim's Progress*, Cambridge: Cambridge University Press.

Cameron, Helen, Bhatti, Deborah, Duce, Catherine, Sweeney, James and Watkins, Clare, 2010, *Talking About God in Practice: Theological Action Research and Practical Theology*, London: SCM Press.

Chang, Heewon, 2008, *Autoethnography as Method*, Walnut Creek, CA: Left Coast Press.

Chopp, Rebecca, 1989, *The Power to Speak: Feminism, Language, God*, New York: Crossroad.

— 1995, *Saving Work: Feminist Practices of Theological Education*, Louisville, KY: Westminster John Knox Press.

— 2001, 'Theology and the poetics of testimony', in D. Brown, S. G. Davaney and K. Tanner (eds), *Converging on Culture: Theologians in Dialogues with Cultural Analysis and Criticism*, Oxford: Oxford University Press, pp. 56–70.

— 2009, 'Reimagining Public Discourse', http://web.uct.ac.za/depts/ricsa/confer/me99/con_paps/chopp.htm, accessed 1 March 2014.

Cixous, Hélène, 1993, *Three Steps on the Ladder of Writing*, New York: Columbia University Press.

— 1998, *Stigmata: Escaping Texts*, London: Routledge.

Coetzee, J. M., 1996, *Giving Offence: Essays on Censorship*, Chicago: University of Chicago Press.

— 2003, *Elizabeth Costello*, New York: Penguin.

Couture, Pamela, 1991, *Blessed are the Poor? Women's Poverty, Family Policy, and Practical Theology*, Nashville, TN: Abingdon Press.

de Beauvoir, Simone, 1972 [1949], *The Second Sex*, trans. H. M. Parshley, London: Pan Books.

de Certeau, Michel, 1984, *The Practice of Everyday Life*, trans. Steven Rendall, Berkeley: University of California Press.

de Certeau, Michel, Giard, Luce and Mayol, Pierre, 1998, *The Practice of Everyday Life*, vol. 2, *Living and Cooking*, Minneapolis: University of Minnesota Press.

Delio, Ilia, 2003, 'Revisiting the Franciscan Doctrine of Christ', *Theological Studies* 64:3, pp. 3–23.

Denzin, Norman, 2003a, *Performance Ethnography: Critical Pedagogy and the Politics of Culture*, Thousand Oaks, CA and London: Sage.

— 2003b, 'Performing [Auto] Ethnography Politically', *Review of Education, Pedagogy, and Cultural Studies* 25:3, pp. 257–78.

— 2006, 'Analytic Autoethnography, or Déjà Vu All Over Again', *Journal of Contemporary Ethnography* 35:4, pp. 419–28.

Dudley, C. S. (ed.), 1982, *Building Effective Ministry: Theory and Practice in the Local Church*, San Francisco: Harper & Row.

Eakin, Paul John (ed.), 2004, *The Ethics of Life Writing*, Ithaca, NY and London: Cornell University Press.

Eliot, T.S., 1974 [1920], 'Gerontion', in *Collected Poems, 1909–1962*, London: Faber & Faber, pp. 39–41.

— 1974 [1935], 'Burnt Norton', in *Collected Poems, 1909–1962*, London: Faber & Faber, pp. 189–95.

— 1951 [1935], 'Religion and Literature', in *Selected Essays*, London: Faber & Faber, pp. 388–401.

— 1939, *The Idea of a Christian Society*, London: Faber & Faber.

Ellis, Carolyn, 2004, *The Autoethnographic I: A Methodological Novel about Autoethnography*, New York: Altamira Press.

Ellis, Carolyn and Bochner, Arthur, 2003, 'Autoethnography, Personal Narrative, Reflexivity: Researcher as Subject', in Norman Denzin and Yvonna Lincoln (eds), *Collecting and Interpreting Qualitative Materials*, 2nd edition, Thousand Oaks, CA: Sage, pp. 199–258.

— 2006, 'Analyzing Analytic Autoethnography: An Autopsy', *Journal of Contemporary Ethnography* 35:4, pp. 429–49.

Ellis, Carolyn, Adams, Tony and Bochner, Art, 2011, 'Autoethnography: An Overview', *Forum: Qualitative Social Research/Sozialforschung* 12:1, http://www.qualitative-research.net/index.php/fqs/article/view/1589/3095.

Etherington, Kimm, 2004, *Becoming a Reflexive Researcher*, London: Jessica Kingsley.

Felman, Shoshona, 1992, 'After the Apocalypse: Paul de Man and the Fall to Silence', in Shoshona Felman and Dori Laub, *Testimony: Crises of Witnessing in Literature, Psychoanalysis and History*, London: Routledge, pp. 120–64.

Felman, Shoshona and Laub, Dori, 1992, *Testimony: Crises of Witnessing in Literature, Psychoanalysis and History*, London: Routledge.

Fiddes, Paul, 2013, *Seeing the World and Knowing God: Hebrew Wisdom and Christian Doctrine in a Late-Modern Context*, Oxford: Oxford University Press.

Forrester, Duncan, 1997, *Christian Justice and Public Policy*, Cambridge: Cambridge University Press.

— 2001a, *Truthful Action*, Edinburgh: T & T Clark.

— 2001b, *On Human Worth*, London: SCM Press.

— 2003, 'The Political Service of Theology in Scotland', in W. Storrar and P. B. Donald (eds), *God in Society: Doing Social Theology in Scotland Today*, Edinburgh: St Andrew Press, pp. 83–124.

Fowler, James, 1981, *Stages of Faith: The Psychology of Human Development and the Quest for Meaning*, San Francisco: Harper & Row.

Frank, Arthur, 1995, *The Wounded Storyteller: Body, Illness and Ethics*, Chicago: University of Chicago Press.

— 2004, 'Moral Non Fiction: Life Writing and Children's Disability', in Paul John Eakin (ed.), *The Ethics of Life Writing*, Ithaca, NY and London: Cornell University Press, pp. 74–194.

Gardiner, Michael, 2000, *Critiques of Everyday Life*, London: Routledge.

Geertz, Clifford, 1973, *On the Interpretation of Cultures*, New York: Basic Books.

Gibson, John, 2008, *Fiction and the Weave of Life*, Oxford: Oxford University Press.

Giddens, Anthony, 1991, *Modernity and Self Identity: Self and Society in the Late Modern Age*, Cambridge: Polity Press.

Gillen, Julia, 2006, 'Child's Play', in Janet Maybin and Joan Swann (eds), *The Art of English: Everyday Creativity*, Basingstoke: Palgrave Macmillan, pp. 157–208.

Graham, Elaine, 1995, *Making the Difference: Gender, Personhood and Theology*, London: Mowbray.

— 2002, *Representations of the Post/Human: Monsters, Aliens and Others in Popular Culture*, Manchester: Manchester University Press.

Graham, Elaine, Walton, Heather and Ward, Frances, 2005, *Theological Reflection: Methods*, London: SCM Press.

Greu, Etienne, 2005, 'Speaking of God and speaking from God', in E. Graham and A. Rowlands (eds), *Pathways to the Public Square: Practical Theology in an Age of Pluralism*, Münster: Lit Verlag, pp. 203–10.

Habermas, Jürgen, Brewster, Philip and Buchner, Carl, 1979, 'Consciousness-Raising or Redemptive Criticism: The Contemporaneity of Walter Benjamin', *New German Critique* 17, pp. 30–59.

Haraway, Donna, 1991, *Simians, Cyborgs and Women: The Reinvention of Nature*, London: Free Association Books.

Harding, Sandra, 1991, *Whose Science? Whose Knowledge? Thinking from Women's Lives*, Ithaca, NY: Cornell University Press.

Harvey, Barry, 1997, 'The Body Politic of Christ', *Modern Theology* 13:3, pp. 319–45.

Hauerwas, Stanley, 1990, *Naming the Silences: God, Medicine, and the Problem of Suffering*, Grand Rapids, MI: Eerdmans.

Heelas, Paul, 2008, *Spiritualities of Life: New Age Romanticism and Consumptive Capitalism*, Oxford: Blackwell.

Heelas, Paul and Woodhead Linda, 2005, *The Spiritual Revolution: Why Religion is Giving Way to Spirituality*, Oxford: Blackwell.

Hill, Christopher, 1988, *A Turbulent, Seditious and Factious People: John Bunyan and his Church*, Oxford: Oxford University Press.

Hillesum, Etty, 1999 [1981], *An Interrupted Life: The Diaries and Letters of Etty Hillesum*, trans. Arnold Pomerans, London: Persephone Books.

Hopewell, J., 1982, 'The Jovial Church: Narrative in local church life', in C. S. Dudley (ed.), *Building Effective Ministry: Theory and Practice in the Local Church*, San Francisco: Harper & Row.

— 1988, *Congregation: Stories and Structures*, London: SCM Press.

Hopkins, Gerard Manley, 1976a, 'As Kingfishers Catch Fire, Dragonflies Draw Flame', in *Poems and Prose*, ed. W. H. Gardener, Harmondsworth: Penguin, p. 51.

— 1976b, 'That Nature is a Heraclitean Fire and the Comfort of the Resurrection', in *Poems and Prose*, ed. W. H. Gardener, Harmondsworth: Penguin, p. 65.

Irigaray, Luce, 1993, *An Ethics of Sexual Difference*, trans. Carolyn Burke and Gillian Gill, London: The Athlone Press.

Ivens, Michael, 1998, *Understanding the Spiritual Exercises: Text and Commentary: A Handbook for Retreat Directors*, Leominster: Gracewing.

Jantzen, Grace, 1998, *Becoming Divine: Towards a Feminist Philosophy of Religion*, Manchester: Manchester University Press.

King, Martin Luther, 1981, *Strength to Love*, Philadelphia, PA: Fortress Press.

King, Ursula, 1999, 'Feminist Theologies in Contemporary Contexts', in D. Sawyer and Diane Collier (eds), *Is There a Future for Feminist Theology?*, Sheffield: Sheffield Academic Press.

Kirmayer, Laurence, 1996, 'Landscapes of Memory: Trauma, Narrative and Dissociation', in P. Antze and M. Lambek (eds), *Tense Past: Cultural Essays in Trauma and Memory*, London: Routledge, pp. 173–98.

Klug, Ron, 2002, *How to Keep a Spiritual Journal: A Guide to Journal Keeping for Inner Growth and Personal Discovery*, Minneapolis, MN: Augsburg.

Kolb, David, 1984, *Experiential Learning: Experience as the Source of Learning and Development*, Englewood Cliffs, NJ: Prentice Hall.

Le Doeuff, Michèle, 2002 [1980], *The Philosophical Imaginary*, trans. C. Gordon, London: Continuum.

Lefebvre, Henri, 1991a [1974], *The Production of Space*, trans. Donald Nicholson-Smith, Oxford: Blackwell.

— 1991b [1947], *A Critique of Everyday Life*, vol. 1, trans. John Moore, London: Verso.

— 2002 [1961], *A Critique of Everyday Life*, vol. 2, *Foundations for a Sociology of the Everyday*, trans. John Moore, London: Verso.

— 2004 [1992], *Rhythmanalysis: Space, Time and Everyday Life*, trans. Stuart Eldon and Gerald Moore, London: Continuum.

— 2005 [1981], *A Critique of Everyday Life*, vol. 3, *From Modernity to Modernism (Towards A Metaphilosophy Of Daily Life)*, trans. Gregory Elliott, London: Verso.

Leigh, David, 2000, *Circuitous Journeys: Modern Spiritual Autobiography*, New York: Fordham University Press.

Louw, D., 2001, 'Creative Hope and Imagination in a Practical Theology of Aesthetic (Artistic Reason)', *Religion and Theology* 8:3–4, pp. 327–44.

Lyotard, Jean-François, 1984, *The Post Modern Condition: A Report on Knowledge*, trans. Geoff Bennington and Brian Massumi, Manchester: Manchester University Press.

MacIntyre, Alasdair, 1981, *After Virtue: A Study in Moral Theory*, London: Duckworth.

Mann, Bonnie, 2006, *Women's Liberation and the Sublime*, Oxford: Oxford University Press.

Maritain, J., 1954, *Creative Intuition in Art and Poetry*, London: Harvill Press.

Marx, Karl, 1990 [1867], *Capital: A Critique of Political Economy*, vol. 1, trans. Ben Fowkes, New York: Penguin.

Miller, Daniel, 2008, *The Comfort of Things*, Cambridge: Polity Press.

— 2010, *Stuff*, Cambridge: Polity Press.

Miller-McLemore, Bonnie, 1998, 'The Subject and Practice of Pastoral Theology as a Practical Theological Discipline: Pushing Past the Nagging Identity Crisis to a Poetics of Resistance', in Denise Ackermann and Riet Bons-Storm (eds), *Liberating Faith Practices: Feminist Practical Theologies in Context*, Leuven: Peeters, pp. 175–98.

— 2012a, *Christian Theology in Practice: Discovering a Discipline*, Grand Rapids, MI: Eerdmans.

— 2012b, 'Introduction: The Contributions of Practical Theology', in Bonnie Miller-McLemore (ed.), *The Wiley-Blackwell Companion to Practical Theology*, Oxford: Wiley-Blackwell.

Miller, Nancy K., 2004, 'The Ethics of Betrayal: Diary of a Memoirist', in Paul John Eakin (ed.), *The Ethics of Life Writing*, Ithaca, NY and London: Cornell University Press, pp. 148–60.

Moon, Jennifer, 2006, *Learning Journals*, London and New York, Routledge-Falmer.

Newtown, George, 1998, 'From St Augustine to Paul Monette: Sex and Salvation in an Age of Aids', in G. Thomas Kauser and Joseph, Fichtelberg (eds), *True Relations: Essays on Autobiography and the Postmodern*, Westport, CT: Greenwood Press, pp. 51–62.

Norton, David, 2000, *A History of the Bible as Literature*, Cambridge: Cambridge University Press.

Novak, Michael, 1965, *Belief and Unbelief: A Philosophy of Self-Knowledge*, New York: Macmillan.

O'Donovan, Oliver, 1984, *Begotten or Made?*, Oxford: Clarendon Press.

O'Halloran, Kerry, 2009, *The Politics of Adoption: International Perspectives on Law, Policy and Practice*, London: Springer.

Owens, Jill, 2006, 'The Epistolary Marilynne Robinson', in PowellsBooks.blog, 24 January, http://www.powells.com/blog/interviews/the-epistolary-marilynne-robinson-2-by-jill.

Parsons, Susan, 2002, 'Feminist Theology as Dogmatic Theology', in S. Parsons (ed.), *The Cambridge Companion to Feminist Theology*, Cambridge: Cambridge University Press, pp. 114–34.

Pattison, Stephen, 2007, *The Challenge of Practical Theology: Selected Essays*, London: Jessica Kingsley.

— 2013, *Saving Face: Enfacement, Shame, Theology*, Farnham: Ashgate.

Peacock, Molly, 2007, 'Why I am not a Buddhist', in Neil Astley and Pamela Robertson-Pearce (eds), *Soul Food: Nourishing Poems for Starved Minds*, Tarset: Bloodaxe Books, p. 110.

Pechey, G., 1998, 'The Post-apartheid Sublime: Rediscovering the Extraordinary', in D. Attridge and R. Jolly (eds), *Writing South Africa*, Cambridge: Cambridge University Press, pp. 57–74.

Picca, Leslie, Starks, Brian and Gunderson, Justine, 2013, '"It Opened My Eyes": Using Student Journal Writing to Make Visible Race, Class and Gender in Everyday Life', *Teaching Sociology* 41:1, pp. 82–93.

Plath, Sylvia, 1990, 'Three Women: A Poem for Three Voices', in *The Collected Poems of Sylvia Plath*, ed. Ted Hughes, London: Faber & Faber, pp. 176–87.

Rhys, Jean, 1975 (1939), *Good Morning Midnight*, London: Penguin.

Richards, Thomas, 1991, *The Commodity Culture of Victorian England: Advertising and Spectacle, 1851–1914*, London: Verso.

Ricoeur, Paul, 1991, *A Ricoeur Reader: Reflection and Imagination*, ed. Mario J. Valdès, Hemel Hempstead: Harvester Wheatsheaf.

Roberts, Michele, Llewellyn, Dawn and Sawyer, Deborah, 2008, 'Getting a/cross God: An Interview with Michele Roberts', in D. Llewellyn and D. Sawyer (eds), *Reading Spiritualities: Constructing and Representing the Sacred*, Aldershot: Ashgate, pp. 15–26.

Rossetti, Christina, 2001, 'Goblin Market', in M. H. Abrams (ed.), *The Norton Anthology of English Literature*, 7th edition, New York: W. W. Norton, pp. 2140–52.

Ruether, Rosemary Radford, 1983, *Sexism and God-Talk: Towards a Feminist Theology*, London: SCM Press.

Saiving, Valerie, 1979 [1960], 'The Human Situation: A Feminine View', in Carol Christ and Judith Plaskow (eds), *Womanspirit Rising: A Feminist Reader in Religion*, San Francisco: Harper & Row, pp. 25–42.

Sandywell, Barry, 1996, *Reflexivity and the Crisis of Western Reason: Logological Investigations*, vol. 1, London and New York: Routledge.

Santmire, H. Paul and Cobb, John Jr, 2006, 'The World of Nature According to the Protestant Tradition', in R. Gottleib (ed.), *The Oxford Handbook of Religion and Ecology*, Oxford: Oxford University Press, pp. 115–46.

Scary, Elaine, 1985, *The Body in Pain: The Making and Unmaking of the World*, Oxford: Oxford University Press.

Schilderman, Hans, 2012, 'Quantitative Method', in Bonnie Miller-McLemore (ed.), *The Wiley-Blackwell Companion to Practical Theology*, Blackwell: Oxford, pp. 123–32.

Schmemann, Alexander, 1965, *The World as Sacrament*, London: Darton, Longman & Todd.

Schön, Donald, 1983, *The Reflective Practitioner: How Professionals Think in Action*, New York: Basic Books.

— 1987, *Educating the Reflective Practitioner: Toward a New Design for Teaching and Learning in the Professions*, New York: Basic Books.

Sheldrake, Philip, 2003, 'Christian Spirituality as a Way of Living Publicly: A Dialectic of the Mystical and Prophetic', *Spiritus: A Journal of Christian Spirituality* 3:1, pp. 19–37.

Schüssler Fiorenza, Elizabeth, 1983, *In Memory of Her: A Feminist Theological Reconstruction of Christian Origins*, London: SCM Press.

Silkin, Jon, 1965, 'Death of a Son', in Francis Turner Palgrave and John Press (eds), *The Golden Treasury of the Best Songs and Lyrical Poems in the English Language*, Oxford: Oxford University Press.

Sisson, Larry, 1998, 'The Art and Illusion of Spiritual Biography', in G. Thomas Couser and Joseph Fichtelberg (eds), *True Relations: Essays on Autobiography and the Postmodern*, Westport, CT: Greenwood Press, pp. 97–108.

Slee, Nicola, 2004, *Women's Faith Development: Patterns and Processes*, Aldershot: Ashgate.

Smart, Elizabeth, 1991, *The Assumption of the Rogues and Rascals*, London: Paladin.

— 1992, *By Grand Central Station I Sat Down and Wept*, London: Paladin.

Spry, Tami, 2011, *Body, Paper, Stage: Writing and Performing Autoethnography*, Walnut Creek, CA: Left Coast Press.

Staude, John-Raphael, 2005, 'Autobiography as a Spiritual Practice', *Journal of Gerontological Social Work* 45:3, pp. 249–69.

Stuart, Elizabeth, 1999, 'The View from the Font', *Theology and Sexuality* 6:11, pp. 7–8.

Taylor, Charles, 2004, *Modern Social Imaginaries*, Durham, NC: Duke University Press.

Taylor, Mark Kline, 1990, *Remembering Esperanza: A Cultural-Political Theology for North American Praxis*, Maryknoll, NY: Orbis.

Tillich, Paul, 1981, *The Shaking of the Foundations*, Harmondsworth: Pelican.

van der Ven, Johannes, 1993, *Practical Theology: An Empirical Approach*, Kampen: Kok Pharos.

— 1998, *God Reinvented: A Theological Search in Texts and Tables*, Leiden: Brill.

Veling, Terry, 2005, *Practical Theology: 'On Earth as It Is in Heaven'*, New York: Orbis.

Wall, John, 2003, 'Phronesis, Poetics and Moral Creativity', *Ethical Theory and Moral Practice* 6, pp. 317–41.

— 2004, 'Fallen Angels: A Contemporary Christian Ethical Ontology of Childhood', *International Journal of Practical Theology* 8:2, pp. 160–84.

— 2005, 'The Creative Imperative', *Journal of Religious Ethics* 33:1, pp. 45–64.

— 2007, 'Fatherhood, Childism and the Creation of Society', *Journal of the American Academy of Religion* 75:1, pp. 52–76.

Walton, Heather, 1984, 'If God is on the Side of the Poor – Why Don't They Win?', *Movement: The Student Christian Journal* 56, pp. 6–7.

— 2007a, *Imagining Theology: Women, Writing and God*, London: T & T Clark.

— 2007b, *Literature, Theology and Feminism*, Manchester: Manchester University Press.

— 2008, 'Staging John Coetzee/Elizabeth Costello', *Literature and Theology* 22:3, pp. 280–94.

Ward, Frances, 2005, *Lifelong Learning: Theological Education and Supervision*, London: SCM Press.

Ward, Peter, 2008, *Participation and Mediation: A Practical Theology for the Liquid Church*, London: SCM Press.

Weaver, Darlene, 2007, 'Embryo Adoption Theologically Considered: Bodies, Adoption and the Common Good', in S. V. Brakman and D. Weaver (eds), *The Ethics of Embryo Adoption and the Catholic Tradition*, London: Springer Science and Business Media, pp. 141–59.

Webster, Alison, 1995, *Found Wanting: Women, Christianity and Sexuality*, London: Continuum.

Whipp, Margaret, 2008, 'Speaking of Faith at Work: Towards a Trinitarian Hermeneutic', unpublished thesis, Glasgow University.

Wiesel, Elie and Beale, Timothy, 2000, *Strange Fire: Reading the Bible after the Holocaust*, Sheffield: Sheffield Academic Press.

Wolfteich, Claire, 2002, *Navigating New Terrain: Work and Women's Spiritual Lives*, Mahwah, NJ: Paulist Press.

Wolin, Richard, 1994, *Walter Benjamin: An Aesthetics of Redemption*, Berkeley: University of California Press.

Woodhead, Linda, 1997, 'Spiritualising the Sacred: A Critique of Feminist Theology', *Modern Theology* 13:2, pp. 191–212.

— 1999, 'Feminist Theology: Out of the Ghetto?', in D. Sawyer and Diane Collier (eds), *Is There a Future for Feminist Theology?*, Sheffield: Sheffield Academic Press, pp. 198–206.

— 2007, 'Why So Many Women in Holistic Spirituality?', in K. Flanagan and P. Jupp (eds), *The Sociology of Spirituality*, Aldershot: Ashgate, pp. 115–25.

— 2008, 'Gendering Secularization Theory', *Social Compass* 55:2, pp. 187–93.

Wright, Terence, 1988, *Theology and Literature*, Oxford: Blackwell.

Pamphlets

For the Banished Children of Eve: Movement, pamphlet no. 24.

The Guerrilla Diaries of Nestor Paz Zamora: Movement, pamphlet no. 2.

Towards a Theology of Gay Liberation: Movement: The Journal of Radical Ideas and Action, pamphlet no. 22.

Name and Subject Index

Academic writing xii, xxi, 57,
97–8
Ackermann, Denise 161
Adams, Tony 3–5
Adoption, theology of 64–76
Adorno, Theodor 168
Albrecht, Gloria 160n
Alter, Robert xxvi
Althaus-Reid, Marcella 97, 153n,
156
Anderson, Pamela Sue xxi, 154
Anxiety 62, 77–88
Apartheid, South Africa 22–4,
26–7, 33, 124–5, 161
Aquinas, Thomas 130, 143–4
Arendt, Hannah 143
Aristotle 143–4, 180
Augustine of Hippo 55–6, 90,
92–4, 96, 130, 143
Autobiography, *see* Life Writing
and Narrative – personal narrative
Autoethnography xii, xxviii,
xxxi–ii, 3–9
analytic autoethnography 6–7
evocative stories 4–5
performance 7–9
examples of autoethnography
10–42

Bachelard, Gaston 33
Bakhtin, Mikhail 26n
Barth, Karl 95, 164, 173

Baudrillard, Jean xv, 182
Bauman, Zygmunt 182
Bedford, Nancy 138–9
Benjamin, Walter 33–4
Bennett, Jane 34, 37–40
Berry, Jan 157n, 175
Bible xiii, xxv–vi, 5, 40, 94–5
Blake, William xxvii
Bochner, Arthur 3–5
Body, embodiment xv–vii, xxv, 3, 5,
17, 20, 64–70, 75, 97, 136, 137,
141, 159, 167, 175–6, 178, 181
Bolton, Gillie xix, xxiv
Bonaventure 40
Bonhoeffer, Dietrich 65, 152
Bons-Storm, Riet 139, 161, 175
Bourdieu, Pierre 35
Breton, André 177
Breytenbach, Breyten 27
Brown, Callum 28
Browning, Don 142–3, 176–7
Buchner, Carl 34

Chang, Heewon xxx
Chopp, Rebecca xviii, 145–7,
161–2
Christ xxvii, 40, 64–5, 69, 93,
141–2, 151, 164–5, 181, 185,
see also Jesus of Nazareth
Church, the xx, 7, 10–20, 21–30,
64–5, 68–9, 72, 75–6, 83, 86,
95, 164, 140–2, 147–8, 149–53,
158–9

CPSIA information can be obtained
at www.ICGtesting.com
Printed in the USA
FFOW03n0927191016
28615FF